BETTER PEOPLE OR ENHANCED HUMANS?

For further engagement with this subject please visit:

www.humanenhancement.org.uk

Justin Tomkins

BETTER PEOPLE
OR
ENHANCED HUMANS?

What it might mean to be fully alive in the
context of Human Enhancement

First published in Great Britain 2013

A Sunnyside Books Publication
www.humanenhancement.org.uk

A CIP record for this book is available from the British Library.

ISBN   978-0-9576718-0-5

To Delana with my thanks

& my love

ACKNOWLEDGEMENTS

I thank God for all those people in Bristol, Poole and beyond who have contributed to this book, each in their distinct and varied ways.

The research upon which this book is based was carried out during my three years of ordination training at Trinity College, Bristol. I am indebted to the Oxford Diocese for helping make that possible, to Andrew Goddard my Supervisor, Emma Ineson and Sonja Arnold my Tutors, David Lloyd and Peter Grimwood my Context Supervisors, and to George Kovoor, our inspirational College Principal. I also owe a debt of thanks to all who journeyed with me during those years as fellow students and other members of the communities of Trinity College, Brentry Church and St Mary's Henbury. I am particularly grateful to those students with whom I served in the BS10 Context and from whom I learned so much: Gabriel Anstis, Lee Barnes, Nikki Bates, Becca Bell, Shelley Billington, Dan Currie, Oli Douglas-Pennant, Simon Durrant, Steve Dyson, James Gibson, Pete Hamborg, Linda Kinchenton, Tim Lewis, Dan McCarthy, Adel Shokralla, Gemma Stock, Suzanne Uttin, and to Gerry Angel and James Stephenson who worked with us.

Whilst this book has its roots in Bristol it was written at Poole, during the first half of my curacy at St Mary's Church, Longfleet (SML). God's generosity in bringing us to Poole has been immense and I am so grateful for all whom we have got to know through doing that. I thank Salisbury Diocese for inviting us to join in serving within this area; all at SML for the generosity of their love and welcome; and Andy Perry, my training incumbent, whose leadership, wisdom and holiness is such a great gift to me and to the church.

I am grateful to all who have read drafts of this book and helped to improve it by doing so: Michael Cuthbertson, Riette Hodson, Mark and Martha McNair, Andy Perry, Mervin Roberts, Delana Tomkins and Lorna Tomkins. I am also grateful to the 'New Covenant' Sunday School class at Franktown Church in Virginia who have trialled the use of this material within the context of a small group discussion and to Martha McNair for arranging that. The mistakes and flaws which remain, for which I take responsibility, would have been far greater had it not been for the generosity of all those who have supported me in this way.

These acknowledgements also provide an opportunity for me to thank my two young children, Tuck and Olivia, for their tolerance of the time I have spent writing. Without my wife, Delana, this book would not have been started, let alone finished, and any value within this writing owes at least as much to her efforts as to my own. I thank God for her love and her support and it is with gratitude and love that I dedicate this book to her.

CONTENTS

PREFACE

This book does not provide all the answers or even ask all the questions concerning Human Enhancement but it does call for active engagement with the subject. Living holy lives in the coming decades will demand prayerful, thoughtful and communal engagement with the world in which we will find ourselves. We cannot know in advance all that such a context will demand of us, yet unless we discuss these issues, unless we identify what it means for us to be human, and unless we do that together, we are likely to find ourselves ill-equipped to face whatever lies ahead.

This call to action is addressed primarily to the Church. I will be delighted if others too are able to benefit from these pages but the arguments within them are made from a Christian perspective. The way we choose to live is shaped by our view of the world and so I expect that this book will be most useful to those who are seeking to follow Jesus in the world of both today and tomorrow.

Whilst this book is focused upon Human Enhancement, it is written in the wider context of technological change. If we wait for a technology to arrive before we start discussing it, our thinking will always be chasing to catch up with new gadgets and scientific possibilities. We will be limited to responding to a world which is shaped in advance by technological designers and engineers. The hope of this book is that we might think about these issues in such a way as to develop some tools or principles which might enable us to engage with future technologies which are as yet unknown. Whilst we do not know what lies ahead, we might think about what it means for us to be human, so that by the time we meet the future we have already considered how we might engage with it. If we do, we may develop enough understanding of ourselves and the world that we will be prepared for engaging with the unexpected and the surprising in the future.

This book is both a warning and a message of hope. It warns that in the fast-changing world of the early twenty-first century, our future is increasingly shaped by our medical, technological and scientific context. Unless we engage wisely with that context we run the risk of waking one day to discover that we have missed opportunities to help shape tomorrow's world. Yet that warning comes in combination with the promised message of hope. That hope lies in the fact that our future is ultimately in God's hands and not in our own. We can therefore face all that comes next with the confidence that the biblical command 'Do not be afraid!' is spoken to us in our context, as it has been to all who came before and to all who will follow after.

Chapter 1

OUR TECHNOLOGICAL WORLD

'And God said to Noah ... Make yourself an ark of cypress wood; make rooms in the ark, and cover it inside and out with pitch.'
Genesis 6:13-14

'Then they said, Come let us build for ourselves a city, and a tower with its top in the heavens, and let us make a name for ourselves; otherwise we shall be scattered abroad upon the face of the whole earth.' Genesis 11:4

St. James's Palace recently released a full list of the gifts which the Duke and Duchess of Cambridge received during their overseas tours in 2012. The presents included a tea service, a traditional Malaysian dagger, a model war canoe from the Solomon Islands and two dressing gown robes; varied but not as quirky as the year before when they received caribou antler snow goggles! The US State Department reported that in that same year, President Barack Obama was given a bicycle made of bamboo. The Queen has given London Zoo a number of exotic animals which she has received during her reign. These include jaguars and sloths from Brazil, two young giant turtles from the Seychelles, and an elephant called Jumbo from the Cameroon. Making good use of gifts can require wisdom. Attempting to keep the elephant at Buckingham Palace might not have been practical!

God is a lavish giver of gifts and he knows just what we need. The gifts which he delights in offering to us have enormous potential for good, yet they can also be misused to cause destruction and to make trouble. Technology is one of many such gifts. Within the first few chapters of the Bible we find two stories of technology, one concerning the building of a boat and the other the making of a tower.[1] One project is carried out at God's command and leads to rescue and a new beginning. The other one leads to community breakdown and the very destruction of relationships which the project had attempted to avoid. The difference in the two cases is the use to which technology is put, whether it is deployed in obedience, or in resistance, to God's plans and purposes.[2]

The building of the Ark was not something Noah set out to do independently or for his own selfish reasons. He did it in obedience to God, at the cost of ridicule, loss of reputation, and surely even the questioning of his own sanity. Consequently the Ark, the result of that technological project carried out by Noah at God's direction, became a haven for Noah, his family, and all those pairs of animals. The technology of boat building led to that family and their animal companions being rescued and offered the chance of a new beginning when the flood waters fell back.

The building of the Tower of Babel was a contrasting project.[3] It was part of a quest, by those made in God's image, to stretch up to be like God. In that regard it was a repeat of Adam and Eve's reaching out to be like God through eating the forbidden fruit in the Garden of Eden.[4] The building of the Tower of Babel was not carried out at God's command but rather it worked against his plans and purposes. It was motivated by a desire of the builders to make a name for themselves, rather than to delight in God and to proclaim his holy name. It was about people attempting to establish their own

4

reputation, in contrast to Noah who was prepared to forsake his reputation in obedience to God.

As these biblical examples demonstrate, technology within human society is nothing new. The names given to particular periods of history point to the significance of the use of stone, iron and bronze within those cultures. Indeed, whilst birds may clasp a stick in their beaks to extract insects from a log, and tool use is reported in numerous other species,[5] the extent of the human use of technology is one of our defining characteristics. Technology is one intrinsic dimension of human experience.

What is new is the pace of technological development. Looking back over the last two hundred years, to before the start of the industrial revolution, it is easy to see how developments in science, medicine and technology have transformed the world in that time. Many of us have relatives alive today who were born almost a century ago, at a time when cars and telephones were rare, when electricity was still not commonly available in the UK, and when space travel was the subject of speculative fantasy. In the last generation developments in mobile phones, personal computers and the Internet have radically changed day to day life across most of the planet.

The speed with which new technologies appear seems to be getting faster and faster and faster, exponentially. So instead of a constant amount of change every generation, the change of the last decade is similar to what was seen in the previous twenty years, and the forty years before that. This exponential pattern of doubling can lead to mind-blowing change.

I love the story of the Chinese Emperor who really enjoyed the new game of chess.[6] He was so pleased with the game that he wanted to reward the inventor. Unwittingly, the Emperor agreed to give the inventor a grain of rice on the first square of his chess board, two grains on the second square, four grains on the third square, and so on, doubling each time in an exponential pattern. To complete that pattern on the sixty four squares of a chess board requires a staggering eighteen million trillion grains of rice. That is an eighteen followed by eighteen zeros, or enough rice to require paddy fields covering twice the surface area of the earth, oceans included. Doubling over just those sixty four squares produces numbers so big they are hard to even imagine.

Computer experts have been looking at the developments in computers over the last fifty years and they have spotted this exponential doubling pattern in many different places. They have looked at the cost of computer memory, and the speed of microprocessors, and the amount of computer memory which has been sold, and all these, and many other measures show exponential growth, doubling every few years.[7]

As the story of the chess board shows, exponential doubling is a powerful pattern, but it is important not to let it confuse us. After all, exponential doubling takes place all around us every day, for example with bacteria. When bacteria grow, they reach a stage at which they can double in number every twenty minutes or so, so that within a few hours, each bacterium has produced thousands of relatives. If this growth continued at this pace the whole earth would be flooded under a solid blanket of bacteria, metres thick. But they do not continuing growing at that rate for ever. Food supplies run out, and their numbers stabilise. Their success and adaptability mean that bacteria do indeed cover much of the earth, but the fact that their exponential growth does not continue indefinitely means that their numbers are limited.

It is possible that technological growth has gone through a similar rapid phase of exponential growth and we may now be about to see it slow down dramatically. If that is the case, we need not be as concerned about the ways in which technology may continue to transform our world. Certainly exponential growth in technology will not continue forever. For example, resources run out, as food supplies run out for bacteria. Yet, if technological growth were to continue at the present pace for even another generation, that would lead to unimaginable change. And it is conceivable that it might do so.

When I was teaching chemistry in a secondary school, students enjoyed making their own playing cards which enabled elements or compounds to be compared with one another. The winning card would represent the element or the compound which beat the other card in relation to some particular criteria, such as proton number, reactivity, or mass. This is similar to the way in which vehicles can be compared in relation to price, top speed, number produced per year, and so on.

If one looks at technologies to do with travel, different types of vehicle have held the 'top speed' record at different times. In that race for speed, trains have been overtaken by planes, which have then seen missiles and interplanetary spacecraft whizz past them in turn. Each of these technologies has seen a short period of exponential growth as it has developed rapidly. What may be more shocking is that when these technologies are considered as a whole, they show a sustained pattern of exponential growth in 'top speed' over a period of almost two hundred years.[8]

We cannot know what impact technology will have upon our world and our lives in the coming decades. Technological development may slow rapidly in the next generation. War, famine, disease, economic collapse or natural disaster might change our world and put a spanner in the technological works. Even without such tragedy it may quickly become apparent that technology contains within itself internal limits to its own growth and development. Nonetheless, it may continue to transform our world at a dramatic rate for years or decades, and if so, it will raise profound questions about what it means to be human, and how we live together in our twenty-first century context.

This book has been written in order to provoke discussion of these and related questions. If technological change proves to be minimal, nothing will have been lost. If it proves to be dramatic we will have had a chance to do some work in preparation. If other events intervene to transform our world so that technological development becomes somewhat irrelevant, at least we will have had the opportunity to remember that we are not guaranteed an unchanging context.

* * *

Considering the impact of technology upon human society raises the question of whether or not it is possible to limit technological development. There have been examples within history of communities saying 'Enough' to technology.[9] These include the Chinese and ship building from the fifteenth to nineteenth centuries, the Japanese and gun use during the sixteenth to nineteenth centuries, the Amish in North America in recent times, and global controls on the use of nuclear weapons.

Near the start of the fifteenth century the Chinese had a mighty navy, said to be significantly larger and more powerful than all of Europe's ships combined. Yet within a few years it had been left to rot and the Chinese turned their backs on ship building for several hundreds of years. No one is certain of the reasoning behind this decision, but it seems to relate to political decisions to focus on events within China rather than upon engagement with the wider world. Whether or not this decision was wise, and how different the world might have looked had it not been taken are interesting questions to discuss, but however we might answer them, one fact remains. This decision is a powerful example of the human ability to be discerning in the use of technology.

In the sixteenth century the Japanese turned their backs upon guns. Having been introduced to firearms by European invaders, Japanese craftsmen had excelled at copying and improving upon the guns that were brought from across the oceans. Guns soon became commonplace in Japan and yet they were not to stay for long. The sense of honour upheld by the Samurai led to guns being rejected in favour of the sword. Their decision was based upon the impersonal death made possible by guns, as opposed to the civility and heroism which Samurai society associated with the sword. Once again one might discuss the wisdom of such a judgement and its consequences, yet it provides a second example of human will restricting technological 'progress'.

A contemporary group of people who demonstrate the possibility of a discerning approach to technology are the Amish of North America. Television documentaries may poke fun at their decisions to remain disconnected from the national electric grid and to apply strict guidelines for the use of cars and telephones, but they too prove that it is possible, even in the twenty-first century, to be discerning about one's engagement with one's technological context.

The development of nuclear weapons in the mid twentieth century changed the possibilities for destruction within war and since that time humanity has faced the threats of living in a nuclear age. Yet, we can celebrate the fact that nuclear weapons have not been used in anger since the bombing of Hiroshima and Nagasaki almost seventy years ago. There have been obvious incentives and motivations for this restraint, and we cannot be certain how long such restraint may last, yet this reality provides another powerful example that access to a technology does not make its use inevitable.

These four examples do demonstrate the possibility of limiting the impact of technology upon society. Yet these examples only relate to specific technologies, particular communities and certain time periods. Even the global example of nuclear weapons only demonstrates the restraint of that community of people who have been able to influence whether or not such weapons are deployed. These examples do not demonstrate human ability to turn back the full technological tide much more than my own personal decisions concerning mobile phone use will affect the development of the next generation of smartphones.

Our personal engagement with technology is important but universal patterns will be determined by social trends rather than individual exceptions. I choose not to carry a mobile phone with me on a regular basis yet I do not pretend that is likely to make technological companies fear for their future profits. My decision is about discerning how to embrace some but not other aspects of technology in order to live in the way I sense God has called me to. For me, this includes seeking to be as fully present as possible with whoever is currently with me. I am not trying to model a use of mobile phones which I hope others will follow. I do not wish or expect others to do as I choose to do. Yet neither do I feel compelled to adopt a particular technology simply because others are doing so.

Technology has a life of its own which goes beyond particular gadgets and the specific decisions of individuals or societies.[10] This book has not been written to argue that technological 'advance' needs to be stopped. Such efforts would be likely to be as futile as attempts to stop the earth rotating about its axis. Yet that is no reason to ignore the impact of technology upon our society today. Whilst we can neither undo technological change nor stop its future impact, we do need to be discerning about our use of technology. The Genesis accounts of the Ark and the Tower of Babel emphasise that point. We are required to use technology, like all God's gifts, for the purposes for which they were given. It is the responsibility of the Church to live as the body of Christ in whatever context we may find ourselves, and in the coming years that environment is likely to be shaped, at least in part, in relation to technology.

Questions for discussion

1. Can you think of valuable gifts you have received which have required careful thought in order to use them well?

2. Are there other biblical passages which come to mind, in addition to those mentioned in this chapter, which may reveal more of how Christians are called to live in a technological world?

3. Do you have a sense of the role of technology within God's plans and purposes?

4. Can you think of times when you have been able to use technology to serve God? If so, can you identify any themes which those times had in common?

5. Have you ever experienced technology taking on a life of its own, despite your own best efforts to use it for good?

6. How does your experience relate to the idea of technology growing exponentially within our society?

7. What are you most excited about, and most fearful about, as you think about the future?

8. Are there aspects of technology to which you would like to say 'Enough'? Do you think it might be possible to do that?

9. Which, if any, boundaries have you already put in place in relation to your own use of technology?

10. Do you have any sense of how God may be calling you to live in relation to him and other people within our technological world in the years ahead?

Notes

[1] Accounts of these two stories may be found in Genesis: 6:5–9:17 and 11:1-9.

[2] Brian Brock is one of many authors to contrast these two technological projects of Noah's Ark and the Tower of Babel. He does so within his 2010 book *Christian Ethics in a Technological Age*, p227. That book offers a rigorous theological engagement with technology as a whole. He draws upon the work of a number of theologians and philosophers to identify how a Christian understanding of subjects such as worship, work, rest, food and sex might illuminate ways of living as a Christian in our technological context. His book provides a good starting point for those wishing to research the theological background of the issues of this chapter.

[3] Pete Moore's book *Babel's Shadow*, published in the year 2000, likens certain uses of genetic technologies to the building of the Tower of Babel. He argues that contemporary human confidence in science, medicine and technology has parallels with the Babylonian tower-builders 'seeking to display their pride in their own capability and self-sufficiency', p10. His book was written at the time when the first draft of the entire human genome was being announced and Moore explores the similarities between our contemporary culture with its successes and accomplishments and that of those tower-builders so many years before.

[4] Genesis 3.

[5] There are numerous reports of tool use amongst other primates. These include the use of sticks by gorillas as aids for walking, by orangutans to measure the depth of water, and by chimpanzees to break into a bee hive to extract honey. Reports of tool use within other species include elephants moving objects in order to stand upon them to access food, otters using stones to break open a shell, and seagulls dropping shells onto roads in order that cars will run over the shells and release the contents.

[6] Ray Kurzweil recounts this legend within his 1999 book *The Age of Spiritual Machines*, p36-9.

[7] Gordon Moore, a leading inventor of integrated circuits is credited with first associating this pattern with technology through his predictions in the 1960s and '70s that computing chips will shrink by half in size and price every year or two. Moore's Law, as it is now known, has continued to hold for fifty years and shows no signs of becoming invalid in the near future. Similar exponential trends have been observed in numerous other technological areas. Ray Kurzweil provides many examples in his 2005 book, *The Singularity is Near*, p66-84. Kevin Kelly also discusses some in his 2010 book, *What Technology Wants*, p157-73.

[8] This is one of the examples which Kevin Kelly uses in the section mentioned in the previous note.

[9] Bill McKibben describes the examples which follow, in more detail, within his 2003 book, *Enough: Genetic Engineering and the End of Human Nature*, p171-9. He acknowledges that these cases do not prove we will be able to hold contemporary technologies in check but he does urge his readers to work towards that goal. His accessible writing puts forward the case that we need to be discerning in our use of technology if we are to avoid it sweeping us along a path we would not choose to travel.

[10] Jacques Ellul discusses this aspect of technology and its impact upon all areas of life in his 1964 book *The Technological Society*. The significance of his concern has only increased since he wrote. Ellul used the word *technique* to express the overarching phenomenon which goes beyond particular technologies to an entire cultural effect. He made a convincing case for the ways in which our society's embrace of *technique* transforms our very nature, p319-427. He associated *technique* with efficiency and saw it as exerting a transformative effect upon society not only through technology but also through the impact of *technique* within politics, institutions and social relationships and all the ways in which being human is sacrificed on the altar of efficient doing.

More recently Kevin Kelly has described a related overarching phenomenon as the *technium*, which he defines as 'the greater, global, massively interconnected system of technology vibrating all around us'. See *What Technology Wants*, p11-7. Kelly understands individual technologies as contributing to this *technium* that affects all aspects of human life; he describes it as having a life of its own and representing a new phase of life on earth. As evolution has led from single-celled organisms to more complex life forms, so too, the emergence of conscious thought has led to technology and now to the *technium*. Kelly's *technium* is more organic than Ellul's *technique* and Kelly views it with far more hope and excitement than Ellul does *technique*, yet they both draw attention to the fact that technology is far more than simply disconnected innovations.

Chapter 2

INTRODUCING HUMAN ENHANCEMENT

'Be perfect, therefore, as your heavenly Father is perfect.'
Matthew 5:48

'Do not be conformed to this world, but be transformed by the renewing of your minds, so that you may discern what is the will of God – what is good and acceptable and perfect.'
Romans 12:2

"That looks better" I declared, and my four year old son looked delighted. He stood before me dressed in brown pyjamas with a tail, and with a cardboard shell upon his back. He had been trying to work out how to dress up as a cross between two different animals. This was his attempt at morphing a monkey with a sea turtle. It was a good attempt and it justified the description 'better', but it would not have been a 'better' way to dress in school uniform or to clothe himself for going out to play football. The word 'better' had meaning when I used it within that one particular context but it would have ceased to express any kind of truth if my son had taken it to mean that such clothing was always 'better' in some universal way.

This book is about Human Enhancement and what it means to become 'better' people. This particular technological quest will be used as a focus for engaging with the wider issues of technological change presented in the previous chapter. The hope is that through detailed engagement with this one specific area of technology, we will gain insights which will illuminate the broader field. We will return to the implications of this exploration for that overarching subject within the final chapters of this book.

Human Enhancement is about using science, medicine and technology, not to make sick people 'better', but to attempt to make 'better' people. Of course, that whole quest depends upon what we mean by 'better'. It raises questions about whether or not it is possible to improve upon the human species and, if so, what that might mean. These questions at the heart of Human Enhancement mean that it is difficult to define the term with any clarity. Nonetheless it is reasonable to think about Human Enhancement as attempts to improve people and the visions which drive those attempts. This technological quest is still in its infancy but it is quickly gathering momentum and fuelled by recent developments in science, medicine and technology, those who advocate enhancement have ambitious plans for the future.

Stating that those who advocate enhancement have ambitious plans is actually something of an understatement. Some see Human Enhancement as offering the means of living to be a thousand[1] or of uploading oneself into a computer network so as to gain electronic immortality[2]. As if that were not enough, some argue that Human Enhancement will bring about genetically engineered children who will go on to become the parents of a myriad posthuman species.[3] Distant parts of the universe will become colonised by various species each descended from genetically engineered human ancestors.[4]

* * *

I recognise the danger in that I may seem to have descended rapidly from the realism of Chapter One to an absurd and unnecessary hysteria in the space of a few paragraphs. Such visions of the future

16

may be seen as no more than science fiction and engaging with them theologically as akin to discussing angels on pinheads.

I accept that those who describe these future scenarios make bold and imaginative leaps from what is technologically possible today to what may one day be possible. These futures may never come about. Yet I think there are two good reasons for taking these scenarios seriously. The first is that there are already many people working towards such goals. Whether or not these teams succeed, their attempts to create these futures are likely to affect our society over the coming decades and I think that means we need to discuss these visions. The second reason is that these visions are not the dreams of lunatics. The vision of an uploaded future, in which we will be able to obtain immortality through forsaking our flesh and bone home, house ourselves within a computer network, and adopt and discard physical and virtual bodies at will is proposed by Ray Kurzweil.[5] Kurzweil is not a naive dreamer. Bill Gates, whose credentials in technology are well-established, has described Kurzweil as the one person best placed to predict the future of artificial intelligence.[6]

Technology is now changing our world faster than ever before. Changes which previously took place over a century may now be observed in a generation or as little as a decade. Were we to describe our contemporary context to someone living in England just before the start of the First World War they might be forgiven for dismissing our description of today's society as laughably unbelievable. My own conclusion is that we need to resist the urge to dismiss these visions too quickly. It is true that they may well never come about. None of us can know the detail of the future. Yet, if we fail to engage with the visions of the future which others are pointing to and working towards, we may miss any opportunity we have to shape the future drawing upon biblical insights and Christian understanding. If we are not aware of the future that others are working towards, we will not be able to speak into that context with the wisdom and love which society may need if the weak and the vulnerable are to be cared for and protected.

* * *

When thinking about Human Enhancement it is easy to blur what is possible now, what is currently being attempted, and what is no more than a dream for the future. Science, medicine and technology move on very fast and published statements on the state of play quickly become out of date. Furthermore, an experiment to achieve one specific objective will often be reported as a small step towards a much larger but less distinct goal. That's why incremental developments in ongoing scientific research can lead to news headlines such as *'Artificial Life' breakthrough announced by scientists*[7] and *Cloning scientists create human brain cells*.[8] The purpose of news headlines is not to convey the specific scientific advance as accurately as possible but to attract the reader's attention to the story. Nonetheless, despite the difficulties of assessing the state of scientific research in relation to Human Enhancement, it is worth attempting to describe an overview of what is possible now, those things which are currently being worked upon, and those projects which are still future dreams.

In relation to which Human Enhancement activities are possible now, plastic surgery and prosthetic limbs are already commonplace. These technologies may be used to restore to health rather than to move beyond it, yet they certainly also involve the possibility for enhancement. A deeper exploration of whether or not it is possible to distinguish healing from enhancement will need to wait until the next chapter but for now it is worth acknowledging that the line between healing and enhancement can be fine and difficult to establish, as followers of Oscar Pistorius will be aware. [Since writing the following section last summer, Oscar Pistorius has been charged with the murder of his girlfriend, Reeva Steenkamp. As this book goes to print his trial has not yet taken place. Whatever the outcome of that trial, Pistorius' involvement in the 2012 Olympic Games laid down a marker in relation to the potential impact of Human Enhancement within competitive sport.]

* * *

As I write, the London 2012 Olympic Games are over, the Paralympic Games have not yet begun and there has been much discussion about the eligibility of Oscar Pistorius to compete against able-bodied runners in the men's 400m. Pistorius, known as 'Blade Runner' was born with a key bone, the fibula, missing in each of his legs. As a result, at 11 months old he needed to have each leg amputated halfway between his knee and his ankle. Nonetheless, he pursued his passion for sport with the use of various prosthetic limbs and he was introduced to running at the age of seventeen. His natural talent and determination, allied with carbon-fibre prosthetics called the *Cheetah Flex-Foot* enabled him to sprint competitively against the world's fastest men.

His prosthetic limbs and his ability forced sporting bodies to explore the question of whether or not his limbs gave him an unfair advantage over able-bodied runners, and so whether or not he ought to be allowed to compete against them. It was decided that he would be allowed to compete in both the 2008 Olympics in Beijing and the 2012 Games in London. Pistorius failed to qualify for the South African team in 2008 but his qualification for the 2012 games prompted much debate. Michael Johnson, the 400m world record holder, argued that Pistorius ought not to have been allowed to compete.[9] The debate included a number of arguments. One was that whilst prosthetic limbs might not yet enable an amputee to beat an able bodied runner, prosthetic technology will develop in the future and decisions now need to look ahead to that time. A second argument was that future athletes who suffer accidents leading to the loss of limbs might discover their times drop when using prosthetics.

As it was, Pistorius became the first amputee to compete against able-bodied athletes at the Olympics. He made it through to the semi-finals of the men's 400m in the London 2012 Olympic Games but then finished eighth and last preventing him from reaching the finals. This achievement, formidable but not threatening for a medal, enabled the world to applaud an athlete who demonstrated the ability to triumph over adversity and to inspire others to overcome obstacles in the way of success. Yet had he obtained a medal, or even set a new world record for the 400m, cries of unfair advantage would surely have been deafening. If such a milestone is witnessed in the future, it may be understood as representing the point when prosthetic technology moves from healing to enhancement.

* * *

When I first started introducing others to the subject of Human Enhancement I got used to people asking me if that meant I was studying cosmetic surgery! The subject does not occupy a prime location within writing on Human Enhancement yet it is a good example of an existing technology which can be used for enhancement purposes. As with the case of prosthetic limbs above, which purposes count as enhancement and which as therapeutic is not always easy to define. Much cosmetic surgery tends to involve changing one's body to get it closer to either a perceived normal or ideal human shape. Nonetheless, it is certainly possible to attempt to use cosmetic surgery to achieve a body shape which is 'better' than human.

I am not aware of any attempts to model one's ears on the Vulcan shape of *Star Trek*'s Mr Spock but such a target might be understood as an enhancement quest. No sooner had I typed the previous sentence than I recognised I had better search the Internet to confirm whether or not such a project had in fact been attempted. Perhaps unsurprisingly, it appears that several people have already succeeded in reshaping their ears in this way. In April 2011 it was reported that 'plastic surgery to achieve pointy ears is gaining popularity among young people'.[10]

* * *

As well as prosthetic limbs and plastic surgery, other existing technologies which might either be understood as enhancement or as pointing towards it include the use of drugs to improve concentration, the selection of embryos for use in in-vitro fertilisation (IVF), and experiments with additional senses.

Ritalin is a drug prescribed to school children who have difficulty concentrating in the classroom. Such a condition has been named Attention Deficit Hyperactivity Disorder (ADHD). Whilst there is a sustained debate around whether or not such difficulty constitutes an illness, or simply represents an increased form of the challenge of any child to settle and study, it is agreed that some children find concentrating harder than others. Providing medical support to these children can easily be understood as therapy and returning them to the state of health which other children take for granted. Yet Ritalin and other drugs which stimulate the brain, such as Modafinil, are finding their way into the hands of some of the world's brightest university students. These undergraduates are using them to cram for finals, in the way that many students of my generation would drink large quantities of coffee.[11] Taking a drug designed to be used by those who have a particular difficulty in concentrating, and using it to increase one's already high ability to concentrate can be understood as enhancement.

Selecting between embryos within IVF treatments so as to choose which embryo will be implanted into the mother's womb and given a chance to develop into a child is also already commonplace. Options for such selection are still fairly basic and include gender and the presence or absence of particular genes relating to disease. Nonetheless, such human influence over the characteristics of a child yet to be born may be considered to be an enhancement of the natural process of procreation. Again, such manipulation raises important questions about how the terms 'better', 'improved' or 'enhanced' are to be understood.

A number of people have decided to use their own bodies to experiment with seeking additional senses. Todd Huffman chose to have a small magnet implanted in his left ring finger and so was able to sense the movement of the spinning hard drive within his computer.[12] He suggests that if computer programmers had his implant they might be able to begin to feel the efficiency of their work.

Kevin Warwick implanted a radio transmitter in his upper arm which triggered doors to swing open as he came near, for lights to turn on around him, and for his computer to welcome him with a greeting of 'Good Morning!' when he approached. In a later experiment Warwick had a 100-pin electrode implanted in a nerve of his lower arm. As well as enabling him to control an electronic hand from a distance, this second implant enabled him to sense his surroundings through sonar signals from a specially developed cap he wore, and to communicate nerve to nerve with his wife who had a simpler implant placed into her own arm for a few hour trial period.[13]

* * *

The restricted access to information concerning developments within military research laboratories means that it is impossible to know what possible enhancements are being worked upon as I write, but much enhancement work can be identified.

The United States Defence Advanced Research Projects Agency, DARPA, sponsors a number of projects which would open up various enhancement possibilities if successful.[14] These relate to military objectives but have possibilities for civilian life too. They include pain vaccines to enable soldiers to carry on working despite what would normally cause unbearable physical pain, drugs to enable soldiers to survive for long periods without sleep, and treatments to enable soldiers to go for prolonged periods without food. They also include drugs to manipulate the emotions and so prevent depression and other emotional responses which might render a soldier incapable of continuing to function.

* * *

What might prove to be possible in the future is unknown and the proposals are limited only by our imaginations. Many of the proposed steps towards the long term dreams of radical life extension, electronic immortality and new species of humans build upon genetic engineering and nanotechnology.

Genetic engineering of humans involves manipulating the genetic material in a person, or an embryo yet to be born, in order to alter the DNA coding of their body. This might affect any aspect of their characteristics. Genetic engineering of plants and other animals is still in its infancy, and in people the science is less developed still. However, a number of proposals hint at what may lie ahead. These include designing a child to excel at one particular sport or in a particular profession.[15] Numerous discussions have involved the selection of embryos on the basis of gender, characteristic and perceived ability. Cloning, a related technology, would allow a 'successful' design of a child to be copied and to be available to others.

Nanotechnology involves the manipulation of small objects on the nanometre level, the scale of the molecular constituents of our physical world, where dimensions are measured in millionths of a millimetre. During the last twenty years or so, techniques of manipulating individual molecules have become more and more advanced and have led to numerous ideas about medical possibilities. These include nanobots, very small devices, within the human blood stream which might increase the capacity of blood to carry oxygen, or might act to repair wounds or diseased tissues.[16] The oxygen carrying capability of such nanobots might enable humans to swim underwater for 15 minutes without external breathing apparatus. Such technology even leads some to suggest that humans of the future might have programmable blood, do without eating, and even do without a heart. For those readers wondering at what point such future beings would cease to be human, they have indeed been described as Humans 2.0.[17]

* * *

As it is hard to define Human Enhancement, so too, it is difficult to say when people began to seek Enhancement. From ancient times, people have written of the quest to live longer, to gain immortality, and to gain power.[18] Yet, it is only with recent developments in science, medicine and technology, that Human Enhancement has started to be discussed as such. In that sense, the subject is only a couple of decades old.

Many of the people who have helped to shape early discussions on Human Enhancement have been scientists and ethicists. Some of those who have been particularly involved have been those who

24

would call themselves Transhumanists. Theologians have also made contributions to the debate, but so far that theological engagement has been fairly limited.[19]

Transhumanists are people who aspire to being more than human, to be what has been called posthuman, by using scientific and technological tools.[20] The idea of a posthuman is a being with vastly greater abilities than human beings currently have.[21] So, a posthuman might live to be thousands of years old, might be able to communicate telepathically with other posthumans, and their brain might be part of a future Internet. They might have been genetically engineered to excel as a runner, or a swimmer, or a dancer. Human Enhancement involves the incredible question of whether the continued existence of human beings might be less important than their changing into a future form, albeit one with what we might consider to be superpowers.[22]

* * *

I used to wear a T-shirt which said 'Go against the flow' and which had an image of many fish, just one of whom was swimming in the opposite direction to all the others. Underneath the image, in small writing, was the reference from Paul's letter to the Romans quoted at the beginning of this chapter: 'Do not be conformed to this world but be transformed by the renewing of your minds'. As a university student grappling with issues of living as a Christian within a culture which seemed to regard Christianity as an unnecessary relic from the past, I found encouragement in the message of not conforming to the world. I look back with real gratitude to so many people around me at the time who helped me and others to think through issues of what it means to be transformed by the renewing of our minds, so as to discern what it means for us to serve God.

My character can include the desire to fit in, and so the encouragement not to be conformed to the world was one that I found usefully liberating at that time. It helped give me the courage to do what I sensed I needed to do in response to God's call without feeling restricted by what others would think of that. Yet, I recognise that there is very little which is unusual about a university student, or any other young person for that matter, not conforming to the world! As well as the need to fit in and to be accepted, many of us when we are young seem driven to cast off the restrictions and impositions of those around us and to establish our own identity. University cities are crammed full of young people experimenting with the freedom of early adulthood and casting off the conforming to parental rules which has often been so restricting in the recent past.

In his letter to the Christians in Rome, Paul recognises that the Church will need to avoid being squashed into the world's mould. Such resistance will not be a sign of immaturity or a petulant desire to avoid doing what one is told, but a necessary protection against losing one's God-given role. Only by resisting the world's pressures will it be possible for God's people to be free to love and to serve in the counter-cultural way to which they are called.

There are different ways to avoid conforming, and so too different ways to seek the transforming of our minds, and different means of seeking perfection. The perfection to which Jesus called his disciples was not the result of steroid-grown muscles, airbrushed beauty, or drug-enhanced psychedelic creativity. It was a perfection of character, sacrificially demonstrated through love of God and love of neighbour. These conflicting understandings of transformation and perfection are central to 'Human Enhancement' and to this chapter.

Human Enhancement raises profound questions about progress, development and the significance of being human. Of the many technological issues which human societies will face in the coming decades, Human Enhancement is likely to be one of the most significant. This is because it reaches deep down into what it means to be human. Many of the other technological issues will influence the shape of the world to come, but few are likely to affect the nature and identity of human beings as much as Human Enhancement.

Human Enhancement makes a good focus for an exploration of issues of technology because it is a relatively new area in which there is still much work to be done in terms of understanding some of the issues involved. Yet it has also been around for long enough that it has already stimulated a flourishing debate.[23] Concerning as it does the human body and mind, it is perfectly placed for exploring issues of what it means to be human in a technological world.

Questions for discussion

1. In what senses is it possible for a person to become 'better'?

2. Are the ideas of people living to be a thousand, or uploading themselves into a computer system so ridiculous as to mean we do not need to consider them? On what basis may we form a judgement about this?

3. What experience do you have of media headlines sensationalising scientific, medical or technological developments?

4. How do you feel when you see an athlete using prosthetic limbs competing against able-bodied competitors?

5. How do you react to the idea of people seeking to modify their ears so as to make them resemble those of Mr Spock or an elf?

6. Do you think the use of drugs such as Ritalin amongst university students needs to be monitored, or regulated or prohibited?

7. Is the idea of gaining an extra sensory experience, such as that offered by having a magnet implanted in a finger, appealing to you?

8. Can you empathise with the Transhumanist quest to become 'better' than human?

9. In what ways, if any, do you experience pressure to conform to the world?

10. What might the benefits be of exploring Human Enhancement as a means of engaging with other issues of technology within our society?

Notes

---

[1] In his 2007 book *Ending Aging*, Aubrey de Grey writes that 'I expect many people alive today to live to one thousand years of age and to avoid age-related problems even at that age', p325. The thinking behind this incredible statement is explored in more detail in Chapter Four.

[2] Within Ray Kurzweil's 2005 book *The Singularity is Near*, Kurzweil describes how what he calls 'software-based humans' will be 'vastly extended beyond the severe limitations of humans as we know them today. They will live out of the Web, projecting bodies whenever they need or want them, including virtual bodies in diverse realms of virtual reality, holographically projected bodies, foglet-projected bodies, and physical bodies comprising nanobot swarms and other forms of nanotechnology', p325.

[3] In his 1999 book *Remaking Eden* Lee Silver imagines how humans might diverge into two species, the GenRich and the Naturals and how in time, these two species would diverge further producing dozens of different species of human descendents, p288-90.

[4] In his book mentioned in the previous note Silver writes: 'Eventually, the descendents of humankind will travel through millions of centuries, explore millions of worlds, and diverge into millions of species with little resemblance to the humans of the twentieth century', p290.

[5] *The Singularity is Near*, p325.

[6] Within the opening quotes praising *The Singularity is Near*, Bill Gates is quoted as saying 'Ray Kurzweil is the best person I know at predicting the future of artificial intelligence' piii.

[7] *'Artificial life' breakthrough announced by scientists* was a headline on the BBC website on 20th May 2010. The article described the removal of genetic material from a bacterial cell, followed by the insertion of a synthetic genome. Thus the phrase 'artificial life' in the headline actually described synthetic genes within a natural bacterial cell. Significant as this accomplishment was, the headline may be read as promising more than was actually delivered by the scientific breakthrough.

[8] *Cloning Scientists create human brain cells* was a headline in *The Observer* Newspaper on Sunday 29th January 2012. The article described a breakthrough in which human skin cells had been turned to stem cells from which brain cells had successfully been grown in a laboratory. Whilst reporting on a significant scientific success, as in the previous note, the word 'create' within the Newspaper headline seems to promise the ability to form from nothing, whereas what was actually described was the, albeit impressive, transformation of one cell type into another.

[9] An article by Oliver Pickup in *The Daily Telegraph* of 17th July 2012, under the headline *Games legend Michael Johnson believes Oscar Pistorius has an unfair advantage* quotes Michael Johnson as stating 'my position is that because we don't know for sure whether he gets an advantage from the prosthetics that he wears it is unfair to the able-bodied competitors'.

[10] On 7th April 2011 the *ABC News* website reported this phenomenon under the headline *Elf Ears Are the Rage Among Quirky Young Adults*. The article described young people choosing the painful and irreversible surgery in order to look like *Star Trek*'s Mr Spock, or elves, such as those from the *Lord of the Rings* films. See http://abcnews.go.com/Health/ear-pointing-surgery-elf-ears-mr-spock/story?id=13317198, accessed 30th April 2013.

[11] In his 2002 book *Our Posthuman Future* Francis Fukuyama explores the increasing use of Ritalin and other psychotropic drugs. An article published on the BBC News website on 23rd October 2008 and entitled *The Ritalin Express* described 'chemical enhancement' spreading through academia as students 'go to extreme lengths to get the right grades'. See http://news.bbc.co.uk/1/hi/7684963.stm, accessed 12th October 2012.

[12] Pete Moore interviewed Todd Huffman about his implant and describes the encounter and the implant in his 2008 book *Enhancing Me,* p117-35.

[13] Moore describes Kevin Warwick and his experiences in the next chapter of the book described in the previous note, p137-59.

[14] In his 2005 book *Radical Evolution*, Joel Garreau describes a number of such projects being sponsored by DARPA at the time of his writing.

[15] Lee Silver imagines a future in which 'One subtype of GenRich athlete is the GenRich football player, and a subtype is the GenRich running back. Embryo selection techniques have been used to make sure that a GenRich running back has received all of the natural genes that made his unenhanced foundation ancestor excel at the position. But in addition, at each generation beyond the foundation ancestor, sophisticated genetic enhancements have accumulated so that the modern-day GenRich running back can perform in a way not conceivable for any unenhanced Natural. ... Another GenRich type is the GenRich scientist'. *Remaking Eden*, p5-6.

[16] Ray Kurzweil describes nanobots as 'small robots the size of human blood cells or smaller that can travel inside the bloodstream' and explores their medical potential in *The Singularity is Near*, p253-5.

[17] Ray Kurzweil states that 'the intertwined revolutions of (genetics, nanotechnology and Artificial Intelligence) will transform our frail version 1.0 human bodies into their far more durable and capable version 2.0 counterparts', in *The Singularity is Near*, p299-300. Steve Fuller explores this subject in his 2011 book, *Humanity 2.0: What it means to be Human, Past, Present and Future.*

[18] The *Epic of Gilgamesh* which dates back to around the twenty-first century BC is one example of an ancient description of the human quest for immortality. In his 2008 book, *The Living End*, Guy Brown draws upon this ancient text as he explores the human search for immortality, p63-9. More recently, Friedrich Nietzsche's writing on the 'Übermensch' or 'overman' and J.B.S. Haldane's 1923 essay on Daedalus provide other examples of the enhancement quest which pre-date the contemporary period in which the quest has been referred to as 'Human Enhancement'.

[19] As the roots of the enhancement quest pre-date its recent emergence as a subject of ethical debate, so the start of theological engagement with the field is difficult to identify. C. S. Lewis' 1943 book, *The Abolition of Man*, Paul Ramsey's *Fabricated Man* from 1970, and Oliver O'Donovan's *Begotten or Made* from 1984 can all be placed within the bounds of theological engagement with enhancement, if one accepts that qualifying works may pre-date contemporary interest in the subject and need not include the phrase 'Human Enhancement' itself.
Recent significant theological contributions to the Christian perspective on Human Enhancement include the 2002 book, *Human Genetics* by Robert Song, and *From Human to Posthuman: Christian Theology and Technology in a Postmodern World* by Brent Waters, from 2006. Celia Deane-Drummond has also been influential, both through her own writing and also in encouraging others to write articles on the subject. Key books which she has been involved in editing include the 2003 book *Brave New World?: Theology, Ethics and the Human Genome* and the 2006 book *'Future Perfect? God, Medicine and Human Identity'*.

[20] This definition comes from the writing of Nick Bostrom in the 2003 document *Transhumanist Values*, p1. Bostrom is a founder of the *World Transhumanist Association*, now called *Humanity Plus*.

[21] This definition is also found in the article by Bostrom mentioned in the previous note.

[22] Ray Kurzweil, in *The Singularity is Near*, p31-2, 202-3, and Lee Silver, in *Remaking Eden*, p4-8, both imagine a future in which natural humans continue to exist alongside their enhanced posthuman neighbours. Yet in both these imagined scenarios there is an acceptance that these unenhanced humans will be unable to compete with or even relate deeply with those who are enhanced. Thus the survival of humans in such scenarios seems to be dependent upon the enhanced choosing to allow the ongoing existence of the unenhanced.

[23] A key introduction to Human Enhancement, admittedly from a decidedly pro-enhancement perspective, is provided by the 2008 book *Human Enhancement* edited by Julian Savulescu and Nick Bostrom. A very different take on the subject is found in Michael Sandel's 2007 short book, *The Case against Perfection*. A Human

Enhancement Study carried out by the European Parliament in May 2009 (IP/A/STOA/FWC/2005-28/SC35, 41 & 45; PE 417.483) argued that the literature on Human Enhancement had reached a critical mass, qualifying it as a major topic of ethical research.

Chapter 3

Key issues raised by Human Enhancement

'Then (Jesus) called the crowd to him and said to them, "Listen and understand: it is not what goes into the mouth that defiles a person, but it is what comes out of the mouth that defiles. ... Do you not see that whatever goes into the mouth enters the stomach, and goes out into the sewer? But what comes out of the mouth proceeds from the heart, and this is what defiles. For out of the heart come evil intentions, murder, adultery, fornication, theft, false witness, slander. These are what defile a person, but to eat with unwashed hands does not defile."' Matthew 15:10-11, 17-20

'When the scribes of the Pharisees saw that he was eating with sinners and tax collectors, they said to his disciples, "Why does he eat with tax-collectors and sinners?" When Jesus heard this, he said to them, "Those who are well have no need of a physician, but those who are sick; I have come to call not the righteous but sinners."'

Mark 2:16-17

My grandfather's birthday is in early July and so it often falls close to the final weekend of the annual Wimbledon Tennis Championships. I remember us gathered together as a family to celebrate my grandfather's birthday in 1981 and to watch the tennis when John McEnroe beat Björn Borg to win a Wimbledon final for the first time. It was during that match that McEnroe famously asserted that the umpire could 'not be serious'. The outburst revealed the passion and the emotion which is as much a part of professional sport as muscle development and hand-eye coordination. As a nine year old boy struggling to control my own emotions there was something wonderfully reassuring about the flawed brilliance of McEnroe and his willingness to let the whole world watch his own growth as a man and a tennis player. In subsequent years, as I grew myself, I watched McEnroe continue to grow too and to do so, not just in one area, but in relation to discipline, ability, character and all those other areas of human growth.

We might consider how such maturing and developing relates to becoming 'better'. An important question concerning enhancement is whether or not such improvement is possible through physical, biological and chemical changes alone. This is the first of three enhancement issues which will be explored within this chapter.

Those who advocate enhancement would see changes which lead to increasing one's life expectancy and one's ability to perform mental and physical challenges as improvements. Those who urge caution in relation to enhancement might argue that whilst we may be able to work to bring the human body back to health when it is diseased, to seek to improve it beyond health is arrogantly to assume that we can remake a human being into something different and better. They might point to less tangible criteria such as patience, generosity and self-control as more significant measures of becoming 'better'.[1] Those who advocate enhancement might counter that physical and chemical changes can lead to such improvements in character. One's understanding of what it means to be human, whether or not there is a plan and a purpose to human life, and if so what they might be, all relate to these issues.

The quote from Matthew with which I started this chapter describes Jesus teaching that matters of the heart are more important than external appearances. Whatever the accepted saying may be about cleanliness and godliness, our holiness is more important than our hygiene. The quote from Mark reveals that Jesus has not come to those without problems, but to those in need. These two biblical texts challenge an enhancement quest which seeks perfection by focusing exclusively upon physical, chemical and biological change.

* * *

A second important issue in the enhancement debate involves the question of whether or not it is possible to distinguish between making sick people well and making well people 'better' than well. In other words, it is possible to distinguish between enhancement and therapy. I understand therapy, or healing, to be about dealing with disease, injury or birth defects, whereas enhancement is about seeking to improve upon those without injuries, diseases or birth defects. However not everyone agrees.

An exhibition on Human Enhancement opened in London recently and a video used to publicise the event included images of glasses, false teeth and a hearing aid.[2] Whilst these objects can undoubtedly improve one's ability to see, eat and hear, it is questionable whether or not they represent enhancements.

Those who seek to advocate enhancement will often attempt to connect it to medical treatments and technologies which are generally accepted and valued such as wearing glasses, having a pace-maker, or using a hearing-aid. They therefore seek to show the continuity between contemporary medical treatment and enhancement quests. Those who urge caution in relation to enhancement seek to distinguish it from healing the sick, in order to demonstrate that whilst helping to make people well is a wonderful activity, seeking to improve upon health is a different thing altogether.

One way that people have tried to distinguish between therapy and enhancement is by using the idea of what is normal.[3] Using this idea, therapy is about taking people who are below the normal level in relation to some capacity or ability, and raising them to the normal level. Enhancement is about taking those who are already at or above the normal level and raising them further. For example, giving growth hormone to children suffering with a growth deficiency would be therapy. Giving the same hormone to children who are already of 'normal' or greater height for their age, but who wish to play professional basketball, would be enhancement.[4]

This idea of normal does allow some kind of line to be drawn between one activity and another but it has been challenged as lacking in real meaning.[5] Lines drawn in this way may be seen as arbitrary and of little use in making ethical decisions. This is an important point. The whole purpose of seeking to distinguish between enhancement and therapy is to make judgements about what is helpful and what is not. If we find a distinction but that distinction does not help us to make decisions it is of little use.

Another limitation with the idea of what is normal is that what is normal changes with time. Over the centuries average human height has changed. Therefore taking today's level and using it to allow some children but not others to receive a growth hormone is somewhat arbitrary. There is nothing wrong with an arbitrary line for certain purposes. For example, when a society needs to decide how to spend money on healthcare, there will need to be lines between who will receive care and who will not. There will be limited funds and so it will not be possible to provide limitless treatment for all. Yet such arbitrary cut off points cannot provide any absolute principles for warning against enhancement activities.

Another example relates to vaccinations. Providing everyone with the chance to be vaccinated against a disease such as chickenpox, might be understood as an enhancement in terms of raising the 'normal' level of resistance to chickenpox in the population, yet it is clearly about fighting disease rather than making people better than human.[6]

These examples serve two purposes. One is to acknowledge the difficulty of defining enhancement, and the challenge of separating it from therapy in a watertight legal sense. The second is to point beyond that, to an intuitive sense that we already know something about how to distinguish between fighting disease, and making well people 'better' than human. This is important because the value of healing is well established within Christianity and whatever we may decide in relation to enhancement, it is important to maintain our innate sense that healing is a good thing.

There are many examples in the New Testament of Jesus healing those who were sick. We are told of him curing the blind[7] and the paralysed[8] as well as those with leprosy[9] and internal bleeding[10]. He even raised those who had died.[11] He understood that healing was an important part of the work which he had been sent to do. In the book of Acts, we read of Jesus' followers being involved in similar healing activities.[12] And throughout the last two thousand years the Church has often been at the forefront of efforts to heal the sick through nursing care, and the establishment of hospitals and health systems, as well as through prayer for healing. Our fallen world contains injury and disease, and we point to future hope when we partner with God in seeking to bring health and wholeness.

Even though it may be hard to pin down a distinction between healing and enhancement, we know that working to bring healing is different from the pursuit of immortality through medical and scientific means. Whilst healing is about a regaining of health, the quest to avoid death involves a reach beyond what is human. We may yearn for life after death, but such hope is placed in God's gift not in human accomplishment. We look forward to future intimacy with God, not because we have a great life insurance policy with exceptional medical cover, but because we believe that through his death and resurrection Jesus has opened the way for us to be with him beyond death.

Seeking a distinction between therapy and enhancement is no mere academic exercise. If we can discern a distinction, it is possible to say that enhancement needs to be viewed differently to the good work of healing the sick. If we cannot, it is much harder to argue that there is anything wrong with enhancement, for if healing is good and we cannot distinguish between therapy and enhancement, it is difficult to argue that anything can be wrong with enhancement.

The fact that so much hangs upon whether or not it is possible to distinguish between enhancement and therapy is just one reason why such a distinction has not been universally accepted. Even those who seek such a distinction recognise the challenge of doing so. Nonetheless, those who caution against enhancement argue that though it may be difficult to define such a distinction, the idea of a fundamental difference between therapy and enhancement needs to be held on to, for in such a distinction lies the difference between caring for God's good gift of human life, and seeking to improve upon that gift.[13]

* * *

A third key issue relating to Human Enhancement concerns its religious dimension. Christians continually seek, through prayer and discipline, to become 'better' people. Yet, that sense of 'better' relates to becoming the people we were created to be, rather than seeking to be different from the way we were created. We seek to become more Christ-like, as the Holy Spirit continues to work in us, celebrating the possibility of the gift we were given when we were created human. In the context of Transhumanists seeking to cast off the restraints of our humanity, the Church can point to a different way of becoming 'better'.

It is particularly important for the Church to engage with Human Enhancement, and to do so soon, for the enhancement quest does not simply raise important moral and ethical questions. Human Enhancement is inherently religious, and offers an alternative to Christian faith. Human Enhancement is not, at heart, a scientific project, but rather a religious quest. It does not point beyond religion; rather it is itself, an alternative, postmodern religion.[14]

There are a number of Transhumanists who are perfectly comfortable regarding Human Enhancement in this way, and some have even described working towards a Transhumanist theology.[15] Others downplay religious associations and, of course, those who advocate Human Enhancement will do so from a variety of perspectives and motivations. Some of those motivations will be religious, others will not. Yet, there is a central religious dimension to the enhancement quest which shapes transhumanism, whether or not one approaches it from a visionary, philosophical approach, or from the perspective of an engineering project. That central religious dimension concerns seeking human salvation through human efforts, without reference to God. It is about placing one's hope and one's faith in human accomplishment rather than in divine gifts.

One way in which the ethical and religious heart of the enhancement quest reveals itself is in relation to attitudes towards the weak and the poor. Julian Savulescu, a key proponent of enhancement, was a PhD student of the Australian ethicist Peter Singer. Singer argues that respect for human beings is dependent upon those humans exhibiting characteristics we associate with people, such as conscious thought.[16] On this basis, he goes on to propose that mentally handicapped humans are less worthy of respect than able-bodied higher mammals such as dolphins and chimpanzees. He argues that a severely mentally handicapped human is not worthy of the term 'person', for to be a person involves qualities and abilities which are missing in certain cases of mental malfunctioning. This argument is fundamentally different to the Christian perspective in which it is not human ability which confers value and identity, but God's gift. That gift is not dependent upon human functioning, but upon the love of the Creator, who fashions people in his image.

Singer's perspective can be seen in the writing of Savulescu, his student, who applies Singer's thinking in relation to unborn children.[17] Assuming this association of ability with value, Savulescu argues that people are obliged to have healthy rather than disabled children and therefore that it is good to select embryos using pre-implantation genetic diagnosis. Whilst it is true that good parents desire good things for their children, Savulescu is not dealing with a situation where a single child might be born with or without a genetic disease. Savulescu is writing of choosing between two embryos, either but not both of which will be given a chance to live, and choosing on the basis of ability. This feels uncomfortably like a child's nightmare of being asked to choose between their two parents. A child ought not to be asked to choose between their parents. There is an assumption in the very question which needs to be challenged. Similarly, the Christian call to welcome children, to love our neighbour as ourselves, and to offer special protection and support for the weak and the helpless within the community, points towards another way of relating to children than choosing which of two embryos deserves the gift of life.

40

The way in which those who advocate Human Enhancement write of God is also revealing in relation to identifying enhancement as a religious quest. One theme in Transhumanist writing involves turning the concept of God as creator on its head. One such Transhumanist writer describes that God will emerge from the universe as it begins to wake up following massive technological developments.[18] This view portrays God as man's creation rather than the other way around. As man continues to learn and progress, knowledge seeps into the universe itself such that God is formed. This is an example of arrogant foolishness which the psalmist warned against when he wrote 'The fool says in his heart that there is no God'.[19]

Another Transhumanist has written of democratic science as being the new religion.[20] The common theme within Transhumanist and pro-enhancement writing is that whatever humankind's problems, solutions will be found through human will and human accomplishment. There is no need of support from an imagined deity. Transhumanism arrogantly rejects the need for God's activity, and that demands a Christian response. We will not know in advance what future technologies will open up as possibilities for Transhumanist projects. Nonetheless, it is possible and necessary to name transhumanism as a religious quest, and to point to Christ and the genuine hope he offers for the present and the future.

This religious dimension to Human Enhancement means that as well as the practical efforts to improve humans, it also involves the visions behind such attempts. The next chapter will explore three such visions.

Questions for discussion

1. Is it important to be able to distinguish between therapy and enhancement?

2. Do you have an innate sense of the difference between making a sick person well and of making a healthy person better than well?

3. Do you consider wearing glasses to be a form of enhancement or therapy?

4. Is the concept of what is 'normal' helpful in terms of classifying an activity as therapy as opposed to enhancement?

5. How do you react to the claim made in this chapter that all forms of Human Enhancement involve an attempt to seek through human efforts a transformation which is only possible as a gift from God?

6. How significant do you feel the visions behind enhancement quests are in relation to the means for achieving those quests?

7. Is it possible to be objective about visions concerning the future of the human species?

8. How important a priority does healing need to be within our world today?

9. Do we have an obligation to have the best possible children? If so, what does that mean to you?

10. Is it fair to claim that transhumanism is itself an alternative religion?

Notes

[1] Paul's description of the fruits of the Spirit in Galatians 5:22-23 offers a specific description of what 'better' means in relation to being human. We are 'better' when our lives are characterised by love, joy, peace, patience, kindness, generosity, faithfulness, gentleness and self-control.

[2] The Exhibition entitled *Superhuman* was put on by the Wellcome Trust and was open from 19th July – 16th October 2012.

[3] Norman Daniels works with the idea of therapy as raising or returning to 'normal' functioning where 'normal' refers to what is statistically normal for the human species. See p25-42 of Savulescu and Bostrom's book *Human Enhancement*.

[4] Michael Sandel explores this distinction in his 2007 book, *The Case against Perfection*, p16-9.

[5] The pro-enhancement ethicist John Harris makes a particularly powerful case against using 'normal' functioning as the basis of a distinction between therapy and enhancement in his 2007 book, *Enhancing Evolution: The Ethical Case for Making Better People*, p36-58.

[6] Norman Daniels and John Harris have debated this issue. See the footnote on p34 of Savulescu & Bostrom's *Human Enhancement*. Their continued disagreement is just one example amongst many of the fact that the debate around whether or not it is possible to distinguish between therapy and enhancement is fraught with conflict and disagreement.

[7] See the following biblical references: Matthew 9:27-31, 12:22, 20:29-34; Mark 8:22-26, 10:46-52; Luke 11:14, 18:35-43 and John 9:1-7.

[8] Matthew 9:2-7, Mark 2:3-12 and Luke 5:18-25.

[9] Matthew 8:2-4, Mark 1:40-42 and Luke 5:12-13, 17:11-19.

[10] Matthew 9:20-22, Mark 5:25-29 and Luke 8:43-48.

[11] Matthew 9:18-25, Mark 5:22-42, Luke 7:11-15, 8:41-56 and John 11:1-44.

[12] Acts 3:1-10, 5:12-16, 9:32-41, 20:7-12, 28:7-9.

[13] In the 2008 book *Design and Destiny: Jewish and Christian Perspectives on Human Germline Modification*, edited by Ronald Cole-Turner, Nigel Cameron and Amy Michelle De Baets write: 'By acknowledging that the line between therapy and enhancement is at many points ambiguous, we do not abandon the need to make this distinction or the extreme importance of our seeking to do so.', p113. They go on to argue that the difficulty of distinguishing therapy from enhancement actually has some benefits, including the fact that it can help us identify what it means for humans to flourish and it can help us consider other reasons why enhancements may be problematic, beyond the fact that we might classify them as enhancements.

[14] As long ago as 1939, C. S. Lewis described 'the scientific hope of defeating death (as) a real rival to Christianity' – see Volume II of his *Collected Letters*, 1931-1949. In *From Human to Posthuman*, Brent Waters expands this point writing: 'The prospect of becoming posthuman is not a profane, postmodern alternative to a modern paradigm, mired and unencumbered by primitive and un-exorcized religious beliefs. Rather, posthuman discourse represents idiosyncratic religious sentiments that have been forged in postmodern and historicist rhetoric ... Posthumanism is not a postmodern alternative to lingering religious beliefs, but is itself a contending postmodern religion', p79.

[15] Heidi Campbell and Mark Walker refer to a 'transhumanist theology' in their 2005 article, *Religion and Transhumanism: Introducing a Conversation*, pvii.

[16] See Peter Singer's 1994 book *Rethinking Life and Death*, p187-222.

[17] In *Human Enhancement*, Savulescu argues that 'morality requires that people have healthy rather than disabled children', p241. On this basis he also argues for the selection of embryos to choose the best children using pre-implantation genetic diagnosis – see his 2002 article *Procreative Beneficence: Why We Should Select the Best Children*.

The September 2012 edition of *Reader's Digest* included an article by Savulescu entitled *It's our Duty to have Designer Babies*, p80-3. This is just one example of the success of ethicists who advocate enhancement succeeding in making their voice heard within the popular press.

[18] In *The Singularity is Near*, Kurzweil writes: 'Once we saturate the matter and energy in the universe with intelligence, it will "wake up", be conscious, and sublimely intelligent. That's about as close to God as I can imagine', p375.

[19] Psalm 14:1.

[20] In *Ending Aging*, de Grey writes: 'Science is in a very real sense the new religion: what individual scientists say can be doubted, but the public scientific consensus is gospel', p312.

Chapter 4

THREE VISIONS OF AN ENHANCED FUTURE

'In the last days it will be, God declares, that I will pour out my
Spirit upon all flesh, and your sons and daughters shall prophesy, and
your young men shall see visions, and your old men shall dream
dreams.' Acts 2:17

The future is both known and unknown. As a father, I know that it is
my daughter's second birthday on Monday, yet I do not know who
will be able to join us in celebrating with her on the day. As a
scientist, I know that the sun will rise and set each day between now
and then, yet I do not know what the weather will hold. As a
Christian, I know that there will be a new heaven and a new earth,
yet I do not know when they will be revealed.

Jesus explained that no one but God the Father knows when the last
things will take place.[1] Such details of the future will always be
unknown to us until they come about. Other aspects of the future
have already been made known. For example, the Bible describes the
fact that Jesus has already won the final victory over sin, death and
the devil, and the outworking of that victory will be witnessed in the
future. The book of Revelation reveals this accomplishment in such a
way that we may find many of our practical questions of detail left
unanswered. Nonetheless, we are left in no doubt about the fact that
God is working out his purposes for humanity and the whole of
creation, and that he has already secured the final victory. That level

of knowledge about the future we can know with certainty. We have a vast horizon of resurrection hope.

My father died of cancer towards the end of 2005 after a few years living with the disease and inspirationally continuing to model the good humour, love for others and trust in God which characterised his life. At one point during his treatment a doctor described a particular therapy as offering a small window of hope. A family friend pointed out that whilst this statement expressed a medical truth it did not realistically express the wider context of hope in which we found ourselves. All of us, my father included, were living in the context of the vast horizon of resurrection hope. No small window can contain hope. We have a vast horizon of resurrection hope.

Further aspects of the future will be revealed by God as he brings about his plans and purposes. For example, both the Old and the New Testaments of the Bible contain descriptions of God revealing future famines in order that appropriate action might be taken in advance.[2] The Bible makes clear that such revelation of the future is to come from God, and that attempting to seek out such details in other ways is both harmful and forbidden.[3] Nonetheless, as the quote at the start of this chapter reminds us, the Bible promises that God himself will reveal dreams and visions of what comes next.

So as we live with both the unknown-ness of the future and also the knowledge that God has achieved the final victory and that we have a vast horizon of resurrection hope, so too we will discover God revealing small details of what comes next. The Holy Spirit is present within all Christians and is constantly leading and guiding. We need to grow in the ability to hear God's voice and to respond to it. As we grow as Christians, God will prompt us about how he is calling us to live, to love and to serve. He may reveal particular details of what comes next as part of his work. Recognising our own frailty and that God's ways are not our ways, we will be wise to be humble and cautious if we attempt to offer to others that which we sense God has revealed to us.[4] Nonetheless, it is important that we maintain an expectancy that God will speak to us. Failing to listen through fear that we will mishear is like seeking to avoid relationships in case they go wrong. The solution to mishearing God's voice is not to stop listening, but to practice listening and to do so in community with wise and mature Christians. Using the Bible, Christian tradition and what others around are sensing as they too listen to God themselves will help us to discern God's voice and to test what we sense him saying to us.

As Christians we can expect God's Holy Spirit to lead us to see visions and dream dreams. The work of the Holy Spirit within us will affect our perspective and vision for all aspects of life, and will give us insights into what God is doing in and around us. The Bible also tells us that, without vision, a people perish.[5] Such visions will be consistent with biblical truths.

Yet not all visions are from God. In the absence of faith in God, we will not be without faith, but will inevitably place our faith in something or someone else. So too in the absence of Godly vision, we will not be without vision, but will turn to alternative visions. Our nature as human beings means that we will seek to find meaning in the world around us. If we reject the reality of acknowledging ourselves as creatures, formed and redeemed by a loving God, we will be driven elsewhere to attempt to make sense of our lives and where we are going. There are myriad alternative visions which attempt to retell the human story without reference to the reality that our identity is rooted in our relationship with God.

Such alternative visions are at the heart of the quest for Human Enhancement. This is because attempts to become 'better' than human are as much about the visions and desires which motivate such attempts as the technologies which might enable such visions to be turned into reality. Visions behind Human Enhancement tend to focus upon living longer, having more control over having children, and upon increasing freedom from bodily limitations. Three authors have been particularly significant in representing these goals and the remainder of this chapter will involve an exploration of their three enhancement quests.

* * *

Aubrey de Grey offers a vision of humans who live very much longer than our current lifespan of up to a century or so.[6] He does not attempt to describe that future in any wider detail but he imagines what human lifespan might be achievable if humans work passionately to resist aging with every effort of dedication. He argues that it is scandalous that one hundred thousand people worldwide die every day from aging.[7] He is determined to do his bit to prevent those deaths and he calls upon others to join him in his fight against aging.[8]

De Grey does not simply offer a dream of living longer. He has written at length of his ideas for defeating cancer, and for tackling six other key causes of aging in the body.[9] He proposes bold and creative possibilities for combating biological aging pathways within the human body. He acknowledges that he does not have the answers to the questions of human aging, yet he offers a framework for wrestling with those questions and he calls upon others to join him in seeking answers, or to provide the funding to allow others to do so.

De Grey's vision for defeating aging grows out of his view that all causes of death are equivalent, and so all equally worthy of being resisted. When he writes of the one hundred thousand people who die each day of aging, he describes this as equivalent to thirty World

48

Trade Centres, or to sixty Hurricane Katrinas.[10] In this way, he writes as if it is the same for an elderly man to die peacefully of 'natural causes' after a happy and fulfilled life, as for a young mother to die at the hands of a terrorist attack.

De Grey's vision of the human body is that it might be maintained much as a vintage car can be kept on the road for as long as desired, so long as enough money is invested in the necessary maintenance and repairs.[11] On the basis of such an understanding of ongoing preservation, aging need no longer be a cause of death, and lifespans will be able to increase dramatically. Furthermore, de Grey believes that the necessary breakthroughs in the fight against aging are within reach.[12] Therefore, as previously reported in Chapter Two, de Grey believes that there are people alive today who will live to be one thousand years old.[13]

De Grey has numerous supporters and his ideas are embraced by many who advocate enhancement. Nonetheless, within the world of gerontology, amongst those scientists who study aging, he is regarded by most as unorthodox, and by some, as a charlatan.[14] His background is in computer science and whilst he has obtained a PhD in gerontology, he did so as an outsider, through his ground-breaking proposals and his substantial and original contributions to the field, rather than through growing in knowledge and understanding from within the discipline. He might be understood as a genius who has had the ability to cross disciplines and to offer clarity to aging research through his fresh perspectives and unusual insights. Alternatively, he might be dismissed as an engaging communicator and captivating character who has bold ideas but little awareness of the scientific realities to which such ideas relate.

It is easy to take issue with de Grey's comparison of the human body with a vintage car, and to his numerical treatment of death. It is simple too, to challenge his scientific credentials and to mock his bold assertions. Nonetheless, his vision is representative of those of a growing number of people who are determined to do whatever is necessary to fight aging and death. It challenges us to engage with the ideas of all who have paid to have their bodies cryogenically preserved in the hope that future technologies will enable them to be resuscitated. Most importantly, it expresses one key strand of the quest for Human Enhancement, namely the desire to live longer, much longer. It symbolises the desire to extend this present life for as long as possible.

* * *

Lee Silver articulates the vision to have greater control over issues relating to having children in his book on human genetic engineering.[15] He describes the lengths to which ordinary men and women have already gone in order to have a child of their own and to give that child the best possible start in life. He then goes on to argue that if those same priorities are able to be allied with 'advances' in medicine and technology over the coming years, we will see parents selecting the genetic make-up of their children so as to enable them to excel in chosen fields such as sport, music, drama, business, or all four.[16] Whilst choices might need to be made about conflicting qualities such as those required to play basketball or to be a jockey, other qualities might happily be combined.

Silver describes a near future in which infertility no longer causes distress,[17] where same sex couples are free to have children which have a genetic connection to both parents,[18] and where cloning is commonplace.[19] He describes a distant future in which the genetically engineered descendents of humans are no longer able to breed with 'natural' humans and thus two, and later more, different species are formed.[20]

Silver's future is not one which he calls others to make real, neither is it one which he describes himself as working towards. Rather he seems to view this future as inevitable, so long as people continue to have the freedom to make their own reproductive choices and the technological resources at their disposal continue to increase. Silver presents himself as a reporter rather than an advocate of such a future. Indeed, whilst he seems to write with some excitement, he is not without nostalgia, and he dedicates the book to his parents, for creating him 'in the old-fashioned way'.[21]

Silver acknowledges that the future he describes carries many echoes of eugenics, the dream of creating a super-race.[22] Such ideas were popular throughout Europe and America in the late nineteenth and early twentieth centuries before their implementation by Hitler within Nazi Germany led to eugenics becoming a dirty word. Silver argues that it was the process of seeking to bring about eugenic goals which was suspect rather than the goal itself.[23] He describes a genetically-enriched population coming about not through social policy or political will but simply as the collective consequences of individual decisions to have a child of one's own and to provide that child with the best possible start in life. Silver argues that this difference in process is important in distinguishing genetic engineering from eugenics. Whether or not this distinction would avoid the subjection of one population to the will of another would depend upon how Silver's natural and genetically-enriched populations related to one another, and whether or not genetic enrichment would be associated with a higher status and value in society. It is hard to imagine that it would not, and that the 'natural' population would not suffer as a consequence.

Silver is a distinguished geneticist and his book is informed by his biological expertise, yet he makes bold and imaginative leaps as he envisages the future. His vision of the future develops as much from his imagination and his creativity as it does from his understanding of contemporary developments in science, medicine and technology. Furthermore, he dates some of the scenarios he describes, particularly those in which the genetically-enriched descendents of humans come to form a separate species to the naturals, over three hundred years in the future.

Whether or not Silver's vision of genetic engineering proves to be an accurate predictor of the future is less important than the fact that it reveals a second key thread of the enhancement quest. Human Enhancement concerns both changing those who are alive today, and also seeking to shape those who have yet to be born. Genetic engineering is a crucial aspect of the enhancement quest for it provides a means of seeking to design the characteristics of future generations.

* * *

If the previous two scenarios are shocking, Ray Kurzweil's vision of the future is more so.[24] Arguing on the basis of continued exponential development in technology over just a single generation, Kurzweil argues that by the mid 2040s a technological singularity will occur.[25] Beyond that point, the world will be changed forever. Genetic engineering, nanotechnology and robotics will reach a stage of development which will mean that it will be impossible to distinguish the biological from the mechanical. In other words, humans and machines will have become so interconnected that it will no longer be possible to distinguish people from robots, nor will such a distinction have meaning.

For Kurzweil such a milestone in the history of life on earth is just the beginning. From the time of the singularity onwards, the universe itself will wake up, and will become suffused with consciousness and meaning.[26] In a dizzy spiral of increasing possibilities, the potential

52

of humans to determine both their own lives and their environment will take off in such a way that human power and influence will be limited only by imagination and creativity. Admittedly, such a scenario does raise the question of whether or not it is still possible to use the term 'human' within this context. Kurzweil himself acknowledges this and recognises that an answer depends upon our understanding of the nature of being human. He argues that 'the essence of being human is not our limitations – although we do have many – it's our ability to reach beyond our limitations. We didn't stay on the ground. We didn't even stay on the planet. And we are already not settling for the limitations of our biology.'[27]

Kurzweil offers a vision of the future in which we continually reassess our understanding of what it is to be human as we transcend previous limits. He proposes that within a generation developments in science, medicine and technology will have reached such a threshold that nothing will ever be the same again. Kurzweil sees this turning point as opening the possibility of immortality itself. He imagines a minority of people choosing not to embrace these technological possibilities but argues that such people will become quaint exceptions.[28] Kurzweil believes that he himself will achieve immortality through caring for his sixty year old body for another few decades until such a point when scientific, medical and technological advances enable him to discard that aging body for a different home.[29] He believes that many others alive today who choose to do so will also achieve immortality. They will do it in the same way, through uploading themselves into a computer network from which they will be able to adopt and discard real and virtual bodies at will.

As with the visions of de Grey and Silver described earlier in this chapter, we cannot know if the vision of Kurzweil will prove to be anything like the future as it will be revealed by the passage of time.

His vision, like theirs, grows out of a deep and informed engagement with science and technology. It would be naive to dismiss it out of hand and without consideration. Yet it certainly places huge and perhaps unrealistic hope in the ability of humans to control and manipulate their environment. A Christian engagement with such a vision cannot be limited to an exploration of whether or not such a vision is realistic. Whether or not such a vision comes about, the fact that Kurzweil and others are working towards it will shape the world in which we live today and tomorrow. Kurzweil's vision is representative of all those enhancement dreams in which humankind takes control of its own destiny and achieves immortality within an earthly utopia. The extent to which our society embraces such dreams is likely to have a huge impact upon the way in which we use our resources and the way in which we treat one another. Kurzweil's vision represents the third and most ambitious of the aspects of the enhancement quest with which we will engage in the remainder of this book.

* * *

These three visions of longer life, of engineering children, and of escaping our aging bodies and achieving an earthly immortality represent the ambitious Transhumanist quest to break free of the restrictions involved in being human. We may be inclined to ridicule these visions as naive fantasies, yet whether or not they prove to have even small glimmers of connection to what the future will actually hold, they are useful in revealing the hopes and dreams of those who advocate Human Enhancement. Whether or not these visions come about, we live in a world where an increasing number of our fellow humans will be making economic, political and personal decisions based upon their desire to see these things come about.

The decisions which will be taken by those who seek a posthuman future will not be taken lightly, nor will they represent hobbies or whims. They represent a faith and hope for which an increasing number of people are prepared to make enormous sacrifices.

Aubrey de Grey argues for investing one billion dollars a day in the war on aging and he has committed his own energies and resources to contributing to that fight. He is not alone. One of the online documents that the Transhumanist community has rallied around is 'The Fable of the Dragon Tyrant'.[30] This fable describes death as a dragon which has been consuming people for as long as anyone can remember until finally, the community says enough is enough and they work to defeat the dragon once and for all.

Ray Kurzweil has invested a great deal of study in learning about the dietary and exercise habits which will maximise his chances of staying alive and healthy for a further three decades. His aim is to place himself in the best possible position for taking advantage of future medical opportunities for further life extension, and eventually for immortality. With his doctor, he has written two substantial books on diet and exercise as part of this process.[31] Kurzweil also ensures that he implements the conclusions of his research within his day to day life. He takes approximately two hundred pills a day, containing various supplements to his diet. He receives an eight hour detox treatment each and every week and undergoes frequent and regular monitoring of various physiological measures. Kurzweil is passionate about his vision for the future.

Ray Kurzweil has an unusual vision but it is hard to dismiss his views as ridiculous. As noted in Chapter Two, Bill Gates, who might be expected to know a thing or two about technology, rates Ray Kurzweil as the person best placed to predict the future of artificial intelligence.[32]

* * *

As the Church seeks to engage within the debate on Human Enhancement these visions are highly significant for they shape the actions of those who seek a posthuman future. They provide the opportunity for Christians to declare that we too yearn for a life which is not limited by death and decay. We can state that we too hope for a future in which our bodies will no longer be subject to the limits and restraints which we presently experience. Christians can also affirm the desire of parents to care for their children. Yet, within the Christian vision, such future hope comes about through the actions of God and not simply as a result of human striving.

These visions are also significant for they are not dependent upon any limits within existing technology. Thus they provide a way of engaging with future issues of technology, even without knowing what those technologies will be, for it is visions such as these which will determine where future funding priorities will lie, and in turn, some of the ways in which people will seek to use technology.

Questions for discussion

1. To what extent is the technological future shaped by dreams and visions?

2. Do you experience hope for the future? What do you understand to be the basis for that hope, or lack of it?

3. What emotions do these visions provoke within you? Which particular aspects of these visions evoke these emotions most powerfully?

4. How do you react to Aubrey De Grey's view that aging and death are scandalous?

5. To what lengths would you be prepared to go, or would you have been prepared to go, to have a child?

6. How do you react to Ray Kurzweil's view that from the mid 2040s the universe will begin to wake up?

7. Whether or not these visions become reality, what difference does it make to our society if some of us are working towards these types of goals?

8. What questions would you most like to ask each of these three men?

9. Is it possible for you to distinguish between aspects of these visions which excite you and those which cause you concern?

10. Are you confident in the scientific credentials of these men? What difference does that make to your confidence in their visions of the future?

Notes

[1] Matthew 24:36 describes how 'no-one knows about that day or hour, not even the angels in heaven, nor the Son, but only the Father'.

[2] Central to the biblical story of Joseph is the fact that God uses Joseph to reveal to Pharaoh that his dream warns of seven years of famine following seven years of plenty. On hearing this warning, Pharaoh then appoints Joseph as his deputy to oversee the appropriate preparation for the challenges ahead (Genesis 37-47). In the New Testament, a report is given of how Agabus stood up and through the Spirit predicted that a severe famine would spread over the entire Roman world. In response, Jesus' disciples took action to support those affected (Acts 11:28-30).

[3] Divination, or the act of seeking to discern the future apart from through God's revelation, is prohibited in Leviticus 19:26 and in Deuteronomy 18:10-12. The word itself expresses the rebellious desire to seek to become like God, the temptation to which Adam and Eve fell prey in the Garden of Eden. However humorously we attempt to dress up modern attempts to predict the future, we can open ourselves up to dangerous and destructive forces if we turn to other means than God's revelation in order to seek to discern the future.

[4] Jack Deere's 1996 book, *Surprised by the Voice of God* explores the experience of God speaking to Christians today. To deny that God speaks today is to discount the experience of the body of Christ and to question the reality of God. God is present amongst us, living and active, and his communicating with us is just one aspect of his activity. As anyone knows who has listened for the voice of God, the challenge is discerning God's voice and distinguishing it from other thoughts, desires, impulses or promptings. I am confident in God's ability to speak, but less confident in my ability to hear. I am glad I am not called to listen alone, but can do that as just one member of the body of Christ, and I am so grateful for all around me who help discern what we need to be hearing of what God is saying, to the Church, to the world, and into our personal lives.

[5] Proverbs 29:18a as translated in the King James Version of the Bible reads: 'Where there is no vision, the people perish'.

[6] *Ending Aging*, p311-39.

[7] *Ending Aging*, p8.

[8] *Ending Aging*, p311-39.

[9] De Grey identifies seven areas of aging which need to be defeated if the fight against aging is to be won. He names these as: cell loss and atrophy; junk outside cells; cross-links outside cells; death-resistant cells; mitochondrial mutations; junk inside cells and nuclear mutations. See *Ending Aging* p32-45.

[10] *Ending Aging*, p8.

[11] *Ending Aging*, p44-5.

[12] *Ending Aging*, p311-39.

[13] *Ending Aging*, p325.

[14] Dr Guy Brown was one of de Grey's PhD examiners. In his 2008 book *The Living End* Brown describes de Grey and his work. He writes: 'De Grey was certainly an exceptionally talented examinee, and very entertaining too. But his unorthodox origins and approach have caused others to raise eyebrows. De Grey wants to stop aging by any means possible, as soon as possible, and is willing to do almost anything to achieve this aim. Thus he is more interested in medical engineering than basic science, and more interested in practical politics and fundraising than academia. ... 28 leading researchers of aging responded to de Grey and denounced his SENS agenda as modern day charlatanism', p229.

[15] The 1999 book, *Remaking Eden*.

[16] *Remaking Eden*, p1-13.

[17] *Remaking Eden*, p78-91.

[18] *Remaking Eden*, p206-222.

[19] *Remaking Eden*, p107-52.

[20] *Remaking Eden*, p4-8, 281-93.

[21] *Remaking Eden*, pv.

[22] *Remaking Eden*, p185-90, 253-5.

[23] *Remaking Eden*, p253-5.

[24] Reading Ray Kurzweil's *The Singularity is Near* had a profound effect upon me and set in motion the train of thought which led to me beginning the research that led to the writing of this book. Kurzweil is a key representative of those who see technology as opening a door to a future in which all dreams may be achieved through human endeavour. In the introduction to his book, Kurzweil describes his love of the Tom Swift Jr. series of books in which Tom would face a terrible predicament before solving the problem using an ingenious idea. Kurzweil describes remaining 'convinced of this basic philosophy: no matter what quandaries we face – business problems, health issues, relationship difficulties, as well as the great scientific, social, and cultural challenges of our time – there is an idea that can enable us to prevail. Furthermore, we can find that idea. And when we find it, we need to implement it. My life has been shaped by this imperative', p2. I hear Kurzweil expressing an idolatrous worship of human ingenuity as opposed to trust in God.

[25] *The Singularity is Near*, p7-33.

[26] *The Singularity is Near*, p390.

[27] *The Singularity is Near*, p311.

[28] *The Singularity is Near*, p31-2, 202-3.

[29] Kurzweil has co-authored two books with the physician Terry Grossman, describing in great detail how to live in such a way as to make it possible to stay alive until the singularity brings immortality within reach. The first of these books, *Fantastic Voyage*, was published in 2004; *Transcend* followed later, in 2009.

[30] *The Fable of the Dragon Tyrant* can be found on Nick Bostrom's website.

[31] *Fantastic Voyage*, 2004 and *Transcend*, 2009.

[32] *The Singularity is Near*, piii.

Chapter 5

FINDING THEOLOGICAL TOOLS WITH WHICH TO WORK

'For it is as if a man, going on a journey, summoned his slaves and entrusted his property to them; to one he gave five talents, to another two, to another one, to each according to his ability. Then he went away.' Matthew 25:14-15

'When the Spirit of truth comes, he will guide you into all the truth; for he will not speak on his own, but will speak whatever he hears, and he will declare to you the things that are to come.' John 16:13

I am not a natural handyman. I remember my father's trepidation when he first let me use his electric drill to put up shelves in my bedroom as a teenager. Yet I still know that using the appropriate tools is important if one is to do a good job and I love watching my young son beginning to learn to use a hammer and a screwdriver. I have great admiration for craftspeople, artists and builders who can create structures of beauty and purpose through using appropriate tools and materials.

We might even argue that the appropriate use of tools is one characteristic that sets humans apart from other creatures and so which relates to being fully human. As noted in Chapter One, humans are not unique in using tools. Nonetheless humans routinely use tools to enable a vast extension of their natural ability. Tool use has developed to such an extent that makers of handheld computers can now boast that 'there is an app for everything'. In this technological context it is as important as ever to keep alert to the tools which God is offering to enable us to make sense of living Christian lives in our society today.

A Christian engagement with technology and Human Enhancement in particular requires God's resources. The technological quest of tower building in Babel reported in Genesis 11 was a quest which relied on human ability rather than God's gifts. The consequences of that quest included the disruption of languages which gives us the English word 'babble'. Unless the Church uses God's gifts to engage with issues of technology, we will be unable to avoid babbling. With the appropriate theological tools and empowered by the Holy Spirit, we can hope to speak with wisdom and with truth.[1] Even speaking in such a way, we may not influence society to act as we recommend. Nonetheless, that is not our responsibility. It is our task to witness to God's work in the world, and to point out the foolishness of acting as if hope for the future lies in human hands. We are resourced with theological tools with which to carry out this task.

The Bible contains the truths we require for a theological engagement with Human Enhancement. Through the work of the Holy Spirit, the Bible provides illumination with which to make sense of God's calling to each of us in our contemporary context. The writing of the Church over the last two thousand years and the wealth of Christian experience are gifts which reveal how those who have gone before us have wrestled with using the Bible to respond to God's call in their own generations and contexts. God is a generous God and we have been given a rich treasure chest of 'talents' to use well.

Using such talents involves Spirit-filled work. We cannot mindlessly look up solutions to questions of genetic engineering or social networking within a biblical index. Asking God to empower us with his Spirit, we need to prayerfully and thoughtfully discover how the Bible provides theological tools with which to engage with Human Enhancement. As in all the work of the Church, such activity is not something we are called to undertake alone, but in community with those around us and resourced with the legacy of those who have gone before us in faith. Work has already begun on this process of engaging with Human Enhancement but very much more work has yet to be done.[2]

I pray that in the coming generation, more and more theological tools, rooted in the Bible and used prayerfully and empowered by God's Spirit, will enable us to engage ever more richly with the subject of Human Enhancement as well as other technological issues. This will help to illuminate these areas and to reveal how we make wise decisions in relation to them. Within this book, I will attempt to work with three key theological tools, those of eschatology, love of God and love of neighbour.

* * *

Eschatology can be an off-putting word. Not only is it a word which is rarely used in day to day conversation but it can also be associated with strange views of the future. Nonetheless, it is important in relation to issues of technology and Human Enhancement for it relates to what comes next and to where we are going. It means the study of the last things, those things which relate to God's final plans and purposes for his creation. It relates to judgement, restoration and a new heaven and a new earth.

As we noted at the beginning of Chapter Three we do not have a complete understanding of the future. We know that God will bring to completion his final victory over sin, death and the devil, but the detail of that is surrounded in mystery. It is therefore perhaps not surprising that we do not always explore eschatology within the Church as deeply as we need to. One result of this is that the area can be unhelpfully hijacked by sensationalist ideas which run the risk of distorting a Christian understanding of the subject or at least overemphasising certain aspects of it. However, as in so many things, accepting that some of our theological engagement with the future has been poor demands not that all engagement stops, but that it improves.

When technology raises questions about the future of the human species, Christian eschatology can offer a long-term perspective on where things are going. Without at least some eschatological framework it is impossible to explore contemporary issues within the wider context of God's activity inside and outside of time.

* * *

When Jesus was asked which was the greatest commandment, he pointed to the two Old Testament commands to love God with one's heart, mind, soul and strength, and to love one's neighbour as oneself.[3] Jesus said that all the law hangs upon these two commands. We are therefore on solid ground if we attempt to engage with issues of technology using these two commands. Of course, it takes work to establish what it means to love God and one's neighbour in the specific and particular situations in which each of us finds ourselves. Nonetheless, focusing upon how a technology raises questions in relation to these two commands is likely to open up important areas for theological engagement with the subject.

The command to love God with heart, mind, soul and strength draws attention to our whole self. However we understand the different dimensions and components which make up who we are, a subject which will be explored further in the next chapter, we are to love God with our entire being. Such love will involve recognising that

God is God and that we are not. It will involve following his commands and seeking to live in accordance with his purposes. It will involve accepting our dependence upon God and trusting him to provide for our needs. It will involve seeking to offer ourselves as living sacrifices, as an act of spiritual worship.[4]

The command to love one's neighbour as oneself draws attention to the various different people who will be affected by each of our decisions. It prevents a restricted view of a situation in which I consider only how my actions will affect me. It reminds me that I am always connected to others, and all that I am and all that I do has an impact upon others.

Whilst love is undoubtedly a central biblical theme it can be confusing, and it is worth noting that it can feed unhelpfully into romanticism and the idea that anything goes as long as it is accompanied by warm feelings. A case has even been made for not including love as a focal image of the New Testament.[5] Nonetheless, as before, the answer to misuse is not non-use but wise use, and love is a central theological tool. The concept of love can be protected against unhelpful contemporary connotations and distortions by ensuring that it is kept connected to God's love for humanity. This love was expressed through Jesus' death and resurrection and it emphasises the place of self-sacrifice within love of one's neighbour.[6]

* * *

These tools of eschatology, love of God, and love of neighbour are not the only theological gifts which God has given to us. There are many other such tools which we might use within our engagement with Human Enhancement,[7] but it is these three tools which will be explored in this book. I pray that they will inspire others, not only to extend the work involving these tools, but to also expand this work by drawing upon additional tools.

Theological tools are vital to engage with contemporary issues of ethics and technology from a Christian perspective but their value lies in relationship with God, as one aspect of seeking a Godly perspective on these issues. They are one dimension of, not distinct from, seeking God's vision for the world and attempting to respond to contemporary issues in the power of his Holy Spirit.

* * *

In early 2012 the cruise ship *The Balmoral* set out from Southampton heading west across the Atlantic towards *The Journey* which had departed from New York. They met on April 14th in order to mark the centenary of the sinking of *The Titanic*. As the band on board *The Titanic* kept up the tune 'Nearer my God to Thee' as the ship went down, so the same music was playing again one hundred years later within two memorial services. The first service marked the collision with the infamous iceberg, and the second commemorated the point at which *The Titanic* sank beneath the waves.

Human history is shaped by the adventuring spirit which led to *The Titanic* setting sail one hundred years ago. Such exploration is intrinsic to our human identity and much of our understanding of previous cultures survives in the form of tales of epic quests and heroic deeds. As with the case of the Challenger Space Shuttle disaster, such pioneering may lead to tragedy, yet that is not a good reason to call for a halt to adventuring. Furthermore, whether or not such a call were justifiable, it would be futile. Humans will always be compelled to reach out in adventure, despite the risks and challenges.

It is right that we celebrate good human accomplishments. It is appropriate that we recognise the engineering excellence which enabled *The Titanic* to set sail. Nonetheless, if we base our hope for the future upon human accomplishments, we are liable to find that we have built upon frail foundations. Furthermore, trusting our future to the work of human hands is both hopeless and unnecessary. God has already secured our future hope, not through human accomplishment but through divine gift. As we remember the sinking of *The Titanic* one century ago, amidst our consideration of the tragic loss of life we will do well to note the fragility of human achievements. The centenary of the sinking of that supposedly unsinkable vessel provides a timely reminder that we will be wise not to place too much faith in the work of human hands.

* * *

The three tools of eschatology, love of God and love of neighbour will be explored in Chapters Seven to Eleven. Before we begin that work, we will consider the significance of a Christian understanding of the human body, in order to draw upon that understanding within future chapters.

Questions for discussion

1. Which tools do you use on a regular basis? How did you learn to use them well?

2. What has been your experience of thinking about eschatology? Have you been put off by any unhelpful engagement?

3. How important do you feel it is to live today in the light of what lies ahead?

4. In what ways is it possible to express love for a God who is all powerful?

5. When do you find it most difficult to express love for others?

6. Is 'love' the central tool for theological engagement with the world?

7. Are there other tools you will use for exploring issues of ethics and technology? If so, what are they?

8. What 'talents' has God given you for use in this area?

9. If God is strong in our weakness, what is the place of developing our competence and growing skill and expertise in using theological tools?

10. To what extent do we need to be celebrating significant human achievements such as the ability to launch ocean-going ships?

Notes

---

[1] The biblical account of the Tower of Babel (Genesis 11:1-9) resonates with many aspects of a Christian engagement with issues of technology. The fact that the consequences of that technological quest led to disruption in relation to language highlights how significant good communication can be. We are not called to babble, like those Babylonian tower-builders, but to guard our tongues and to speak well, with wisdom and truth, remembering the significance of wisdom, affirmed throughout the Bible, and that Jesus described himself as the 'truth'. This requires the Spirit's activity. The outpouring of the Holy Spirit at Pentecost has been seen as a reversal of Babel and we need the Spirit's empowering if we are to communicate with wisdom and truth.

[2] Note 19 of Chapter Two described a few key theological contributions to the enhancement debate.

Celia Deane-Drummond has drawn upon a theological understanding of 'virtue' in order to engage with Human Enhancement. She advocates considering how the theological virtues of faith, hope and charity, as well as the cardinal virtues of prudence, justice, fortitude and temperance might illuminate explorations of what it means to seek perfection. See *Future Perfect*, p178-81.

In *From Human to Posthuman*, Brent Waters draws upon a theological engagement with postmodernism in order to explore how a postmodern perspective contributes to the enhancement quest. He thus draws upon theological tools which have been developed within the engagement with postmodernism and deploys them within the task of engaging with Human Enhancement.

In his 2008 PhD dissertation, Thomas Daly explored the issue of life extension drawing upon the writing of the Desert Fathers, including Athanasius and St Anthony. He demonstrated how the experience and theology of Christians many centuries earlier offer profound insights into our contemporary context. In particular he explored how the ascetic practices of fasting, central to the lifestyle of the Desert Fathers, not only relate to contemporary discoveries about calorie restriction as a means of possible life extension, but point beyond life extension to preparing our bodily selves for their ultimate purpose through resurrection. See *A Theological Analysis of Life Extension via Aging Attenuation with Particular Reference to Ascetic Practice in the Desert Fathers* by T. Thomas Woodford Daly, Edinburgh University, 2008.

One other key theological tool which has been used within the engagement with enhancement includes the weight of theological work exploring the relationship of science and theology. D. Gareth Jones is one Christian writer who uses his skills and experience as a professional scientist to engage with issues relating to the wider context of Human Enhancement within his 2005 book *Designers of the Future*.

[3] Jesus' comments on the greatest commandments are described in Matthew 22:37-40, Mark 12:29-31 and Luke 10:25-28, and draw upon the Old Testament commands found in Deuteronomy 6:5 and Leviticus 19:18.

[4] Romans 12:1.

[5] Richard Hays has argued, in his 1996 book *The Moral Vision of the New Testament*, that the concept of love has 'become debased in popular discourse' and that it may therefore 'produce more distortion than clarity', p200-3.

[6] Gene Outka explores this in some depth in his 1972 book, *Agape: An Ethical Analysis*.

[7] Other tools which might be explored include areas of systematic theology such as creation; thinking of particular theologians such as Aquinas, Barth or Calvin; the application of particular books of the Bible to the area; drawing upon the illumination of particular theological communities such as liberation theologians, and so on.

Chapter 6

SOME BODY TO LOVE

'You shall love the LORD your God with all your heart, with all
your soul, and with all your might.' Deuteronomy 6:5

'If the Spirit of him who raised Jesus from the dead dwells in you, he
who raised Christ from the dead will give life to your mortal bodies
also through his Spirit that dwells in you.' Romans 8:11

I watched a fascinating car advert on the television recently which
involved an actor playing two people. One was the character, and the
other 'their body'. The point of the advert was that if your body
could choose a car, it would be the one advertised. It picked up on
contemporary ideas of our bodies as being somehow separate from
whom we really are. We feel young inside and are surprised when
we see an older person staring back at us in the mirror. The fact that
our body is currently overweight does not reflect the real person
inside. Sex changes are even available for those men or women who
find themselves trapped inside a body of a different gender.

The advert made me smile, but it represents a dualistic idea of the
human person, which is different to that which is described in the
Bible. Dualism involves two separate elements and viewing humans
dualistically, as consisting of two parts, involves thinking of them as
one part soul and one part flesh. In dualism, the all-important soul is
housed inside the transient flesh. In contrast, the Bible describes a
more united view of the human person, where spirit, mind and body

are connected within a single human form. According to this biblical view, my body is as much a part of who I am, and as integral to my identity, as are my mind and my spirit.

A Christian theological engagement with Human Enhancement involves taking the human body very seriously. This means both valuing the body as an awesome gift of God, and recognising the deep connection between one's body and one's identity. It is not possible to make sense of who I am without recognising that I am as much an ensouled body as an embodied soul.[1]

The significance of human bodies is complicated. We know only in part and we disagree on details. It can be hard to reach consensus on the subject. One reason for our lack of understanding is that the reality of what it is to be human touches upon mysteries of creation which will always be beyond human comprehension this side of the grave. Realities of soul and spirit, and what it means to have God's Holy Spirit within us, relate to who God is and to his creative work, and at present we only 'see in a glass darkly'.[2] We deceive ourselves if we pretend to understand God and his works completely.

One matter relating to human bodies which is the subject of contemporary theological discussions relates to the way in which our human form can be understood as a unity. Theologians tend to agree that the dualistic understanding of humans as souls within bodies is rooted not within the Bible but in Greek thinking and Gnosticism.[3] Nonetheless, some of these theologians understand our body-soul unity to be formed in such a way that our soul may exist for a period in a disembodied form after death. John Cooper makes a convincing case for this position drawing upon both the Old and the New Testaments as well as upon writings from the early Church and the intertestamental period.[4] Others argue that our bodies are a fundamental unity in which our identity can never be understood apart from our physical presence.[5]

* * *

As in so many situations when we are struggling to explain mysteries which are beyond human understanding, language can be confusing. The use of the word 'dualism' is an important example. There is widespread Christian consensus around the fact that the dualistic thinking of the Greeks and the Gnostics is inconsistent with a biblical understanding of the human form as an essential unity. Confusingly, though, the word dualism is also used within a theological debate concerning whether or not it is ever possible for human identity to exist in a disembodied form. This has been named the Monism-Dualism debate.

Whilst we might discuss whether the human form is comprised of body, mind and spirit, or body, mind, soul and spirit, there is theological agreement around the idea that the human form is a unity made up of various aspects. Our body is not an optional extra to who we are, but a key component of our nature and our identity. What is under discussion within the Monism-Dualism debate is whether or not that unity can ever be separated without a complete loss of human identity, and that question comes out of consideration of the biblical promise of everlasting life.

The promise of everlasting life is central to a Christian understanding of the future, yet this belief raises complex questions in relation to the human body. We know that the bodies of those who die are not preserved. They may be cremated soon after death, or slowly break down after burial. Even during life, they may have been ravaged by disease or have suffered the effects of injury. Our future hope cannot be based on the literal preservation of our earthly bodies in this corrupted state.

This makes good sense, for not even our earthly existence depends upon the fixed preservation of our bodies at a molecular level. There are all sorts of statistics quoted about the number of atoms in our body which were once part of the body of Julius Caesar, or some other famous historical figure. The reality behind such statistics is that our body is made up of millions upon millions of cells, most of which are dying and being replaced on an ongoing basis. Thus most of our cells will be significantly younger than our own age. Most of the molecules making up those cells will have been derived from the food and drink we consume and will have fascinating histories which will almost certainly have included being part of numerous other living systems, some of which are likely to have been human.

Recognising that our bodies are in this state of constant flux with molecules coming and going makes clear that it is not a particular set of molecules which can define our human identity. So when we argue that our physical form is a crucial aspect of who we are, our nature and our identity, we raise the question of how our physical form can be available to us within everlasting life. We may be prompted to reflect upon how our bodily existence might be preserved the other side of the grave.

Within the Monism-Dualism debate, Monists argue that however God preserves our identity beyond death, we will never exist within a disembodied form for our physical body is intrinsic to who we are. Dualists on the other hand, such as John Cooper mentioned above, argue that it is possible for us to exist in a disembodied form for a temporary period between the time at which we die and the time at which we gain our resurrection body. Both Monists and Dualists agree that our ultimate embodiment takes the form of a resurrection body.

Whilst the Monist-Dualist debate focuses upon whether or not it might be possible to exist in a disembodied form after death, it relates to accounts of out of body experiences whilst alive. I find Gordon McPhate's account of his own experience particularly interesting. Gordon is both a physician and an Anglican priest, he is qualified in medical ethics and in neuroscience, and was Visiting Professor of Theology and Medicine at the University of Chester as well as Dean of Chester Cathedral. He acknowledges he has a problem, for he is intellectually persuaded by the idea of psychosomatic unity, or the sense that the mind and the brain cannot be separated, yet he himself has experienced a profound out of body experience.[6] He writes that he 'was subject to a near-death experience in which my mind was temporarily dissociated from my body, such that I observed my own cardiopulmonary resuscitation following cardiac arrest, from above'.[7] In other words, his intellect leads him to conclude that it is not possible for him to experience anything from outside his body, yet his senses persuade him that he has done just that. We are in mysterious territory!

* * *

Theologians will continue to debate these matters as we struggle to understand more of how God has created us. However, whatever we make of these questions, there is an underlying theological consensus around the issue of resurrection and this challenges many visions emerging with Human Enhancement. As there is theological consensus regarding the significance of the human body and a rejection of a Greek dualistic understanding of the body as simply a container for one's essential soul, so too there is consensus around the hope of resurrection bodies. The Bible describes Jesus himself, after being raised to new life, having a physical resurrection body which was similar to his previous body but also somehow different.

Having risen from the dead, Jesus demonstrated that his body was physical. He ate fish.[8] He invited Thomas to place his hands in his side and to feel the marks of his wounds.[9] Yet Jesus' body was also significantly different. His disciples, those who had spent the previous three years living and travelling with him and who might well be expected to know his appearance particularly well, did not always immediately recognise him.[10] Furthermore, when they did recognise him after his resurrection, it was often by what he said or did, not by his appearance itself.[11] Jesus appeared amongst his disciples within a locked room, a further indication that this body was somewhat different to his previous human form.[12]

The Bible also describes how Jesus' own bodily resurrection both points towards and makes possible our own bodily resurrection in turn. As the first fruits of a harvest reveal what is yet to come in greater measure, so we in turn will experience resurrection as Jesus already has.[13]

This understanding of bodily resurrection, both for Jesus and for ourselves in turn, is a building block of Christian understanding and is deeply rooted within the Bible and Christian tradition. Nonetheless, there is a mythology of souls and bodies which is markedly different to this orthodox view and yet which still permeates discussions of life and death, even within Christian contexts. It is not unusual to hear people within churches speaking of our souls departing our bodies at death and 'going to heaven'.

Whatever happens to us after death, our ultimate identity is not that of disembodied souls but of people with resurrection bodies. We are embodied beings and speaking of our souls departing our bodies at death may reflect more of the Greek dualism which still permeates our culture than of biblical faith. Furthermore, whilst the Bible does indeed promise life beyond death, it does not mention us going to reside in heaven. The Bible describes a new earth and a new heaven. It seems strange to promise a new earth if we will not spend time on that new earth. It is hard to read the Bible without a clear sense that on both sides of death we will experience embodied life within physical creation.

This Christian understanding of embodied life before and after death is in marked contrast to visions of the future found within Transhumanist writing. As described earlier, Aubrey de Grey writes of preserving the human body through maintenance and repair much as a vintage car may be kept in good working order.[14] Chapter Four also described Ray Kurzweil's vision for disembodied existence through uploading one's identity into a computer network.[15] It is important to note that these visions are based upon a very different understanding of human identity to that of Christian theology.

* * *

Whilst recognising the dangers of opening up a whole new kettle of fish so soon after references to the resurrected Jesus eating fish, it would be remiss to end a chapter on the significance of the body without at least touching upon the biblical concept of the body of Christ. A number of New Testament passages describe those who follow Christ as forming his body on earth today.[16] Similarly, the bread and wine of communion are described as Christ's body and blood.[17]

As members of the body of Christ, it is that body which is central for our life and wellbeing. Taking communion on a regular basis is a central act of Christian faith, expressing our dependence upon God for all that we need. The body of Christ is more significant than our own. However, rather than devalue our own physical bodies, this membership of Christ's body emphasises even further the significance of our own embodiment. Christ himself embraced the embodiment which we ourselves have received as a gift. At the incarnation, Christ took on human flesh. After his resurrection, Jesus appeared to his disciples and revealed to them his resurrection body. After his ascension into heaven, he sent his Holy Spirit that his body, the Church, might continue his work, enlivened with the power of the Spirit.

Our bodies have become no less than temples of the Holy Spirit.[18] Thus once again, through the action of God, as we draw close to God our physical form becomes more, not less, significant. At creation, God blessed humanity with the gift of human form. At the incarnation, Jesus affirmed the value of the human form yet further by taking it upon himself. Filled with God's spirit, our flesh and blood becomes a temple of the Holy Spirit. At communion, our flesh is embraced by God as we eat his body and drink his blood, however shadowlike may be our understanding of that mystery. Together, as members of the Church, our bodies are formed into the body of Christ, to bring about his plans and purposes.

For Christians, the human body is of profound significance and engaging with Human Enhancement will involve testifying to the value of the human form and its awesome reality as created and redeemed by God.

Questions for discussion

1. What are the most significant factors which shape your identity?

2. How does your body affect your identity and your understanding of who you are? Does this change with time and in relation to changes in your body?

3. Is your body a true representation of who you are?

4. How do you react to the claim that we are what we eat?

5. How do you picture those you have loved who have already died? For example, at what age and in what state of health?

6. Does your understanding of what happens to your body beyond death affect your thinking of your body today?

7. What do you make of reports of 'out-of-body' experiences?

8. Do you think of yourself as a member of the body of Christ? If so, what does that mean to you?

9. Do you consider your body to be a temple? If so, what does that mean to you?

10. What do you think Jesus meant when he invited us to eat his body and to drink his blood?

Notes

[1] In his 1970 book, *Fabricated Man* the theologian and ethicist Paul Ramsey writes: 'We need rather the biblical comprehension that man is as much the body of his soul as he is the soul of his body', p133.

[2] 1 Corinthians 13:12.

[3] Gnosticism was a heresy within the early church which, amongst other things, devalued the significance of the human body through overemphasising the importance of the spiritual at the expense of the physical.

[4] John Cooper's 2000 book, *Body, Soul and Life Everlasting: Biblical Anthropology and the Monism-Dualism Debate* explores how we might understand the nature of the human form in relation to everlasting life.

[5] Nancey Murphy is a key advocate of the position that human beings are a fundamental unity and that our existence is inherently connected to our physical form. See, for example, her 2008 article *Nonreductive Physicalism and Free Will* available online via metanexus.net.

[6] Gordon McPhate describes his near-death experience within a chapter entitled *Ensoulment Revised in Response to Genetics, Neuroscience and Out-of-Body Experiences* within *Future Perfect*, p100-112.

[7] See *Future Perfect*, p110.

[8] Luke 24:40-43 specifically described the resurrected Jesus eating a piece of broiled fish. John 21 does not mention the resurrected Jesus eating but it does describe him inviting his disciples to have breakfast with him after they caught a miraculous catch of fish.

[9] See John 20:24-31.

[10] John 20:15 describes how Mary Magdalene thought that the resurrected Jesus was the gardener, until he spoke to her.

[11] Luke 24:13-34 describes two disciples on the road to Emmaus who recognised Jesus when he broke the bread.

[12] John 20:19-23.

[13] 1 Corinthians 15:12-58, particularly verses 20-23.

[14] *Ending Aging*, p44-5.

[15] *The Singularity is Near*, p324-5.

[16] Biblical passages referring to the body of Christ include: 1 Corinthians 12:12-31; Ephesians 4:1-16; Colossians 1:18; 3:15.

[17] 1 Corinthians 11:17-34.

[18] 1 Corinthians 6:19.

Chapter 7

NOW AND NOT YET

'Now faith is the assurance of things hoped for, the conviction of things not seen.' Hebrews 11:1

'Then I saw a new heaven and a new earth; for the first heaven and the first earth had passed away, and the sea was no more. And I saw the holy city, the new Jerusalem, coming down out of heaven from God, prepared as a bride adorned for her husband. And I heard a loud voice from the throne saying, "See the home of God is among mortals. He will dwell with them; they will be his peoples, and God himself will be with them; he will wipe every tear from their eyes. Death will be no more; mourning and crying and pain will be no more, for the first things have passed away."' Revelation 21:1-4

The phrase 'Are we nearly there yet?' is familiar to anyone who has travelled on a long car journey with young children. The child feels as if the journey has already been going on for days and they need encouragement that we really will reach the promised destination. I love the scene in the second *Shrek* film where the three companions are travelling to *Far, Far Away* and Donkey is continually asking 'Are we there yet?'! As Christians journey through life we too await what comes next, and with faith we cling on to the conviction of what we have not yet seen.

A Christian engagement with Human Enhancement will be shaped by the fact that we already have a hope for the future. We trust in the promise of intimacy with God beyond death. Jesus himself has promised that in his father's house are many rooms and that he is going to prepare a place for us.[1] As the above quote from the book of Revelation promises, we await a time when there will be no more mourning, or crying, or pain. How awesome!

Ambitious quests to extend life on earth look different in the light of whether or not one has this hope beyond death. The quest to seek immortality through uploading oneself into a computer network emerges from the perspective of those who understand death to be the end of existence. If we have hope of life beyond death, this life is not the be all and end all. Without that hope, we may be left clutching at any possibility of extending this current life for as long as possible, through whatever means might be, or become, available.

A significant contribution which Christians can make to the debate on Human Enhancement is to demonstrate empathy with those who hope for more than a lifespan of 'three score years and ten'. Yet, as well as empathy, Christians can point to a hope for the future which makes it clear that quests to seek within this life for what is on offer in the next, are unnecessary. We do not need to settle for a pale imitation of resurrection life through our own efforts when the real deal, surround sound, full colour, high definition version, is already available through God's generosity.

Christian hope for the future affects life today for it involves living in the present with the understanding that God's future plans and purposes are already beginning to break in upon the present. There is an element of both now and not yet about the coming of the Kingdom of God. Through his death and resurrection Jesus has already won the final victory over sin, death and the devil. Even though that victory has not yet been brought to completion and we live in between times, when the Kingdom of God is both here and not yet fully present, God's victory has already been accomplished.

It is a bit like a child waiting for Christmas and seeing packages laid out under the tree. There may be another day or two to wait until Christmas arrives and the parcels can be opened but it is certain that Christmas will arrive and the presence of the gifts is evidence of that. The Church and the sacraments, such as baptism and communion, point towards Jesus' final victory even though the outworking of that victory is not yet fully within sight.

The fact that God has already secured the ultimate victory offers liberation in the present. Our present experience can be embraced as the awesome gift which it is, yet we do not need to cling possessively to this present life, for we have hope for the future too.

It is this eschatological perspective which is the subject of this chapter and the next. Dietrich Bonhoeffer offers a means of engaging with one aspect of this perspective. Bonhoeffer was not only a brilliant German theologian but a passionate Church leader who was committed to worshipping God and to caring for others.[2] Rather than take the easy option of staying away from Germany during the rise to power of the Nazi party in the 1930s by working as an academic in the relative safety of America, he chose to return to his home country. His commitment to live and to work as part of the Confessing Church in Germany eventually led to his execution in Flossenbürg concentration camp on 8th April 1945, just a few short weeks before Hitler's death and the German surrender.

* * *

Bonhoeffer wrote of the importance of living in the present, recognising the full value of the time in which we live, but without underestimating the significance of what is yet to come.[3] He used the terms 'ultimate' and 'penultimate' to write about the final things which make sense of all that has gone before, and those things which are happening now, which will only make sense when we know the end of the story. He knew as well as anyone that it was important to make sense of the present time. He was writing during the rise of Nazi Germany. He knew that things were going on which were wrong. Evil forces were causing suffering and threatening freedom. In that context, as in ours, we might be tempted to feel that good is losing the battle with evil. Yet, Bonhoeffer pointed to the future, and argued that the present only makes sense when understood in the context of what comes next.

It is as if we are walking along a tightrope and that if we slip off on either side we are in trouble. On one side lays the temptation to take this present context too seriously. If we do that, we will take our eye off the significance of intimacy with God beyond death. Yet equally dangerous is the temptation to slip off the other side of the tightrope by becoming so pre-occupied with life beyond death that we do not take seriously enough the significance of our life today, and the needs and concerns of those around us.

A landscape painter will switch perspective between the foreground, the horizon and their canvas as they work to capture the image of what they see. Bonhoeffer argued that each of us needs to be working with two perspectives at once if we are to live in the present in the light of what comes next. He used the example of being with someone who is grieving for the death of a loved one to illustrate this.[4] If we only point to future hope we risk missing the significance of the present experience of loss and grief. Yet, if we are only caught up in present loss we can lose touch with the hope of resurrection life. Focussing upon the two together enables an appropriate and helpful companionship in the sorrow of now, not risking trivialising that with flippant words, yet with an awareness that this is not the end of the story.

This balance which Bonhoeffer calls us to maintain provides a useful tool with which to engage with Human Enhancement.[5] It gives us one specific way of working with the wider tool of the biblical theme of eschatology.[6] In the remainder of this chapter, the visions of Lee Silver, Aubrey de Grey and Ray Kurzweil described in Chapter Four will be explored with the aid of this tool.

There are numerous other ways in which eschatology might be used within a Christian engagement with Human Enhancement. As in other aspects of this work, my hope is that this engagement might inspire others to try different ways of using Christian theology to illuminate the realities and assumptions within the Human Enhancement debate, and to point to what it means to live well as human beings, created and redeemed by God, living in today's technological context.

* * *

Ray Kurzweil describes a vision of an uploaded future in which humans will be able to discard their fleshy body at will, in order to opt for a less restricting container to their essential self.[7] He invites us to imagine posthuman possibilities involving us becoming software run on various real or virtual bodies. Kurzweil's vision of future hope beyond the failing of our fleshy home, of avoiding death to continue some form of earthly life, is very different to the Christian hope of life beyond death. It represents a desire to escape from the material world and therefore relates to Bonhoeffer's warning about focusing exclusively upon ultimate concerns and losing sight of the importance of the physical world of today. Kurzweil's vision reveals his thinking in relation to the ultimate and the penultimate and so we are able to challenge it on that basis.

Whether or not Kurzweil's vision of an uploaded future proves to be technically achievable it represents a lack of respect for the physical world. Even though Kurzweil writes of being able to make use of real and virtual bodies at will, the idea that our essence might be preserved in a disembodied form this side of death expresses disregard for the significance of being created as embodied beings. Kurzweil is writing as if our bodies are of little value.[8]

* * *

Lee Silver's vision is of genetically engineering future generations of children. This will give parents the chance to select characteristics for their offspring which will provide them with the potential to excel at a chosen field such as sport, music or business.[9] This represents a desire to subject the physical world to our wills, using whatever means are necessary to do so. As such it reveals the same disregard for the material world as is shown by Kurzweil's visions, just expressed in a different way. Instead of a desire to escape from the material, Silver represents a vision in which the material world is dominated in order to force it to conform to human will.

Whatever else we may think of Silver's vision, it is challenged by Bonhoeffer's concepts of the ultimate and the penultimate for it represents an unhealthy disregard for the value of the penultimate and the present nature of the physical world. Silver's future, like Kurzweil's, grows out of an unhealthy focus upon the ultimate. As Bonhoeffer argues will always be the case, rather than affirm the value of the ultimate, such disconnection between the ultimate and the penultimate devalues both.

We might expect that it is particularly important to see the goodness of the future. If such a perspective is balanced by recognising the goodness of the present is too, such a view is certainly healthy. The problem appears if we start to get so excited by the future that we lose touch with the value of today. It is this distorted perspective which Bonhoeffer warned against. He argued that it is only when we think about the present and the future in relation to one another that we can fully appreciate each of them for what they are.

By disregarding the significance of the material world of today, Silver and Kurzweil devalue both the ultimate and the penultimate.[10] By his exclusive focus upon an ultimate goal, Silver misses the possibility of ultimate hope growing out of the penultimate. In other words, he fails to see how resurrection bodies express both how good the physical world is now, and also point to an even more wonderful physical reality in the future.

* * *

Aubrey de Grey's vision, by contrast, represents a tendency to reduce everything to the material and so it relates to an exaggerated focus on the penultimate. By considering the human body as no more than a material object such as a car or a house, de Grey reveals a perspective which misses the deeper reality of living creatures.[11] Christians affirm the value of the physical but they also recognise that it is just one aspect of a world which also involves spiritual realities.[12] De Grey by contrast views life as no more than the physical and in doing so he denies the value of the ultimate.

Bonhoeffer has warned that getting too focused upon the present actually leads us to devaluing both the present and the future. Therefore de Grey's sense of human life as no more than physical existence does not affirm the physical; instead it degrades it by trying to separate it from its ultimate future significance. From a Christian perspective the physical world, with which de Grey is concerned, has value as part of creation. That is wonderful. But it also has value in relation to Jesus' incarnation and to the new creation. If we truly want to celebrate the physical world we need to recognise its significance now and also as part of God's ultimate purposes. De Grey's vision fails to do that.[13]

* * *

In this way, Bonhoeffer's concepts of the ultimate and the penultimate provide a useful means of critiquing enhancement visions such as those of Chapter Four. They also offer a means of considering how versions of such visions might be adapted in such a way as to avoid a distorted focus upon either the ultimate or the penultimate. For example, Kurzweil's vision of attempting to upload one's human identity into a computer network expresses a disregard for the penultimate. Considering this uploading attempt raises questions about other forms of uploading.

Uploading aspects of one's identity such as personal photographs, journal entries and personal details is commonplace in the early twenty-first century. Yet not all uploading of this kind necessarily expresses disregard for the material world. After all, such embrace of the virtual world can complement deep and genuine engagement with the physical world. However, if we wish to protect against behaviour which might begin to express an unhealthy and distorted focus upon the ultimate, we might choose to keep alert to when our uploading begins to lead us to increasingly disconnect from the physical world. If we notice such a disconnection, alarm bells might usefully start to ring, for it might reveal an unhealthy move away from engagement with the physical world around us.

Questions for discussion

1. What are you waiting for with the greatest passion?

2. Do you feel drawn to think most about the past, the present, or the future? Which influences cause you to live in this way?

3. Do you recognise within yourself a tendency to live excessively within either the present or the future? How does that express itself and what might you do about it?

4. What hope do you have for the future?

5. How does that future hope affect the way you live day to day within the present?

6. Which feels most real to you, physical or spiritual realities?

7. Which tempts you most, the idea of escaping from the world or of taking it too seriously?

8. Do you ever feel as if you need the physical world to bend to your will? If so, when?

9. Do your commitments to family, friends, colleagues and others demonstrate the significance of both what is ultimate and penultimate, the now and the not yet?

10. Are there aspects of the visions of Kurzweil, de Grey and Silver which you feel able to affirm in the light of this chapter?

Notes

[1] John 14:2-3.

[2] Eric Metaxas' 2012 biography of Bonhoeffer, *Bonhoeffer: Pastor, Martyr, Prophet, Spy* offers an inspiring account of his life.

[3] Within his book *Ethics*, Bonhoeffer considers *The Last Things and the Things Before the Last*, sometimes translated as the 'ultimate' and the 'penultimate', p120-185.

[4] See *Ethics*, p125-6.

[5] This tool can be framed in terms of the question: 'Is this enhancement quest, or the vision behind it, inconsistent with Bonhoeffer's concepts of the ultimate and the penultimate?'

In his 2011 book, *Respecting Life* the contemporary theologian and bioethicist Neil Messer has described how Bonhoeffer's writing on the ultimate and the penultimate can be applied to bioethics, p38-40. Messer proposes the use of the question 'What attitude does the project manifest towards the material world (including our own bodies)?' as a means of exploring medical projects in the light of Bonhoeffer's understanding of the ultimate and the penultimate, p38.

Messer relates Bonhoeffer's idea of exclusive focussing on the ultimate with hatred of the material world, expressed either through a desire to escape from the material world or to subject it, violently if necessary, to our wills. He relates Bonhoeffer's idea of an exclusive focus on the penultimate to a tendency to reduce everything to the material.

Messer is arguing that getting too caught up in either the present or the future will express itself in how we think about physical objects, our bodies included. If we give up on the value of life today, in this moment, we will stop treasuring the physical world around us. We may then want to escape from this world, maybe through suicide or escaping into computer games or virtual reality, or through losing ourselves in drink or drugs. Alternatively we may want to do everything we can to manipulate this world so that we prove that we are in control. This might involve an obsessive attempt to control our own weight and fitness levels and to work to shield oneself from the mess and chaos of the world within sanitised artificial environments.

Similarly, Messer argues that if we are so focused upon present reality that we lose touch with the future, then we are likely to become fixated by the physical world. We may place all our hope in coming up with physical solutions to our problems. We may be tempted to reduce emotional and spiritual complexities to physical issues which may seem easier to understand and to relate to. We may relate to the world around us and our fellow humans as no more than physical objects obeying rational laws. We are likely to deny the reality of evil and sin and will speak instead of flawed logic and of irrational behaviour.

Messer's point is not that penultimate realities are material and ultimate ones are non-material. That would be to deny the ongoing significance of the physical world and the reality of resurrection bodies. Instead, Messer emphasises the importance of valuing the present material world 'properly and proportionately in the light of God's promised good future'.

Within this chapter, I have drawn heavily upon Messer's insights, applying his proposals to the specific field of Human Enhancement.

[6] The tool framed in note 5 above in relation to the question of inconsistency with Bonhoeffer's concepts is actually a specific example of a wider tool which might be framed in terms of the question: 'Is this enhancement quest, or the vision behind it, inconsistent with Christian eschatology?'

[7] See *The Singularity is Near*, p198-203.

[8] Bonhoeffer's thinking has therefore given us a theological tool with which to challenge Kurzweil's vision. We have been able to show that Kurzweil expresses a disregard for the penultimate and the physical world. Even though Kurzweil's vision is so different to a Christian vision of hope for the future, it is still valuable to be able to use Bonhoeffer's thinking in this way. We did not need to rely on gut instinct. Instead we have challenged Kurzweil's vision not on the basis of it sounding strange, but because it denies the value of the physical world which God has already proclaimed as good. Furthermore, as we have used the ideas of the ultimate and the penultimate here, they might also be used in relation to less straightforward enhancement quests. Some such imagined quests will be considered at the end of this chapter.

[9] See *Remaking Eden*, p4-8.

[10] Bonhoeffer warns against distorted thinking which focuses too much upon either the ultimate or the penultimate, not because it risks valuing one at the expense of the other, but because both are devalued if they become disconnected from the other.

[11] See *Ending Aging*, p44-5.

[12] De Grey's reduction to the physical is very different to the perspective of Christians, such as Nancey Murphy, who argue that human identity is dependent upon our physical nature. Murphy and others express the enormous value of the physical within life and the impossibility of considering life without that physical aspect. See *Nonreductive Physicalism and Free Will* available online via www.metanexus.net

[13] De Grey hopes that human aging and death can be solved by appropriate maintenance and repair of our bodies. Yet our problems cannot be dealt with that

easily. We are fallen creatures and we require more significant attention. By viewing human life as no more than physical existence, de Grey has no place for a concept of sin within his understanding of people and so too no means of perceiving the significance of the incarnation and the resurrection of Christ for future human hope. He therefore describes a futile vision to tackle the suffering of aging and death through human efforts alone, without reference to Jesus.

It is this ignoring of sin which means that de Grey does not identify moral differences between causes of death. The horrific consequences of human sin express themselves in terrorist fatalities and cause a level of pain and misery over and above that which is experienced by those grieving the loss of an elderly loved one who has died of 'natural causes'. Yet, within de Grey's vision, these two causes of death cannot be distinguished, for to do so would involve an understanding of meaning which is not accessible when human life is understood as no more than physical.

Chapter 8

MAKING IT UP AS WE GO ALONG

'Therefore my beloved, just as you have always obeyed me, not only
in my presence, but much more now in my absence, work out your
own salvation with fear and trembling; for it is God who is at work in
you, enabling you both to will and to work for his good pleasure.'

Philippians 2:12-13

As a child I remember being very grateful for the fact that no matter
what surprises life seemed to present, my parents always seemed
prepared for them. It was as if they had learned in advance exactly
what needed to be done in every conceivable situation. We returned
home one evening when I was about 8 or 9 years old to find that our
house had been burgled. Very calmly, working together, my parents
took stock of the situation, informed the police and others who
needed to know, whilst continuing to care for me and my younger
sister. Once the necessary tasks had been completed at our house
they drove us all off to my grandparents for the night. I never
questioned their ability to respond to the unexpected yet they did not
have any special parental file in which to look up 'Burglary
response' under entries beginning with the letter B.

As an adult now myself, I recognise that coping with the unexpected
is more about forming habits, priorities and perspectives, than about
learning what to do in every possible situation. My parents did not
know in advance how to respond to each unexpected event yet they
had developed ways of living and being which enabled them to make

instinctive judgements and actions in a crisis. As we reflect upon them we may or may not be pleased with our instinctive responses, but it is certain that those responses will grow out of our previous thinking and our earlier experiences. A decision that may be taken in the blink of an eye will reveal the sort of person we have become over a period of many years.

The Duke of Wellington is reported as observing that the Battle of Waterloo was won on the playing fields of Eton.[1] In other words, the way in which we cope in the heat of the moment is shaped by those habits we have formed over long days and months of preparation. The character and the identity of the officers who led at Waterloo were not established in the midst of battle, they were forged years earlier through lessons on the rugby field and through sustained cooperation and competition with school friends. Olympic athletes do not acquire the ability to win gold medals during the Olympic Games themselves. Instead the Games reveal that winning ability which was gained earlier through a sustained period of dedicated training and preparation.

All humans face the challenge of so shaping our lives that we are content with our instinctive responses to the events of each day. Not all events demand an instinctive response, and in some situations we can take stock and consider before deciding how to act. Indeed there are times when we are not responding at all but initiating a new situation. Yet it is those aspects of life, such as crises, which demand an instinctive response that often reveal most about how our character is being shaped, for in those cases we get just one chance to respond as we wish, and our response needs to be immediate. We are not able, as happens in certain films and television programmes, to pause reality, to comment upon our experience of it, to consider our response, and then jump back into time's stream well prepared to take action. Neither can we travel back in time to change responses we come to regret.

As Christians we face the further challenge of ensuring not only that we are pleased with our instinctive responses but that they are consistent with what it means to live as a Christian in our particular context. At one level it is clear what this involves: we need to live in the light of the biblical story, to keep the Ten Commandments, to love God with all of our heart, mind, soul and strength, and to love our neighbour as our self. Yet, applying this to our own context is not always easy. New Testament writers were not living in the age of the Internet, genetic engineering and games consoles. We cannot simply copy the actions of those Christians who lived in earlier times. Life is not that simple. No one has yet lived the particular life to which each of us is called. No one has yet modelled the particular way that God calls you or me to be fully alive and to be holy, as a member of the body of Christ, within our own unique skin.

This need to work out how to live well without simply copying those who have gone before has led a number of Christians to turn to the skill of improvisation within music and drama for inspiration. Tom Wright has described the Christian call to live holy lives today, as like the challenge for an actor to improvise the ending to an unfinished Shakespearean play.[2] The task involves looking carefully at what has gone before, and working out how to behave now, in the light of what has already happened. For the actor, this involves studying the earlier part of the script, identifying unfinished themes within the play, and understanding one's character well enough to be able to predict how they might behave in different contexts.

For the Christian, successful improvisation means understanding how God has already revealed himself to the world and living now in the light of that earlier revelation. It involves taking account of creation, of God's relationship with Israel and of the life, death and resurrection of Jesus. The Christian also has access, through the book of Revelation and other biblical texts, to a glimpse of what comes next, to the final part of the action, to God bringing all things right at the end of the world. We need to take account of this too.

Samuel Wells has built upon Wright's idea and he proposes that we live today, as members of the Church, within Act Four of a Five Act play.[3] This is a wonderfully liberating place to be. The key action, within the third and central act, has already taken place. That was the life, death and resurrection of Jesus. Furthermore, the end, the Final Act, has not yet come to pass. We live in the freedom of Act Four. We simply need to carry on living and loving in the light of what has gone before, knowing that God will make all things right in his own time. That will take place in Act Five which is yet to come. Wells names the five acts in order as Creation, Israel, Jesus, Church and what he calls the 'Eschaton', the bringing together of the last things.

We live in the time of the Church and our responsibility is to respond to Jesus' commands to love God and neighbour, which of course involves making disciples of all nations. We need to tell others about Jesus through our actions and our words but whilst we are called to proclaim we are neither called to offer the world salvation nor to make all things new. Jesus, through his death and resurrection, has already performed the key action in history. He has already achieved the salvation of sinners. We do not need to achieve that. Neither do we need to take all the broken elements of God's creation and transform them into a new heaven and a new earth. God will bring that about in the next act but that act is yet to come. Furthermore, it will be accomplished by God's hands and not our own.

Loving God and neighbour and making disciples of all nations is challenging enough. Exploring what it might mean to follow these commands in the context of Human Enhancement will form the subject of the next two chapters. We do need to work out what this means in our own particular contexts, yet the fact that we do not need to save the world, or make all things new, is liberating. It is also a message which is particularly important for our society today.

Science, medicine and technology have developed to such an extent that it is easy to get carried away with the possibilities of human action. We look to medicine to protect us from disease, and to remove more and more aspects of the threat of death. People have even argued that we look to medicine in the twenty-first century as a means of salvation.[4]

* * *

The claim that we look to medicine to save us is not as strange as it may sound. Consider how emotionally we discuss systems of health care within our societies. We desperately want to know that when we need it most we will receive all the benefits that modern medicine has to offer. We respect the authority of doctors as much, if not more, than any other professional. We might even argue that hospitals are the modern temples in which we worship that which we depend upon most deeply: science, medicine and technology.[5]

To those of us living in the twenty-first century it might seem obvious that it is medicine to which we turn at times of life and death. Yet, as Stanley Hauerwas has pointed out, our architecture reveals that things have not always been this way.[6] Cathedrals had a prime location amongst great buildings of the past. Our dependence upon God was symbolised by spires and towers on the skyline. It is often hospitals which provide the iconic architectural images of contemporary times. Medicine is an awesome gift from God and it is right that it is celebrated. Yet, if we find that we are in a society which is placing a trust in medicine which rightly belongs to God, we need to challenge those priorities and question how far we ourselves have absorbed some of those social views.

To those who look to medicine to fix the ultimate problems of the world, we can affirm that such a task will only be brought to completion at God's hands. We are called to work and pray for healing but not to place our hope for the future in the power of medicine. Human Enhancement may be seen as a tool for ending aging and death, yet that is not a task which Christians have been called to accomplish. We live in Act Four, and we await the end of death by God's hand within Act Five. Transhumanists look to make all things new through bringing about the emergence of new species, from our human root, which will spread through the stars and populate distant galaxies. Yet it is God who will make all things new. Recognising that we are in the penultimate and not the final act of the Five Act story of God's activity in the world releases us from the need to bring about the end.

Becoming better people rather than enhanced humans involves living with a sense of how our own callings relate to the wider activity of God himself. It involves trusting God to bring about his plans and purposes and not anxiously seeking to take control of what he has already put in place.

Christians have work to do but we are called to carry out that work of love in the context of God's own greater activity. History is not determined by human actions alone. In fact, our burden is light and our yoke is easy,[7] for God himself has not only already accomplished the pivotal act of history but he will also bring about the end, in his own time and in his own way. We simply need to improvise our roles in the meantime with love. The subject of loving God and loving neighbour in relation to Human Enhancement will be explored in the next three chapters.

Questions for discussion

1. Which aspects of your life seem predictable and which aspects have taken you by surprise?

2. How have you responded to the unexpected elements of your life?

3. Can you identify themes and resources within those times when you have been pleased with your instinctive response to the unexpected? If so, what are they?

4. Does the concept of living within Act Four of a Five Act drama seem realistic? If so, is it helpful?

5. Does the idea of living in Act Four liberate you to live any differently?

6. Working with Tom Wright's model, what does the Bible tell us about the fifth and final act? What is known and what is unknown?

7. Have you ever experienced medicine being treated as if it can solve all human problems?

8. What are the similarities and differences between the ways doctors and church leaders have been treated in your experience?

9. What do the buildings in your local area, such as schools, churches, hospitals or banks, indicate might be most highly prized in your neighbourhood?

10. Can you identify other artistic skills, in addition to improvisation, which might provide us with inspiration for living well in a technological world?

Notes

[1] Samuel Wells uses this quote from Wellington within his 2004 book *Improvisation*, p73. (He references the 3rd Edition of *The Oxford Dictionary of Quotations* from 1979 as his source, p567). This chapter draws heavily upon the thinking of Wells as described in *Improvisation*.

[2] Tom Wright describes his Five Act framework of Creation, Fall, Israel, Jesus and Church in a number of his writings, including his 1992 book *The New Testament and the People of God*, p140-3.

[3] Within Chapter 3 of *Improvisation*, Wells describes both Tom Wright's use of a Five Act play and his own amendments to Wright's model.

[4] Gerald McKenny has written of the way in which medicine can be seen as a means of dealing with all human suffering as the Baconian Project. He describes it as the quest to win control over the human body and 'to eliminate whatever anyone might consider a burden of finitude'. The name comes from McKenny's identification of the root of this project in the writing of Francis Bacon and René Descartes. McKenny's writing on the subject can be found in the 1998 edition of *On Moral Medicine* edited by Stephen Lammers and Allen Verhey, p308-23. A number of theologians, including Robert Song and Neil Messer have built upon his ideas. For example, see Song's 2002 book *Human Genetics*, p8, 114-8, 120-6 and Neil Messer's 2011 book *Respecting Life*, p6, 12, 26-8, 112, 155, 165, 179.

[5] Stanley Hauerwas explores this idea within his essay *How Christian Ethics became Medical Ethics: The Case Against Paul Ramsey* within his book *Wilderness Wanderings*, p124-40.

[6] Hauerwas contrasts the great cathedrals of Europe with modern major medical centres. See *Wilderness Wanderings*, p126-7.

[7] Matthew 11:30.

Chapter 9

LIVING WITH LIMITS

'Three times I appealed to the Lord about this, that it would leave me, but he said to me, "My grace is sufficient for you, for power is made perfect in weakness." So, I will boast all the more gladly of my weaknesses, so that the power of Christ may dwell in me.'

2 Corinthians 12:8-9

The song *Reach* by pop group *S Club Seven* climbed to number 2 in the UK singles charts in the summer of the year 2000. Its popularity lay in its upbeat tune and its lyrics which encouraged listeners to 'reach for the stars'. I remember attending a Christian camp that summer at which it was played frequently! There is something very human about wanting to challenge ourselves, to aspire to what is out of reach, to stretch out to touch the stars.

I worked at a school whose motto, shared with, amongst others, the Royal Air Force and the state of Kansas, was *Ad Astra per Aspera*. It can be translated as 'to the stars, through adversity'. The motto acknowledges that there will be challenges associated with stretching ourselves. Yet, it also seems to suggest that those who aspire to greatness will be prepared to push through those difficulties.

Human beings have an instinctive desire to stretch, to reach and to grow. My children love to recognise themselves getting taller as we periodically mark their height upon a doorframe. They enjoy pointing out how much shorter they were a year before. God called us to stretch ourselves when he commanded us to be perfect as he is perfect, yet he also points out that his grace is sufficient for us and that his power is made perfect in weakness. Christian faith challenges the human instinct to stretch at all costs. It involves recognising limits and being wise in relation to them. We need to be discerning about which limits we need to seek to overcome and which we may need to accept.

The Babylonian attempt to build a tower reaching to the stars met with God's judgement.[1] It seems that as we grow and strive, there are certain limits it is right to accept, and not to seek to change. As the contrast between the building of the Ark and the Tower of Babel reveals, such discernment relates to the purpose of the growth and striving. Attempts to be like God and to exert our independence from his rule and authority are likely to result in disastrous consequences. Embracing this reality involves recognising certain human limits.

An acceptance of inherent human limits is another gift which the Church can offer to the Human Enhancement debate yet, it can seem counter-intuitive. Athletics events inspire us as we see people stretching themselves to run faster and to jump higher than humans have ever done before. This makes inspirational viewing. The Olympic motto is: 'faster, higher, stronger'. It is good to celebrate the potential within the awesome creation of the human body.

The final of the 100m sprint is one of the most popular events of any athletics completion for good reason. There is such beauty within a human body which is so fully alive. Eric Liddell, that great Christian hero of the 1924 Olympics, said that God made him fast and 'when I run I feel his pleasure'. We too sense that pleasure when we see human beings stretching themselves towards the limits of what is possible. In a similar way, we cheer on the sick patient who fights to overcome their disease. We applaud the accident victim who resists death and struggles toward recovery. Yet the Church offers a related wisdom about the value of accepting inherent human limits, and of recognising the power which lies in weakness.

* * *

This chapter will explore the subject of living with limits and it will do so as one aspect of loving God, the second of the theological tools with which to engage with Human Enhancement that was identified in Chapter Five. Our lifetime provides an opportunity to grow in love and, of course, this side of the grave there will always be more to learn. In order to begin to explore what it is to love God in relation to Human Enhancement, I will focus on one tiny aspect of that goal within this chapter. That small part involves embracing limits.

It may seem strange to jump from the idea of loving God to embracing limits, yet I believe there is a link and I will set out to explain why. Loving God involves delighting in who he is, and that involves recognising him as, amongst so many other things, our Creator God. Of course, God is so much more. He is also our Redeemer, our Lord, our Judge and our King. Nonetheless, one aspect of God's identity is that he is the Creator of the world. What's more, his creation is good. He asserted that fact himself, as we can read in the first chapter of the Bible.[2] Loving God involves delighting in God as Creator, and so valuing how we have been created.

I know that love does not necessarily mean having a high opinion of the abilities of those we love. My wife and I love our children but the fact that our fridge is covered with their artwork is not because we mistakenly believe them to be the world's greatest artists. We love our children for who they are, and we delight in their growing skills in drawing and painting. Indeed, their natural ability is far greater than my own but that is not why I appreciate their artwork. I love their drawing and painting because it has been done by them. Its quality is less important than the fact that it is their work. Yet in relation to God, I do believe there is a link between loving God and recognising his ability. Loving God involves recognising him for who he is. It involves facing reality. And the truth is that God is an awesome Creator. Surely, failing to recognise that God is a good Creator must involve a failure to love him as well as we can, for it involves failing to see such a fundamental truth of who he is and of our relationship with him.

I loved my time learning about science in school, studying and researching it at university, and then returning to the school context to teach. The more I discovered about atoms and molecules, cells and organs, forces and laws, the more I sensed the beauty of the way God has made the world. The corner of the scientific world which I was able to explore in most depth was that of organic chemistry, particularly some of the molecular building blocks of deoxyribonucleic acid, DNA. Each new insight left me in awe of the beauty of creation. God has created an awesome world and whether we look at the very large, the very small, or anything in between, we can find signs of his breathtaking artistry.

I know that recognising the scale of the universe demands humility in relation to the place of humans within the cosmos. Nonetheless, the creation of human beings is no insignificant act by God. The Bible affirms the fact that we are made in God's own image.[3] God is the artist beyond all artists and he has created the universe. All that creation is good. Human beings are no less good than anything else in creation; indeed, we are particularly good for we have been created in God's image. Therefore, loving God and respecting his creative work demands that we value the way that he has made us.

Loving God leads to delighting in the way that he has created his people, you and me. Loving God involves delighting in who we are, with all the complexities that being an embodied creature involves. God created us, and he knew what he was doing. Furthermore, delighting in how God has made us as embodied creatures involves accepting the limits that are an inevitable part of such embodiment. Therefore as this chapter explores embracing inherent human limits, it does so as one aspect of obeying the command to love God with all our heart, all our soul, all our mind, and with all our strength.[4]

* * *

The wisdom of accepting inherent human limits derives from the fact that, as discussed in Chapter Six, humans are embodied creatures. We do not just happen to have bodies. Our identity is inherently connected to our bodies. Our bodies are as much who we are as our mind and our emotions. These different elements of ourselves are fundamentally connected and they make up our very self. Recognising human embodiment demands a recognition of inherent human limits for without an acceptance of such limits it is not possible to celebrate the fact that we are defined, at least in part, by our bodies.

The fact that I have a body means that I cannot be in two places at once. That is a limitation yet it is one which is an inevitable consequence of having a body. It makes no sense for me to delight in being created as an embodied being and yet to object to the fact that I cannot be in two places at once, for the two facts are intertwined. Similarly, having a body means that there is a boundary between what is me and what is not. That is another limitation which is the result of being an embodied creature. It makes no sense to celebrate God's creation of human bodies and yet to object that we have a sense of separation from what is 'other'. Inevitably, being embodied creatures means we will experience being distinct from what is around us.

Celebrating human embodiment and accepting inherent human limitations involves the same reconciling of connected realities that we face throughout life. It is wonderful to walk in the mountains, yet doing so involves accepting the reality of being exposed to the weather and of being up high. It is a joy to form close relationships with other people yet doing so involves accepting that this may cause us to get hurt. Some aspects of life are fundamentally connected and we cannot hope to have the benefits without the cost from one particular gift. Human embodiment is such a gift and learning to embrace the inherent limitations that come with that gift is part of accepting the reality of the world.

I have a good friend who will sometimes ask those he is with what superpower they would most like to have! It is a good question and it often enables those who do not know one another well to learn more about one another's priorities and values. People may suggest flight, or strength, or x-ray vision, or any of the myriad possibilities we encounter in the heroes of comic books, films and television programmes. Whilst we may not have these abilities within our bodies, technology has already given us access to these powers through aeroplanes, mechanical systems and x-ray scanners. Our dreams and visions do shape our technologies.

God has gifted us with the ability to understand the world around us and to shape it for our own purposes. Jesus himself made use of the technology of boat building to travel upon water, whilst also demonstrating the fact that as Sovereign Lord of creation, he did not need to do so![5]

Accepting inherent human limitations does not mean rejecting all technological means with which to work around those limitations.

106

Yet unless we discern a distinction between those technological means which provide further freedom for inherently limited human beings, and those which harmfully remove such limitations, we are in danger of rejecting the good gift of human embodiment. To use a telephone to speak to a relative on the other side of the globe provides freedom yet does not fundamentally reject my inherent human limitations. To seek to give up my body and to upload myself into a computer system so that I may simultaneously be present at any point within that system is to seek to reject an essential aspect of who I am and so to reject the value of my own identity.[6]

* * *

The fact that Jesus was born as a human being gives further weight to the claim that we need to accept inherent human limits. If they were good enough for God surely they are good enough for us. In his letter to the church in Philippi Paul explains that Jesus 'did not regard equality with God as something to be exploited but emptied himself, taking the form of a slave, and being born in human likeness. And being found in human form, he humbled himself and became obedient to the point of death – even death on a cross'.[7] Surely if there was something inherently unacceptable about the limits of the human body God would not have subjected himself to them. Paul's words acknowledge the emptying of himself that Jesus experienced when becoming born in human likeness. Jesus was prepared to do that.

The fact that Jesus walked upon the water might be used as a case for arguing that inherent human limitations need not be embraced, for Jesus was able to transcend them at will. I think it is hard to back up such a claim for despite that fact that Jesus walked upon water he fully embraced the human form with all its limitations. Furthermore, it is possible that it was not so much Jesus' own actions which led to him walking on the water as much as creation itself recognising his presence. John Polkinghorne, in conversation on this subject, remarked that the laws of nature were not suspended at that time but that creation might be expected to behave differently when in direct contact with the Creator himself.[8] In that case, Jesus was not rejecting his own inherent human limitations, but rather his full divinity caused creation itself to respond differently to his presence. As the 'not yet' of the Kingdom of God seems to break into the 'now' giving glimpses of what is to come, this idea seems to suggest that Jesus' body in contact with creation pointed ahead to the richer physical reality of new creation.

If the human form is good enough for God, we stand on very shaky ground indeed if we argue that we need a better home. We can rightly aspire to the resurrection bodies which we have been promised for the future, but we cannot say we are too good for the human form in the meantime.

It might be argued that Jesus only experienced a particular human form. That form was male and not female. It was young and never had a chance to grow old. It was strong and healthy. Nonetheless, Jesus experienced all the inherent limitations which are common to all humans. And the fact that Jesus has done that provides a powerful argument against any who would argue that we need to fight to overcome those limits. Furthermore, Paul reminds us in his letter to the Galatians that in Christ there is neither Jew nor Greek, slave nor free, male nor female.[9]

So, accepting that our nature as embodied beings is a gift from God, and that Jesus was willing to take on human form, both point to the need to accept at least those limits which are inherent to being a human. Acceptance of intrinsic human limits seems to be fundamental to a Christian understanding of human identity.

* * *

Acceptance of inherent human limits is important, but it is not the end of the story and on its own it is not sufficient. A Christian perspective on human limits involves the understanding that we live in the hope of experiencing future resurrection bodies. This is not all there is. We can empathise with all who dream of something more. Inherent human limitations can be embraced in the present because they will be transformed in the future. We do not need to fight to overcome these inherent human limits now because we can trust that these limits have already been overcome. We simply need to wait to experience that reality in due course.

The perspective provided by the hope of resurrection bodies means that embracing inherent human limits is not the end. It is for a fixed period. Yet we sense that we were made for more than this. We have a sense of eternity within our hearts.[10] The task of overcoming inherent human limits has already been achieved but it has been achieved through divine gift and not through the work of human hands. The resurrection provides further reason to embrace inherent human limits for now, because it points beyond now to a time when those limits will rightly be no more.

Chapter Six has already explored how accounts of Jesus' appearances to his disciples after his resurrection revealed something of the nature of his resurrection body and the promise of our own. We have only small glimpses of the nature of resurrection bodies but we have good reason to be confident in their goodness. God's plans and purposes are good and the necessary limitations of embodied life in the present are not lasting. As God makes all things new, we will discover even more of the richness and the goodness of his creativity, his generosity and his love. C. S. Lewis points to this in his description of the new earth in *The Last Battle* where he describes a reality which is more real than that which we now experience.[11] Our present world is revealed to be a *Shadowland* in comparison to what lies ahead, which is more colourful, richer and more real than that which we have yet experienced.

To Transhumanists, who seek to overcome the limits of human lifespan and ability, the Church can offer the alternative of learning the value of embracing human life as it has been presented to us, as a gift. The gift of human life contains inherent limits. Those limits, when embraced, can provide the means of recognising just what an amazing gift it is to be human, and what potential lies ahead, not through overcoming our humanity, but by following God's plans and purposes for our future, a future which leads to resurrection bodies.

* * *

We have noted the distinction, difficult as it is to pin down, between enhancement and therapy. So too we may note the difference between those limits which are inherent to all humans and those faced only by certain individuals. For example, my eyesight is poor. Without my glasses I cannot see any objects clearly which are not very close to my face. Others have very good sight without the use of glasses or contact lenses. Yet all of us share certain limits in relation to how long we may live and how fast we may be able to run. These limits are not due to disease or injury but fundamental limits representing the fact that we are human. If we were a jaguar we would be able to run faster, but we are not. We can use a car, a skateboard, or a rocket to travel faster, but unaided there is an upper limit to the speed at which human beings can run.

There is a meaningful difference between the fact that all humans share an upper limit in relation to lifespan and top running speed, and the fact that some people are limited due to injury, disease or birth defects. Our valuing of healing leads us to seek to overcome those limits which are due to personal difficulties. While we may find ourselves able to learn from the experience of sickness or injury, as many people do, we tend to choose to be made well. We do not embrace all limits without discernment.

Whilst we tend to want to overcome personal limits due to disease or injury this is not always the case. Some blind people have described their blindness as a key element of their identity and one which they would not wish to have taken from them.[12] Similarly, there is a case of a deaf couple who have said that they would choose to have a deaf child in order that they could welcome that child into the deaf community of which they are a part.[13] These may be extreme perspectives, yet they are examples of people discerning that overcoming human limits is not always more important than other considerations, even in the case of personal limits.

Whatever we feel about overcoming personal limits, the Church points clearly to the value of accepting and even embracing inherent human limits, and it is this perspective which presents such a challenge to transhumanism. For whatever reason, and theologians have spent much energy debating why, God has created a world in which humans experience certain limits in relation to lifespan and other mental and physical abilities and characteristics. Attempting to overcome these limits through our own efforts represents a denial of the goodness of the way in which we have been made. Furthermore, God has already pointed towards the way in which these limits will be overcome, not through our work, but through his own. We are promised resurrection bodies.

* * *

Embracing inherent human limits involves an acceptance of the goodness of God's good creation, and a trust in God's plans to work all things together for good. God has created us with a yearning for

111

more than we now experience, a 'God-shaped hole' that longs for intimacy with him. We sense that this world is not all there is. We feel the wrongness of life being cut off before we have fulfilled that for which we were created. Yet we face the choice between seeking to make things right ourselves, and trusting God to achieve that same purpose in his way and in his time. Choosing to trust God is one way in which we may express our love for him.

Questions for discussion

1. If you could have a superpower what would it be and why?!

2. Have you experienced yourself enjoying limits in any situations?

3. Are there human limits which you find particularly difficult to accept? If so, what are they?

4. Do you feel differently about limitations you share with all humans and those which are distinctive to just some of the population?

5. Which sense do you most value? Can you imagine what it would be like to live without it?

6. What failings in yourself and in others do you find most frustrating?

7. What emotions arise within you when you contemplate aging and death?

8. Do you feel human limitations something to be accepted or celebrated? Why?

9. What connections do you sense between the way we love God and the way we delight in how we have been made?

10. What would you most like to say to God in relation to these subjects? On what issues would you most like to hear him speak to you? Do you need to bring these things to God in prayer?

Notes

[1] See Genesis 11:1-9 as well as the discussion of both the Ark and the Tower of Babel as two contrasting technological projects within Chapter One of this book.

[2] In the account of God's creation of the world within Genesis 1 there are six occasions upon which God observed his creation and declared that 'it was good', (verses 4, 10, 12, 18, 21 and 25). Furthermore, on the sixth day, after the creation of human beings, God looked at all that he had made and declared it all to be 'very good' (verse 31).

[3] Verse 27 of Genesis 1 states: 'So God created humankind in his image, in the image of God he created them; male and female he created them'. Much writing and study has been devoted to exploring what it means that God has made human beings 'in his image'. One point of consensus within that exploration is that being made in God's image gives human beings a particular value and place within God's creation, all of which is of very great value through having been named as 'very good' by God himself. One recent book on the 'image of God' which may be helpful to those wishing to explore the subject further is *The Liberating Image* by J Richard Middleton, published in 2005. Middleton explores the meaning of image within the Ancient Near Eastern context and discusses the authority involved in imaging our Creator God.

[4] Deuteronomy 6:5 as well as Matthew 22:37, Mark 12:30 and Luke 10:27.

[5] Jesus walking on water is described in Matthew 14:22-34; Mark 6:45-53 and John 6:15-21.

[6] I acknowledge that the difference between using a telephone and uploading oneself into a computer system involves quite a leap. It would be interesting to explore some of the steps in-between and to make judgements about the consequences of such steps upon our attitudes to our own embodiment and inherent limits. Such an exploration is one of many projects involving technology which might grow out of a discussion of Human Enhancement.

[7] Philippians 2:5-11.

[8] Discussion after a student gathering in Cambridge in the early 1990s.

[9] Galatians 3:28.

[10] Ecclesiastes 3:11.

[11] The last two chapters of *The Last Battle* entitled *Further in and Further up* and *Farewell to Shadowlands* describe Lewis' imaginative engagement with the depth and richness of new creation.

[12] Discussion on ability and disability at Trinity College, Bristol, 2011.

[13] Referred to in, amongst other places, *Enhancing Evolution* by John Harris, p89.

Chapter 10

LOOKING AFTER NUMBER ONE?

'You shall not take vengeance or bear a grudge against any of your people, but you shall love your neighbour as yourself: I am the LORD.' Leviticus 19:18

'One of the scribes came near and heard them disputing with one another, and seeing that he answered them well, he asked him, 'Which commandment is the first of all?' Jesus answered, 'The first is, "Hear, O Israel: the Lord our God, the Lord is one; you shall love the Lord your God with all your heart, and with all your soul, and with all your mind, and with all your strength." The second is this, "You shall love your neighbour as yourself." There is no other commandment greater than these.' Mark 12:28-31

We are steeped in a culture which repeatedly tells us that we need to 'look after number one'. It is suggested that if we do not look after ourselves, no one else will. We are encouraged by cosmetics companies to care for our appearance, 'because we are worth it'. We are used to hearing behaviour justified in terms of the benefits it will provide for the person taking that action. It is unlikely to have been long since we last heard someone say 'It was time to indulge myself'.

This selfish prioritising of our own interests is embedded within our consumer culture. Marketing campaigns frequently refer to indulging, to giving into temptations, and to succumbing to desires.

We are even pressured to mould our relationships with others into ones shaped by our shared roles as consumers when advertisers suggest we recommend a product to a friend. This recommendation is unlikely to mean paying for them to delight in what we have enjoyed, but rather encouraging them to pay for the experience themselves. What is more, businesses will often encourage us to recommend others to try what we have enjoyed by offering us a financial incentive for doing so. In this way our consumer society attempts to squeeze the idea of friendship, where each friend cares for the other, into a pattern of mutually self-interested consumers, making use of one's contacts for one's own interest and the subsequent benefit of a commercial organisation.

It is right to care for ourselves. Jesus recognises that most of us will do this, when he upholds the Old Testament command that we love our neighbour 'as ourselves'.[1] When the apostle Paul commands husbands to care for their wives, he tells them to love those spouses as they love their own bodies.[2] It is right and proper that we look after ourselves. Yet the Bible makes clear that we also need to love our neighbour, and to treat that task as significantly as we do the need to care for ourselves. Therefore our care for ourselves cannot come at the cost of our neighbour's wellbeing. The Church is to model a way of life which challenges our cultural assumption that we can look after number one at the cost of another.

If we are to know how to love our neighbours as ourselves we will need to be discerning about competing needs, differing requests and limited resources. We may need to make tough choices and decisions.[3] There is no question about whether or not this command to love our neighbour as ourselves will face us with a demanding challenge. The Bible makes clear that loving our neighbour will involve costly sacrifice on our part. Jesus spoke of turning the other cheek[4] and of walking the extra mile.[5] We are not called to be doormats but we are called to express the type of sacrificial love shown by Jesus who emptied himself, humbled himself and who became obedient to death, even death on a cross.[6] Paul teaches that we need to regard others as better than ourselves.[7]

It will not always be easy to know what it means to love our neighbour as ourselves. Some of us may even need to learn to love ourselves as part of that process. We will need to keep alert to the ways in which the concept of 'love' has become distorted in our society.[8] Books, films and television shows provide us with myriad images of the meaning of love. The Beatles have told us that 'Love is all you need' and countless pop songs before and since have offered us messages about love. If we are to relate these messages to the biblical commands to love God and to love our neighbours as ourselves, we need to know what we mean when we speak about love. Unless we hold onto love as that which Jesus showed when he died on the cross and rose again for us, we will be vulnerable to the sentimental, romantic, sexualised and parasitic images of love which are so readily available within our culture.

* * *

The command to love our neighbour as ourselves raises two important sets of questions in relation to Human Enhancement. The first relates to considering enhancements in relation to their impact upon all peoples, not just their consequences for ourselves and our close circle of family and friends. The second relates to how enhancements will impact the ability of neighbours to relate to one another and particularly to express love for one another.

Considering the impact of enhancements upon all peoples raises a further range of questions, including issues of justice and the subject of self-defeating enhancements.

Issues of justice are prominent in various ethical questions relating to medicine. Societies need to make important decisions about how the costs of health care are paid for and how that relates to who will be entitled to benefit from them. Such decisions are important in shaping how a society feels about itself. It was interesting to see the way that a tribute to the National Health Service (NHS) formed a key component of Britain's presentation of itself to the world within the opening ceremony of the 2012 Olympic Games.[9] Even within a welfare system such as the NHS decisions need to be taken about how transplant organs are allocated, how waiting lists are managed, and how limited funds are divided between the costs of competing treatments and procedures.

It is not surprising that, as within other medical contexts, Human Enhancement involves questions of justice. Science, medicine and technology may determine whether or not a particular enhancement is available to the few, but politics and economics will determine whether or not it is available to the many. Whilst it may be technically possible to develop tools and resources with the aim of enabling a person to live longer, run faster, or to remember more, it will be a very different issue to explore whether or not such benefits will be made available to all who may wish to benefit from them.

Loving our neighbour as ourselves demands that we consider not just the effect of an enhancement upon one person, but also how its use will impact on society as a whole, and in particular on the weak and the poor. For example, if a certain combination of diet, drug and lifestyle factors is found to significantly extend human lifespan, it will be important to consider whether or not such foods, medicines and ways of life can be made available to all or whether they are inherently only ever available for a privileged minority. Working for no more than two hours a day and being bathed in champagne may be found to have life extending properties, but in a world where some toil down mines and where many lack clean drinking water, such activities are not options for all. If Human Enhancement leads to an even less fair division of the world's resources, loving one's neighbour as oneself will demand that Christians speak into that debate on behalf of the poor and the needy.

The issues of justice touched upon above assume that an enhancement might be understood as being a benefit to all, if only it were made available to all, as in the case of life extension. Yet not all enhancements work in this way and some would be collectively self-defeating so that if everyone had access to them, no one would benefit from them. A good example is that of increased height.[10] For a man to be of above average height can be a benefit both socially and economically. Thus a treatment which increased a man's height or a genetic enhancement which increased the height of his son might be of value, with the proviso that the treatment was not available to others. If all men raised their heights by two centimetres, there would be no overall benefit and the enhancement would be collectively self-defeating.

If love for one's neighbour is to be central to our consideration of Human Enhancement it becomes very difficult indeed to justify collectively self-defeating enhancements. This is not because the Church is not concerned about personal wellbeing. God adores every person in their own unique situation and works for their good, and the Church needs to value each person as God does. What is at issue here is keeping alert to the fact that each person's good is inevitably connected to the good of others. Love of neighbour involves being aware of the good of the whole community, which will not be possible if each person seeks only their own good.

It may be unrealistic to expect the world to legislate against collectively self-defeating enhancements but the Church can model what is possible in a community where each person is loved regardless of his or her height. In such a community, not only is there no advantage in everyone being two centimetres taller, but there is no disadvantage in being of below average height in the first place. The Church can point towards a world in which those enhancements which only grow out of selfishness and competition are revealed to have no worth.

* * *

As well as matters of justice, consideration of love of neighbour also raises issues about how enhancements will affect neighbours relating to one another and their ability to express love for one another. Of course it is not possible to know in advance how a technology or a medical procedure will affect the way in which people relate to one another. Nonetheless, the impact of a given technology is crucial in determining whether or not the technology will be experienced as a benefit to society as a whole. Furthermore, whilst it is not possible to know what the future will hold, we have a wealth of cultural experience with which to predict how technology will shape the world of tomorrow.

Countless novels and films describe how social and technological changes will affect our lives in years to come. Some have even found themselves occupying a prominent place in our cultural imagination. For example, the title of Aldous Huxley's novel *Brave New World* has become synonymous with a world in which technology and politics remove personal choice and freedom.[11] Similarly, Isaac Asimov's imagined laws of robotics, presented through works of science fiction, have captured the imagination of others and found their way into wider conversations.[12] The fact that the impact of technology upon society is not determined by the technology itself but by its interaction with society, means that novels and films provide a significant means of exploring these issues. What is required is not simply a scientific analysis of the technology but an imaginative exploration of human society and how our behaviour is affected by a changing technological context.

Scientists who are willing to offer such an imaginative exploration present a valuable gift for they are able to combine their scientific insights with their own artistic perspective. Susan Greenfield is one such writer. She has imagined our future world by drawing upon her professional expertise as a neuroscientist.[13]

I have written *our* future world yet the world Greenfield describes is an isolated one, with very few if any interactions with other people. A key reason for this is that she describes a future in which we will all have a variety of virtual contacts, most significantly a virtual butler, but also including a wealth of cyber friends.[14] In such a world, where these electronic others are programmed to respond to our own whims and demands, Greenfield describes us becoming increasingly selfish and disconnected from one another. Considering a cyber-butler named Douglas, she writes: 'casual conversations are not as central to your, literally, selfish life as Douglas, who is not only in charge of your home but in charge of you. Douglas is effectively an extension of you, or more accurately of your thoughts and desires and needs – your mind.'[15]

Greenfield's imagination leads her to a vision of society in which social interactions have broken down completely and been replaced by a dependence upon technological companions. She continues to describe the world of the future which she imagines will come about: 'Traditional real relationships in real time atrophied. And the family unit as it used to be, even in its most liberal form, slowly vanished, just as the medieval feudal system, once the bedrock of social organisation, faded in the face of new technologies and progress.'[16]

Greenfield proposes that with any information we desire being freely available electronically and with our various needs met through virtual contacts we will be uninterested in interacting with other humans. She writes: 'Able to access any information we wish, and capable of choosing from a variety of cyber-companions, what would be the worth in seeking out real-life human individuals? If you were to find them, would they be interested, or interesting? They too would be busy talking with their cyber-friends or their butler.'[17]

Like so many visions of the future, we may be tempted to dismiss Susan Greenfield's as a fantasy which will bear no relation to what really lies ahead. Nonetheless, as with the visions of Chapter Four, the values they represent are as important as the question of whether or not they are likely to come about, for they reveal cultural values which are already shaping our future context. If technology continues to develop over the coming years as it has during the previous decades, there is no reason to question Greenfield's view that we will indeed have the option of building our lives around cyber-friends and butlers if we so wish. What is questionable is whether or not we might find an alternative way of living within such a technological context.

Greenfield's vision is made more disturbing by the way in which she does not argue either for or against such a future but simply points towards it as inevitable. She seems to have become so influenced by the self-centred behaviour she has observed around her that she appears unable to imagine a world in which that selfishness does not define one's existence. Her imagined future is the inevitable outworking of growing dependence upon technology, in which human selfishness is not held in check.

I believe that the Church faces the challenge of demonstrating what is possible when human behaviour is not defined by such selfishness but by love of one's neighbour. If we had done a better job of demonstrating that possibility to date, Susan Greenfield's imagined future might already have looked different. If the world is to see beyond selfishness, the Church needs to show what it looks like to love one's neighbour as oneself. We in the Church cannot look at the world and tut disapprovingly at worldly expectations of selfishness. Such expectations need to motivate the Church to demonstrate a better way of living.

My aim in writing the above paragraph is not to encourage us to beat ourselves up or to wallow in feelings of guilt. God is aware of our sinfulness and whilst we were still sinners he died for us.[18] Whilst we need to acknowledge all the wrong that we have done, God is compassionate and quick to forgive. My aim in writing the previous paragraph is to encourage us to look kindly upon those who expect selfishness to dominate our society. If others expect that, it is my fault for not having done enough to model an alternative, more loving way of life. It is my fault as a member of the body of Christ. Each time that selfishness goes unchallenged in the world is a call to the Church to be more visible in demonstrating a better way.

Greenfield's vision seems to be based upon a presumption of fundamental selfishness. Yet it is frighteningly and compellingly believable. Which of us, if we were free to do so, would not be tempted to accept the care and concern of an ever attentive powerful and able cyber butler whose only aim was to pander to our every desire? Yet the fact that such a service leads so smoothly into the self-absorbed life that Greenfield describes, in which such a person becomes detached from all human neighbours and immerses oneself ever more deeply in a virtual world, needs to act as a warning. Using technology to meet our every desire threatens our very identity.

We are created as social creatures to be in relationship with one another and with God. If the purposes to which we put our technology feed the worst of our desires and drives for selfishness and comfort we are in danger indeed. Our selfishness and laziness are threats enough at the best of times, without allying those forces with technological weaponry to destroy oneself through an internal civil war. The command to love one's neighbour is not only about showing care for others, it offers a means of protecting ourselves from the selfishness which might otherwise destroy our very identity.

* * *

We started this chapter acknowledging those social pressures to look after ourselves before others. Some of those forces come from advertisers keen to persuade us to 'treat' ourselves and in doing so, to help them to make a profit. Others come from a culture which values the individual and seeks to 'divide and conquer'. Such cultural forces may seem to affirm our own identity but may sometimes do so at the cost of being in community with others. For example, in relation to ideas we are often reminded that whilst we are free to think what we like, it would be intolerant to impose those ideas on others.

On a daily basis we find ourselves prompted to consider those things which separate us from others and which keep us focused on our own situation and perspective. Both *Brave New World*, mentioned earlier, and George Orwell's novel *Nineteen Eighty-Four* describe a future in which human society is diminished through pressures to limit the relationships which one person will have with another. Like the selfishness pointed to by Susan Greenfield, these pressures to limit our relationships with others are present around us today. They take the form of pressures to keep our faith privatised and to think of ourselves as individuals rather than people.

Bruce Reed was an inspirational Australian priest who founded *The Grubb Institute*.[19] I was privileged to work there, under his leadership, for four years. He would often say that when he thought of himself as an individual he thought of what separated him from others: his skin, his geographical position in space and his own thoughts, feelings and perspectives. When he thought of himself as a person he thought of everyone, living and dead, who had influenced him in becoming the person he was, and who held a sense of him within their own heart; all those whom he thought of and knew himself to be connected to. I love that sense of remaining aware of myself as a person rather than an individual.

In a world in which I often feel tempted to think of myself as an individual, I am committed to giving thanks for all those who have helped me to become the person I am, those I am aware of and those I am not. I am grateful to all those who love me and pray for me, and in some real but profound way, in doing so, define at least some aspect of who I am. I will attempt to keep remembering those around the world, and those not yet born, who will be shaped for better or for worse by my choices about how I use resources, how I give gifts, and by what I say and do. This is part of what it means for me to love my neighbour as myself. I realise I cannot do it in my own strength but I pray that God will equip his Church to demonstrate what is possible when we, as people, really do love our neighbours as ourselves.

* * *

There are many different contexts in which we might explore further how love for one's neighbour illuminates the debate on Human Enhancement. One particularly important context relates to loving the unborn child as our neighbour and it is this subject which will be explored within the next chapter.

Questions for discussion

1. What do you find most difficult about Jesus' command to love others as ourselves?

2. What helps and hinders you in the challenge of loving others?

3. What social pressures do you experience to focus on yourself at the cost of showing love to others?

4. Which experiences of loving others have you found to be most significant? Why?

5. What challenges have you experienced in attempting to show love for others?

6. What have you found to be a support in nurturing community with others?

7. Which issues of injustice in our world do you find most concerning? Why?

8. Can you identify experiences involving technology which have drawn you closer to others or separated you from them?

9. If you could have a cyber-butler of the type described by Susan Greenfield, what would you most appreciate about it? How do you imagine it would affect your relationships with others?

10. Is there anything you feel God calling you to do in relation to caring for those in need and keeping connected to others in our technological world?

Notes

[1] The biblical command to love one's neighbour as oneself is first found in Leviticus 19:18. Jesus' reference to the command constituting, together with the command to love God with one's heart, mind, soul and strength, the greatest commandments is reported in Matthew 22:39, Mark 12:31 and Luke 10:27.

[2] Ephesians 5:28

[3] In his 1972 book *Agape*, Gene Outka explores the greatest commandments, loving God and loving neighbour. He notes the importance of such love being modelled upon the love of God for humanity, and explores the place of self-sacrifice within the love of neighbour, p24-34, 44-54, 77. He also notes that there are three reasons for drawing back from understanding loving one's neighbour as meaning 'writing a blank cheque', p21-2. He describes these as being for the sake of the neighbour, the sake of third parties, and the sake of oneself.

[4] Matthew 5:39

[5] Matthew 5:41

[6] Philippians 2:6-8

[7] Philippians 2:3

[8] Richard Hays, in his 1996 book *The Moral Vision of the New Testament* argues that the concept of love has 'become debased in popular discourse' and that it may therefore 'produce more distortion than clarity'. He therefore argues that love needs to be understood in relation to the love which Christ showed upon the cross, p200-3.

[9] The Opening Ceremony took place on Friday 27th July 2012 in the Olympic Stadium, London, and was directed by Danny Boyle. One section of the ceremony celebrated the NHS, which the programme described as 'the institution which more than any other unites our nation'. This section involved children on 320 hospital beds, some of which functioned as trampolines.

[10] Michael Sandel discusses the possibility of enhancing height in *The Case against Perfection*, p16-19.

[11] *Brave New World* was first published in 1932 and warned of the dehumanising aspects of scientific and material 'progress'. It has since become a core text for students and has established itself in the cultural consciousness.

[12] Asimov's three laws of robotics were first published in his 1942 short story, *Runaround*. The 2004 film, *I, Robot* is just one of many contemporary creative projects which have drawn upon these laws.

[13] Baroness Susan Greenfield is Professor of Synaptic Pharmacology at Lincoln College, Oxford and was Director of the Royal Institution from 1998 until 2010. Her

2003 book, *Tomorrow's People* explores the impact of twenty-first century technology upon the ways we think and feel.

[14] *Tomorrow's People*, p38-44.

[15] *Tomorrow's People*, p40.

[16] *Tomorrow's People*, p41.

[17] *Tomorrow's People*, p43.

[18] Romans 5:8.

[19] Bruce Reed worked to establish *The Christian Teamwork Trust* as part of the follow-up work after the Billy Graham missions in London in the 1950s. This led to the formation of *The Grubb Institute* in the 1960s, which was named after Sir Kenneth Grubb. Bruce Reed used tools from theology and the social sciences to work with others to explore the reality of the world. This thinking enables *The Grubb Institute* to offer courses, consultancy and conferences. Whilst Bruce Reed died in 2003, *The Grubb Institute* continues and details of its current work is available on www.grubb.org.uk

Chapter 11

IT'S LIFE, JIM, BUT NOT AS WE KNOW IT!

'For it was you who formed my inward parts; you knit me together
in my mother's womb. I praise you, for I am fearfully and
wonderfully made. Wonderful are your works; that I know very well.
My frame was not hidden from you, when I was being made in
secret, intricately woven in the depths of the earth. Your eyes beheld
my unformed substance. In your book were written all the days that
were formed for me, when none of them as yet existed.'

Psalm 139:13-16

The title of this chapter, popularised in the 1987 pop song *Star
Trekkin*, may not be a real quote from the original television series of
Star Trek, but it does relate to the discovery by the crew of the
Starship Enterprise of strange alien forms.[1] It also resonates with our
struggle to describe the nature of the unborn child. There is no doubt
that the unborn child is a living being but there is also something
'other' about it.

We can find ourselves both mesmerised and confused by what is
taking place as we consider the formation of a new human life.
God's awesome creativity is on display as he forms a new human
being from a single fertilised egg, but that creativity can leave us a
little ill at ease. As we consider a human embryo we see both
ourselves, but also something not quite familiar. In the presence of
that mystery we may find ourselves unable to draw clear boundaries
or to rely upon our own understanding of what it means to be human.

That can be disconcerting and uncomfortable territory. It can raise confusing questions about what constitutes life.

The human egg and sperm are living human cells with the potential to be joined. These germ cells are living, in the sense that muscle cells and skin cells are living, yet they are not living creatures. Therefore it makes sense that we tend to grieve neither the loss of an unfertilised egg in a woman's monthly period, nor the loss of human sperm. However, when a human egg is fertilised to form a zygote, a fertilised egg with the potential to divide and to grow to form an embryo, the key event on the pathway to the birth of a child has occurred. The way in which we might describe the unfertilised egg as being a living cell is inherently different to the way we might associate life with the zygote.

Despite being unable to control or even completely comprehend the growth of a new human life, scientists have worked hard to observe and to describe the different parts of the process. When a human egg is fertilised by a sperm it forms a zygote which divides repeatedly to form a small ball of cells, called a morula. As that morula continues to grow and divide, it forms a fluid filled sack known as a blastula. Inside this sack a human embryo begins to form, in which cells start to develop in specialised ways and go on to form foetal organs. Fertilisation triggers a process which, when all goes well, leads to the birth of a child. Nonetheless, there is significant disagreement about when human life begins.

Numerous medics, scientists, ethicists, and theologians have pointed to different stages of development in order to draw a line to differentiate biological material from human life. The process by which a zygote develops to form a baby can indeed be understood as comprising of stages. Yet, attempting to identity a single event by which life is separated from nonlife can fail to appreciate the beauty of that process by which God shapes each new precious human form. Such attempts to highlight one part of the process and to over-emphasise its importance in relation to other parts can be to misunderstand the significance of the process as a whole. Seeking to understand aspects of the process in order to understand the whole is valuable, but seeking to reduce the process to discrete events is to fail to appreciate its fundamental unity.

* * *

In some sense it is strange to question whether life starts at the moment of fertilisation. That is clearly the point when the process of growth begins. Yet it is also true that this starting point leads on to numerous other steps, each of which needs to be successfully completed in order for a child to be born. Furthermore, our minds seem to find it hard to think about processes of growth. We will sometimes seek to re-imagine a process as a series of steps in order to grasp it more easily. We tend to speak of falling in love rather than a lifetime of learning to love a spouse. We may seek to define who is on 'our side' as opposed to 'their side' rather than live with the ambiguity of more complex relationships. In relation to sport we can be so focused upon who won and who lost that we can lose sight of an ongoing process of development as a team or a sportsperson.

I wonder if our pre-industrial ancestors living two or three hundred years ago might not have done a much better job than we do today when describing the growing child. Admittedly they would not have had access to modern scientific descriptions of development, yet they would have been familiar with what it was to live according to the coming and going of seasons. They would have been used to watching crops grow and would have known that satisfying their hunger depended on keeping alert to the need to respond to changes in the climate and the environment. They would have been familiar with watching sheep and cattle give birth and with watching the newborn animals grow and develop. Theirs was an analogue age.

Within the digital world of today we can be tempted to think too much in black and white, on or off, present or absent, rather than of the flow of growth and development. When we are in danger of being more familiar with computers than cornfields, and gizmos than goats, then we may have lost the alertness to nature which provides insights into living processes. Such lack of sensitivity to the living world may leave us ill-equipped to make sense of the process of growth of an unborn child. If we reach instead for the artificial world of individual pixels and binary code it is no wonder that we may struggle to comprehend the subtleties and nuances of living systems.

Recognising our difficulty in understanding the process of embryonic growth and development, we will be wise to tread carefully in this territory and to be slow to risk harming that which has a beauty and a potential which we do not fully comprehend.

* * *

In the year 1990, the United Kingdom's Human Fertilisation and Embryology Act ruled that the fertilised human egg, or early pre-fourteen day embryo, is not an individual human being until at least fourteen days from fertilisation. On that basis, the Act allows research on embryos which are less than fourteen days old. This is one example of a line being drawn in relation to the development of an embryo for the purposes of a legal ruling. Whilst key events do occur fourteen days after fertilisation, embryonic development is a process and placing too much significance upon certain events within that process runs the risk of imposing external and arbitrary meaning upon that natural progression.

There are four main arguments for placing particular emphasis upon what takes place fourteen days after fertilisation.[2] The first is that all the cells in the very early embryo are pluripotent. This means that no cell has yet specialised and that it can still develop into any kind of tissue. Some cells will therefore develop into the foetus itself and others will form the supporting tissues of the amniotic sac, the placenta and the umbilical cord. Therefore, the argument goes, until it is possible to know which parts of the early embryo will go on to form the embryo proper it is too early to consider the pre-14 day embryo as an individual organism.[3]

The second argument for the fourteen day limit is that the early embryo is merely a cluster of cells which may or may not go on to develop into an embryo proper. It has yet to face many challenges, any of which might prevent it from going on to fulfil its potential. For example, it might fail to implant in the lining of the womb or it might simply fail to grow normally. Therefore, one may argue, until the early embryo has succeeded in overcoming more of the challenges ahead, it would be premature to grant it the status of an individual life.

The third argument is that up until about fourteen days after fertilisation the early embryo may develop into twins. Therefore it is not possible to regard the early embryo as an individual life for it may go on to form more than one individual embryo.

The fourth argument for the fourteen day limit is that until about fourteen days after fertilisation, it has been impossible to tell which end of the early embryo is which. It is only from about day fourteen onwards that it has been possible to identify a head end and a lower end.

Whilst the above four arguments indicate that deciding upon day fourteen of embryonic development was a far from arbitrary choice, they are not a convincing reason to devalue the early embryo. It is true that some cells of the early embryo will develop into heart and lung tissue and others into the umbilical cord, but to the embryo, all are of value. The embryo still has challenges ahead in relation to survival but so does a young child and so does an adult. We do not tend to challenge the value of an adult or a child on the basis of the fragility of life. It is correct that an early embryo may go on to form twins, but again that is no reason to devalue what may be twice as precious as we once dared hope. Finally, the inability to distinguish parts within a structure is no reason to devalue it. I cannot yet tell whether my young daughter will prefer music or sports. That fact does not mean I value her less, or that she will not in time develop an identity in which both music and sport are key characteristics.

As our understanding of embryonic development grows, we are likely to form new appreciation for key events within that developmental process. Whether or not future insights affirm the significance of what occurs fourteen days after fertilisation, the fact that key events occur within a process does not mean that what comes before or after is of less value. The very nature of a process is that it cannot be simplified into a single key event. Furthermore, a scientific understanding of development is not enough to answer ethical questions about the value of living cells, whatever we may define their status to be or not to be.

* * *

The key issue of status in relation to the human embryo is that of personhood. There have been numerous discussions about whether or not a human embryo qualifies to be classified as a person. The reason for such discussions is the assumption that persons need to be treated differently to those who are not persons. Therefore, if it is established that embryos are persons, they need to be treated with appropriate care. If they are not, we might justify treating them less well. For example, Peter Singer argues that personhood involves conscious thought and therefore dolphins and chimpanzees are worthy of more respect than mentally-impaired humans.[4] From his perspective, greater ability to think deserves greater respect and better treatment.

On this basis, Singer argues that we have less responsibility to care for mentally-impaired humans than for we do for chimpanzees. Similarly he relates a newborn child to a fish, as he writes: 'A being that is not a person does not have the same interest in continuing to live into the future that a person usually has ... Since neither a newborn human infant nor a fish is a person, the wrongness of killing such beings is not as great as the wrongness of killing a person.'[5] This is a staggering claim and Singer is writing, not of the unborn child, but of the newborn human infant. With perspectives like this influencing our ethical and philosophical debates, it is little wonder that our society questions our responsibility towards the unborn child.

Challenging Peter Singer's views involves questioning the whole issue of classification and there are at least two good reasons for doing so. Firstly, our classifications will be dependent upon the terms we use. As each of us is free to reinterpret how we wish to use a term such as 'person' each of us might come up with a different boundary between who is in and who is out in terms of personhood. Therefore, discussions of who is worthy of care will never be conclusively resolved on this basis. Secondly, the idea that how we classify a person or an object justifies the way we treat them bears no relation to the absolutes of God's perspective and God's commands. God asked Adam to name the animals.[6] There seems to be a beautiful link between this task and the work of botanists and zoologists in classifying plant and animal species. Yet, God has not asked humankind to decide whether or not to value his created world. We are commanded to work as stewards of creation.[7] That involves caring for it, not making a decision about parts we will and will not care for.

As we are commanded to work as stewards of all creation, so too, we are called to place a particularly high value on human life. The Bible teaches us that humans are made in the image of God[8] and it is not our place to seek to restrict that description to only some humans. The biblical command to love one's neighbour as oneself reaffirms the significance of particularly valuing all human life. Dolphins and chimpanzees are awesome creatures, yet humans hold a special place in God's creation, not through ability or skill, but through the gift they have received of having been created in God's image.

We can therefore relieve ourselves of the burden of struggling to answer the question of whether or not an embryo is a person. Not only is it impossible to answer, but it fails to appreciate two important truths. Firstly, humans are called to be stewards of all creation and to value it as God's handiwork. Secondly, human worth is derived not through functional value but through the God-given gift of having been created in the image of God. Yet, whilst we will do well to let go of the need to classify embryos or others as persons, the idea of what it means to be a person can nonetheless be illuminating in relation to our own behaviour.

* * *

A number of writers have found it useful to consider Jesus' parable of the Good Samaritan[9] in relation to our treatment of human embryos.[10] When Jesus was asked to identify a man's neighbour, Jesus turned the question on its head and told the story of the Good Samaritan, before then asking who had acted as a neighbour in the story. Jesus' change of question turns the matter at issue from who is

136

worthy of my care, to what care is demanded of me in my role as neighbour.

In the same way, it has been noted that it may be far more helpful to ask how we behave as a person towards a human embryo than to debate whether or not the embryo itself is a person. Such a change of question focuses the issue on the demands which my own personhood makes upon my behaviour towards others, rather than whether or not someone else is a person. If I accept that my own personhood demands that I treat any object which may possibly be understood as a person well, I will need to treat an embryo well without needing to determine whether or not it is a person. This perspective disentangles our treatment of embryos from the thorny philosophical question of personhood. In doing so, it offers a solid basis for protecting embryos which avoids getting lost in unhelpful academic questions of categorisation.

This perspective does not offer a watertight case for protecting embryos at all costs, but it does establish a firm emphasis upon care and protection if I am to preserve my own identity as a person. It is that identity which means that I need to behave with love. Such a perspective demands, at the very least, profound caution in relation to any temptation to use embryos for our own purposes or those of others. There needs to be a presupposition in any discussion of these issues that our treatment of embryos will demonstrate the love for them which is demanded by our own personhood as humans.

Neil Messer suggests that one minimal requirement of such love must be to obey the biblical command 'You shall not murder'.[11] Restraining oneself from murdering is a foundational platform upon which to express love. After all, murdering makes the expression of subsequent love profoundly difficult. Messer draws upon Karl Barth's consideration of this command, in which Barth argues that whilst we might debate exceptions to such a command, 'a definite No must be the presupposition of all further discussions'.[12] In other words, we live in a complex ethical world in which we will need to ask challenging questions, but one foundation upon which we will explore those questions needs to be that we will not murder.

Messer follows Barth's lead to propose that expressing love of neighbour for the embryo will involve 'a definite No' to the destruction of human embryos for treatment or research, but that it may not be an exceptionless No.[13] Barth and Messer, in turn, are daring to take us into the uncomfortable territory in which we face the realities of our complex ethical environment. We might wish for a black and white world in which there are no exceptions, but that may be to seek to simplify the world which God has in fact created and to reduce the complexity which makes sense from God's perspective to our limited comprehension.

As Messer points out, this issue is complicated by the fact that there are different neighbours to whom we are called to show love. We have already mentioned embryos themselves but those patients who might benefit from treatments involving the use of embryonic stem cells are also neighbours. We are commanded to love them too.[14] Thus an ethical tension exists between expressing love for our neighbours who need treatment and expressing love for embryos, showing our neighbourliness to them too.[15] We need to work out how to handle these two competing needs and there is no easy way to know how to do that. There is no consensus within the Church, but the weight of theological opinion does lie firmly on the side of avoiding embryo destruction.

Neil Messer identifies a solid basis upon which to build a case for arguing against destroying embryos by reference to the biblical accounts of Abraham and Isaac,[16] and of Jesus' own death and resurrection.[17] God tested Abraham by asking him to sacrifice his own son, Isaac. Yet, when Abraham showed that he was indeed willing to follow God's call, even if that meant sacrificing his only son, God commanded him not to lay a hand on Isaac.[18] As Messer argues, this account, together with that of Jesus' willing acceptance of death upon the cross, signals an end to the project of saving human life by sacrificing human life. They point us away from attempts to destroy embryonic life in order to save or improve the life of others.

This ethical consideration of competing needs can be confusing.[19] Nonetheless, if the above argument is accepted, the theological tension between expressing love to patients in need of treatment and embryos from whom such treatment might be derived needs to be viewed firmly from the perspective of protecting embryos. Messer makes the convincing argument that at the very least, the burden of proof is on those who would argue that a situation provides an exception to the 'definite No' to embryo destruction.[20] In other words, in the absence of any compelling reason to do otherwise, we need to work on the basis that we will never destroy embryos.

The use of embryos for therapeutic purposes is therefore very difficult to justify, despite the clear affirmation for healing work expressed within the Bible and the Christian tradition. Any case for using embryos within enhancement quests is very much weaker for we cannot appeal to the call to heal. Therefore, all the theological work considering whether or not it is possible to justify using embryos for therapy points away from using human embryos for enhancement. Obeying the command to love our neighbours as ourselves seems to rule out the possibility of destroying a human embryo for the purposes of enhancement.

* * *

The subject of the treatment of human embryos provides a good example of how an issue such as Human Enhancement relates to other bioethical topics. Much ethical and theological work has been done on the status of embryos, largely in relation to abortion. Work in one area can helpfully illuminate another. That is one reason why theological engagement with Human Enhancement is so important, for principles may be discovered in this area which will help the Church to engage with a future technological discussion which has not yet appeared over the ethical horizon.

As with the theological engagement with abortion, the above considerations raise challenging practical questions for the Church. If, as I think we need to, we understand the biblical command to love our neighbour as ourselves to mean that we need to work from the position of saying 'No' to abortion and to the destruction of embryos, we need to point to other means of responding to what is needed within these situations.

Stanley Hauerwas has written about how the Church needs to be the sort of community in which all children can be welcomed.[21] This means working together to build that community. We have more authority to encourage someone else not to have an abortion if we are prepared to stand alongside them, as a community, in meeting the costs of such a decision. Similarly, if we speak out against the destruction of embryos we need to be able to model the type of community which offers another way of dealing with the diseases and other needs which draw people to call for embryonic destruction. The Church needs to be a place in which those in need find love expressed in action. It is right that we speak theological truth into ethical debates but such speech demands that we also model how the Church community offers a new way in which such issues can be addressed.

* * *

This chapter completes this section on using the three theological tools of eschatology, love of God and love of neighbour, to engage with Human Enhancement. It also leads us into questions of how the Church lives and speaks in order to model an alternative to those who advocate enhancement. Such practical questions will shape the content of the remaining chapters, which includes the consideration in the next chapter of how the Church is perceived within society.

Questions for discussion

1. Some people argue that much depends upon when we decide that human life begins. Do you believe that it does? Why?

2. Do you consider a key change occurs in the identity of the embryo fourteen days after fertilisation? Why?

3. Do you feel a need to understand the nature of embryos to make wise decisions about how to behave towards them?

4. What might it mean to treat a human embryo as a neighbour?

5. Do we have an obligation to do whatever we can to have the most healthy and able child possible?

6. How might the biblical command to love one's neighbour as oneself illuminate the abortion debate?

7. Can you identify ways to speak into the abortion debate in the light of this chapter?

8. How does thinking about being a neighbour to others impact the way we need to treat animals?

9. Can you see ways that the Church needs to act if it is to be possible for people to behave as neighbours to others, embryos included?

10. Can you identify practical ways in which God is calling you to be a better neighbour to others?

Notes

[1] The song *Star Trekkin* by The Firm was released in 1987 and was a Number One hit in the UK Singles Charts for two weeks. One of the lyrics, 'It's life, Jim, but not as we know it' did not occur in the original Star Trek series, but has been so popularised by the song that it has been commonly misattributed to the original series since the song's release.

[2] Agneta Sutton explains these four arguments in more detail than there is space for within this chapter, in her 2008 book *Christian Bioethics: A Guide for the Perplexed*, p8-22.

[3] The appearance of the primitive streak within the embryo at about fourteen days after fertilisation marks the beginning of the emergence of the embryo proper from the group of pluripotent cells which will go on to form both the embryo proper plus supporting structures.

[4] See Peter Singer's 1994 book *Rethinking Life and Death*.

[5] *Rethinking Life and Death*, p219-220.

[6] Genesis 2:19-20.

[7] Genesis 1:28.

[8] Genesis 1:26-8; 5:1-2; 9:6.

[9] Luke 10:25-37.

[10] Oliver O'Donovan drew upon the parable of the Good Samaritan in his 1984 book, *Begotten or made?*, p49-66. He argued that discerning 'Who is a person?' involves expressing our own personhood. Some years later Ian McFarland proposes a similar focus upon what it means for us to behave as a person to others. See his chapter within the 2002 book, *Theological Issues in Bioethics* edited by Neil Messer, p76-84.

[11] Exodus 20:13, quoted in Messer's book *Respecting Life*, p123.

[12] Barth, *Church Dogmatics*, vol. III.4 quoted by Messer in *Respecting Life*, p124.

[13] *Respecting Life*, p124-7.

[14] *Respecting Life*, p124.

[15] In his 2001 book *Reproductive Technology*, Brent Waters argues that within this tension the needs of patients sometimes outweigh those of embryos and that the instrumental use of certain embryos is indeed permissible for particular therapeutic purposes, p125. I am inclined to disagree but I recognise that the Church itself is not of one mind on the issue.

[16] Genesis 22:1-19.

[17] *Respecting Life*, p127.

[18] Genesis 22:12.

[19] This consideration of sacrificing human life to save life raises challenging questions, not least about the use of violence in war.

[20] *Respecting Life*, p127.

[21] Writing on how the Church needs to be the sort of community in which questions such as those of abortion can be understood differently is a recurring theme within Hauerwas' work. See, for example: *Abortion: Why the Arguments Fail* within *A Community of Character*, p212-29 and *Abortion, Theologically Understood* within *The Hauerwas Reader*, p603-22.

Chapter 12

COMMUNICATING WELL

'I came that they may have life, and have it abundantly'.
John 10:10b

'For God's foolishness is wiser than human wisdom, and God's
weakness is stronger than human strength'. 1 Corinthians 1:25

'Finally, beloved, whatever is true, whatever is honourable,
whatever is just, whatever is pure, whatever is pleasing, whatever is
commendable, if there is any excellence and if there is anything
worthy of praise, think about these things.' Philippians 4:8

It is no secret that Christians are often caricatured in the media. From
Christians within soap operas, to the Vicar of Dibley and Rowan
Atkinson's on-screen portrayals of bumbling clergy, the Church is
presented in some rather strange ways. We do not need to be overly
concerned by this fact. All groups and professions will at times find
themselves explored through some distorting artistic lenses. Yet it is
worth paying attention to these images for they can contain valuable
information about how the Church is perceived by society.

Some of what the world dismisses as ridiculous, we may choose to
embrace and affirm. After all we are called to be fools for Christ.[1]
God's wisdom can appear foolish to the world yet that is no reason to
cast it aside. It is more valuable than silver and gold, more precious
than jewels.[2] However well we engage with the world as Christians,
we risk ridicule and disrespect. That goes with the territory. We do

not need to avoid such inevitable consequences of following Christ. Furthermore, the role of the fool and the jester within society is valuable for speaking truth in the face of power and popping dangerous bubbles of pompous delusion.[3] Nonetheless, the world's images of us may also illuminate our failings and so encourage us to change for the good and to become more like the Church that God is calling us to be.

* * *

The 2012 American presidential election was a close race. Whilst polls had predicted a victory for Barack Obama, it appeared to be neck and neck and looked as if it might go either way. Furthermore, pre-election polling data indicated that it might not take much to cause a significant shift in public opinion.

I was interested to note how tracking polls moved up and down significantly in the weeks and months leading up to the election. These shifts followed events such as Obama's leadership in the face of Hurricane Sandy and the relative performance of the two candidates in the three pre-election debates. Of course, whether or not Obama is able to lead in a crisis is an important criterion for deciding upon his ability as President, yet the polls indicated that the timing of Hurricane Sandy in the days leading up the election meant that Obama's response to that particular crisis counted for more within voters' minds than other similar behaviour over the previous four years. Similarly, the candidates' performances in the debates seemed to count for far more than their communication in countless previous speeches, discussions and presentations.

There is nothing particularly surprising about this. Our minds are unable to process large quantities of data and when we attempt to make choices we will be swayed by particular details, including those events which have occurred recently. What is significant is that

146

within such a context trivial details can have enormous implications. Both Barack Obama and Mitt Romney wore badges of the US flag during their debate appearances. These prompted discussions about the how the relative badge sizes might affect the outcome of the election. In our television age, the shade of a candidate's suit and the nature of their facial hair seem capable of having a profound effect upon an election and so upon leadership throughout the world.

There is much which might be questioned within political campaigns including cost, transparency and integrity, yet they also offer lessons from which to learn. Content may be more important than style of presentation, yet if a message becomes drowned out by a distracting presentation, the content is unlikely to be appreciated. In this context, the Church needs to be aware that being sensitive to how we are communicating will help ensure that our society is able to hear the hope of the gospel.

We will never be able to control how others perceive us or react towards us and we do not need to do so, yet unless we are alert and sensitive to how we are being labelled we will not be able to judge whether or not what we say is having any kind of impact upon society. If we are able to recognise the labels which others are placing upon us, it may be possible for us to avoid behaving in such a way that we are unnecessarily misunderstood. Jesus calls his disciples to be both wise as serpents and gentle as doves.[4] Our gentleness will help us to tolerate being misunderstood but our wisdom will help us to avoid such misunderstandings where it is possible to do so.

One danger the Church faces when speaking into social issues is that we can be dismissed as being out-of-touch and viewed as prudes who do not know how to enjoy themselves, as seeking to return to the past, and as gloomy citizens who seek to prevent others from having fun. One who simply questions the expansion of technology can be misunderstood as being a stick-in-the-mud who needs to stop whining and catch up with what is going on in the world. Yet Christians engaging within the area of Human Enhancement are neither out of touch nor are they intent upon preventing a good healthy enjoyment of life. Nonetheless, recognising the threat of being perceived in this way gives us an opportunity to challenge this image. Unless we do so we may find the wonderful gifts we can offer to society on God's behalf are rejected and wasted.

* * *

The Church might quite fairly be accused of sometimes being too caught up in its own affairs to take the necessary action to help others. We may sometimes be out of touch with those who most need pointing towards God's love and forgiveness through our internal squabbling over trivial issues of style and comfort. We need to apologise for these things and to seek to do better, in God's strength, in the future.[5]

Nonetheless, pointing towards the realities of the enhancement quest and the desires upon which it is built is far from out of touch. It is precisely through being in touch with what is going on in society that the Church is able to engage with Human Enhancement. This is a key contemporary issue within society and the Church is in danger of being out of touch if it fails to address the subject, not if it does engage. Yet it is important to note that being in touch does not involve accepting popular ideas simply because they are fashionable.

Being in touch involves contributing to discussion in these important areas, but the integrity of the Church demands doing so with a voice which speaks challenge as well as recognition. Engaging with Human Enhancement involves seeing beyond the dreams and aspirations to what is really possible. Society may not enjoy being

148

shown itself in the mirror, yet it is a gift to recognise ourselves as we really are, and real development can be made possible through a realistic understanding of the current situation.

* * *

Jesus repeatedly used the imagery of parties and celebrations when describing the Kingdom of God.[6] Yet, the Church does not always behave with the hospitality and love which this demands. Sadly, we have sometimes failed to affirm the goodness of all God's gifts and have missed opportunities to lead others in celebrating and in partying. Yet Jesus came to bring life and life in all its fullness[7] and he calls his Church to live with the same love, joy and freedom. Nonetheless, living with those wonderful characteristics does not mean unthinking permissiveness which condones any behaviour.

If the Church speaks prophetically into this debate so as to reveal dangerous outcomes which may lie ahead, we are not creating those dangers but warning against them. Messengers bringing bad news are rarely popular but they can be useful, particularly if news of an impending disaster arrives with time enough to avert the tragedy. A daughter may feel her parents limit her fun if they prevent her from doing exactly what she wishes, but they may be acting from a good desire to protect and nurture. Naming the dangers of transhumanism is not about preventing society from experiencing what is good, but about pointing towards the true pathway to abundant life. Seeking transformation through Human Enhancement is to seek through a transient thrill what can only genuinely be experienced through the result of discipline, patience and God's generosity.

Christians can empathise with the Transhumanist dissatisfaction with the idea that this world is all that there is. The Church can affirm the human instinct that yearns for something more. What is at issue is not whether or not we were made for more than our present experience, but the means of accessing that something more. Christians can point to the fullness of life which is possible now through embracing God's good gifts for today, and to the hope for the future which is available through embodied resurrection life. As Christians we delight in the good. Seeking the good involves discerning what is sustainable and what is accessible for all.

To the Transhumanist who seeks an end to aging and a means of immortality, the Christian can reply that we too yearn for such a time. It is the route to such a destination which needs to be the topic of discussion. Such goals cannot be accomplished through the work of human hands but have already been secured through the gift of God. The Church is not seeking to prevent the embrace of such hopes and dreams but rather to ensure that they are sought in such a way that they really will be found.

* * *

We face many challenges as we engage with technological issues in our society in the coming years. One of those is to be aware of how we are perceived by society and to adapt our presentation accordingly, not for the good of our reputation, but for the benefit of those who may close their ears to our message if we present it in too careless a fashion. The Church needs to do what is right in relation to Human Enhancement but also to be discerning about how that action is perceived by others. We need to work to demonstrate that our intention is to enable each of us to experience life in all its fullness.

Questions for discussion

1. Which issues does society tend to demand that we keep in touch with?

2. What experiences have you had of being outspoken? How have others responded?

3. Which issues or situations have prompted you to speak out even if that meant risking being misunderstood?

4. What importance do you place upon what others think of you?

5. Do you feel it is important for the decisions and perspectives of organisations to be understood by others?

6. How is your local church and the wider Church viewed by those you know?

7. Which areas of the media most shape your understanding of others, such as politicians? Do you feel these influences are trustworthy?

8. How might your friends and others describe you? What would the place of faith be within that?

9. How would you like to be remembered by others after your death?

10. What do you perceive to be the main costs of standing up in public for a particular cause?

Notes

[1] 1 Corinthians 3:18, 4:10.

[2] Proverbs 8:10-11.

[3] Enid Welsford explores this subject in her 1968 book *The Fool: His Social and Literary History*. I am grateful to Revd Canon Eric Woods, Vicar of Sherbourne, for using this theme within the retreat he led in June 2012 as he helped me and others to prepare for our ordination as priests.

[4] Matthew 10:16.

[5] Without the willingness to accept and to own one's faults, and those of the communities to which one belongs, it will be impossible to speak with authority into the lives and communities of others. Russ Parker, in his 2001 book *Healing Wounded History* is one of a number of writers who explores the healing possibilities of seeking forgiveness for past wounds. If the church seeks to engage more deeply with the issues which will shape society in the coming generations, and such engagement is critical in the light of the pace of technological developments, it will be more important than ever to face our own sinfulness and to seek God's forgiveness.

[6] Matthew 22:1-14; Luke 15:11-32.

[7] John 10:10.

Chapter 13

Avoiding the Idolising of Efficiency

'When you reap the harvest of your land, you shall not reap to the very edges of your field, or gather the gleanings of your harvest. You shall not strip your vineyard bare, or gather the fallen grapes of your vineyard; you shall leave them for the poor and the alien: I am the LORD your God.' Leviticus 19:9-10

Since the 1980s, the expression *Vorsprung durch Technik*, used in car advertisements, has captured the public imagination and been quoted in pop songs, films and television shows.[1] It can be translated from the German to mean 'advancement through technology', and it boasts of the efficiency and competence of German engineering. Good engineering is not limited to Germany, of course, but we do recognise the achievements of particular countries in certain areas and may joke about heaven involving German engineers, Swiss administrators and French cooks.

The idea of 'advancement through technology' is a powerful one and expresses the widespread cultural assumption that science, medicine and technology are leading us ever forwards and upwards into the benefits of technological progress. From this perspective the world's problems are seen as challenges to be overcome. There can be value in this positivity, yet it also contains elements of naivety which unrealistically ignore the effects of human sin. Even the two World Wars seem not to have punctured this optimism rooted in technological 'progress' coupled with human passion and ability. Such 'progress' drives a search for ever greater efficiency.

Vorsprung durch Technik expresses something of technology and efficiency going hand in hand. Technology is more than gadgets and machines; it is primarily an approach to problems. It involves a mindset which seeks to overcome a challenge as efficiently as possible. The French philosopher Jacques Ellul wrote about this more than sixty years ago.[2] He warned that technological development does not simply represent an increase in e number of machines, but also a growth in the way in which we prioritise efficiency within our thinking.

If we grow as a technological society we tend to look at social issues from a limited perspective that expects a single solution to any problem, namely that which is the most efficient. For example, schooling might be understood technologically as the process for equipping the next generation of parents and workers as efficiently as possible. Those who view education in this way will fail to appreciate the significance of schooling as a tool for personal growth and development. They will risk reducing children to potential parents and workers rather than people of value in their own right.

The key danger of technological development is not so much the introduction of new gadgets and equipment, but the expansion of this mindset which prizes efficiency too highly. Our mindset is remarkably powerful. We recognise this whenever we jokingly warn ourselves that for a person with a hammer, every problem can begin to look like a nail. When we are immersed in a technological culture it can be easy to get caught up in its assumptions and priorities. Few of us are immune from the desire to travel as swiftly as possible from place to place, to make good use of each hour of the day, and to manage our financial resources well. These goals are not wrong in and of themselves, yet if they represent an unholy preoccupation with efficiency we will need to reconsider what it is that is governing our behaviour. Our actions need to be determined by holiness rather than by efficiency.

* * *

The playfulness of children offers a wonderful demonstration of the freedom and joy which is available when efficiency is not a priority. Whether it is the extravagance of running up and down stairs simply because one has energy to burn, of jumping for the sheer pleasure of jumping, or the exuberant creativity of a fertile imagination, these activities point not to efficiency but to fullness of life. We were not created as machines for a task but as people for a purpose. That purpose was relationships, the experiencing and expressing of love with God and with one another. Good relationships will always defy efficiency.

Efficiency finds a single optimised way in which to carry out a task. Good relationships produce beauty, variety, freedom and creativity. Efficiency assumes a bottom line and measures everything else in relation to that one absolute. Relationships enable people to dive ever deeper into an expanding network of care, support and mutual appreciation. Efficiency points towards a single desired outcome. Relationships work towards no single endpoint but offer unfolding growth and development.

Part of my children's recent playfulness has involved planting a small vegetable garden, caring for it, and then enjoying our little harvest of green beans, carrots and tomatoes. This project has not been the most efficient way to grow vegetables or to acquire food for the table, yet it has been a good use of time and energy and has been a delight to us as a family. Neither we nor the vegetables themselves are ruled by efficiency.

There are good scientific reasons for the colours, shapes and tastes of vegetables, however they are not determined by efficiency but rather by the beauty and the creativity of the natural world. It is not efficiency which produces the splendour of a peacock's tail but the outworking of the innate creativity and beauty of the natural world. In other words, by the selection of genes over countless generations as peacocks have competed for the attention of peahens. God has created a breathtaking world of incredible artistry and intricate subtlety. I believe that evolutionary science provides us with a wonderful tool for understanding God's creation and his creativity. That creation is not one of efficiency. It is a world of extravagance, diversity, richness and colour. Where efficiency would point to a single way, the natural world displays countless possibilities, each one a different but wonderful expression of life.

* * *

The natural world does not uphold efficiency as all important. Neither does the Bible, and so it poses provocative challenges within a technological society. In the quote from Leviticus with which this chapter was started, the Bible deliberately commands against efficiency for the benefit of the poor and the alien. Finding the most efficient way of harvesting a field or a vineyard will involve considering the cost and reward of harvesting each part of the crop. Yet the Bible seems to challenge that approach in order that part of the harvest is left over for the benefit, not of the landowner, but of the poor and the alien who are then able to come and gather what they need.

This passage points to God's concern for the poor. It also demonstrates realism in relation to human behaviour. The Bible did not proscribe the gathering in of the entire crop and subsequent distribution to those in need, a method which might be expected to be more efficient. It commanded leaving a portion of the crop which might then be gathered by those in need. The biblical model not only offers resources to those in need but it does so in a particular way. It values the dignity and effort of the poor who were thus enabled to gather for themselves rather than receive what had already been gathered by others. It protects those in need from finding themselves at the mercy of an organisation which controls the distribution of harvested crops. History points to the way in which such human organisations can be corrupted by selfishness and thus fail to provide for the poor. These are examples of concerns which may sometimes need to be given a higher priority than that of efficiency.

* * *

Modern literature too points away from prizing efficiency too highly. As we read Aldous Huxley's novel *Brave New World* we enter into a world of mechanical reproduction, passionless sex and drug-induced comfort.[3] Life has been deliberately structured for control and efficiency and such structuring comes at a cost. The price which Huxley's society pays for its order includes the loss of passion, freedom, intimacy and meaning. Infertility may have gone, but so too has the intimacy of the bond between parent and child. The coupling of transient sex is freely available, but gone is the enduring joining together of one person with another in marriage. Pharmaceuticals remove anxiety and depression, but they also steal passion and emotional life.

The power of Huxley's writing can be in enabling us to see not just the specific details of a society but also over-arching themes and characteristics. The generation of so much creative art exploring themes of science and the future indicates how very many questions are raised by developments in science, medicine and technology. It also reveals our shared desire to engage with these issues. Fiction points to the dangers of idolising technological efficiency. It can be easier to identify the characteristics of fictional worlds than those of our own culture, nonetheless it is hard to dismiss the sense that efficiency has been placed upon a pedestal within our own technological context.

* * *

Recognising that efficiency has become an idol in our society today is an important step in addressing the issue, but identifying the problem needs to be followed by appropriate action. Part of that action will involve the acceptance that there will be costs to be paid if our prioritising of efficiency is to be challenged. To leave areas of a field un-harvested for the benefit of the poor and the alien has a cost for the landowner in terms of reduced yields. Forsaking certain technological methods today will involve accepting that such resistance comes at a price.

If the Church is to model an alternative to the enhancement quest, we will face the reality of seeing others benefit from life extension techniques which we may not wish to embrace. We may see our own children growing up amongst 'enhanced' contemporaries with 'superior' abilities. We may find ourselves outsiders in a world in which involvement in a virtual world holds the key to financial and social rewards. Such modelling of an alternative way will be costly indeed.

It is no easy task to model an alternative to worldly ways but it is one to which the Church in every generation has been called. In our contemporary context such an alternative includes the ways in which we engage with issues of Human Enhancement. The consequences of our choices may mean that we do not live as long as our neighbours, but our lives will nonetheless point to our hope of eternal life. Our children may lose competitive struggles with their contemporaries,

158

but their very identity, like ours, will express dependence upon God rather than upon human ability and efforts. We may find ourselves helpless and in need in terms of financial resources and social riches, yet we will point to a greater treasure and to reliance upon God's generous provision.

The costs of living as if there are more important concerns in the world than efficiency will be enormously high. The consequences of modelling an alternative to a world of enhancement will be profoundly life-changing both for us and for our descendents. Yet, unless we make such a choice, the world is in danger of seeing no alternative to an ever-increasing drive for efficiency and to placing our hope in human efforts rather than divine gift.

Questions for discussion

1. In what ways, if any, can you identify technology to be embedded within our society today?

2. What evidence can you find to suggest that efficiency is a key characteristic of our society today?

3. Can you identify other important characteristics of our society which it will be important to monitor over the coming years, and possibly to resist?

4. What importance do you place upon efficiency within your own life? Why?

5. Have you experienced engaging with particular technologies whilst remaining isolated from the deeper ways in which technology shapes society?

6. What do you most value about our society today?

7. Are there ways in which you feel drawn to fight against social pressures?

8. In what ways can you see our society expressing cultural values and perspectives through its use of technology?

9. How might one make wise decisions in relation to which costs are acceptable for living distinctively as a Christian in a technological society?

10. How do you feel living as a Christian in your context today relates to the costs and challenges of living as a Christian in other times and places?

Notes

[1] Cultural references to the phrase *Vorsprung durch Technik* include its use within the 1993 song *Zooropa* by the band U2, the 1994 song *Parklife* by Blur, and in the television series *Only Fools and Horses* and the film *Lock, Stock and Two Smoking Barrels*.

[2] Jacques Ellul's 1954 book was translated into English from its original French by John Wilkinson and published in 1964 as *The Technological Society*.

[3] Huxley's 1932 novel *Brave New World* famously describes fertilisation of human eggs within laboratory containers in the *Central London Hatchery and Conditioning Centre* as well as socially engineered sexual promiscuity and emotional control throughout society through the use of the drug 'soma'.

Chapter 14

RECOGNISING RISKS
WITHOUT BEING AFRAID

'And you will hear of wars and rumours of wars; see that you are not alarmed; for this must take place, but the end is not yet. For nation will rise against nation, and kingdom against kingdom, and there will be famines and earthquakes in various places: all this is but the beginning of the birth pangs.

'Then they will hand you over to be tortured and will put you to death, and you will be hated by all nations because of my name. Then many will fall away, and they will betray one another and hate one another. And many false prophets will arise and lead many astray. And because of the increase of lawlessness, the love of many will grow cold. But anyone who endures this to the end will be saved. And this good news of the kingdom will be proclaimed throughout the world, as a testimony to all the nations; and then the end will come.

'... Heaven and earth will pass away, but my words will not pass away. But about that day and hour no one knows, neither the angels of heaven, nor the Son, but only the Father. For as the days of Noah were, so will be the coming of the Son of Man. For as in those days before the flood they were eating and drinking, marrying and giving in marriage, until the day Noah entered the ark, and they knew nothing until the flood came and swept them all away, so too will be the coming of the Son of Man. Then two will be left in the field; one will be taken and one will be left. Two women will be grinding meal together; one will be taken and one will be left. Keep awake therefore, for you do not know on what day your Lord is coming. But understand this: if the owner of the house had known in what part of the night the thief was coming, he would have stayed awake and would not have let his house be broken into. Therefore you also must be ready, for the Son of Man is coming at an unexpected hour.'

Matthew 24:6-14, 35-44

There is no shortage of predictions about when the world will end. Even when previously published times of the end have come and gone, those who released them have often amended their prediction to a later date. The prophet wearing a sandwich board proclaiming that 'the end is nigh' is a popular figure in films and cartoons. It is easy to get carried away looking for signs around us to match to biblical prophecies as a means of working out how close we are to the end of the world. Yet if we rush to the other extreme and lose all awareness that, one day, this world will come to an end, then we will be at risk of being unprepared when that day does arrive.

It is not difficult to imagine how the end of humanity might come about. Countless films portray the dangers of nuclear war, biological catastrophes, asteroid collisions, dramatic climate change, terrorist attack, and numerous other global threats to human life. We are used to seeing New York and London devastated in movies by snow, flood, earthquake and fire. We are invited to contemplate the terror which might be unleashed by scientists who unwittingly release a nano-technological threat into the environment or by villains who hold the world hostage with the weaponry of a new and deadly microbe.

It is not only film makers and authors of science fiction who point to these risks, so too does the scientific world. Each edition of the

Bulletin of Atomic Scientists features a clock on the cover.[1] The closer the hands of the clock are to midnight, the greater the risk of nuclear war as perceived by the bulletin's editors. The time on this Doomsday clock shifts forwards and back in response to international events.

Martin Rees is a research professor based at the University of Cambridge and a former President of the British Association for the Advancement of Science. He has argued that the odds are no better than fifty-fifty that our present civilisation on Earth will survive to the end of the present century without a serious setback.[2] In the prologue of the book *Our Final Century* in which he sets out this claim he writes:

'We still live, as all our ancestors have done, under the threat of disasters that could cause worldwide devastation: volcanic super-eruptions and major asteroid impacts, for instance. Natural catastrophes on this global scale are so infrequent, and therefore so unlikely to occur within our lifetime, that they do not preoccupy our thoughts, nor give most of us sleepless nights. But such catastrophes are now augmented by other environmental risks that we are bringing upon ourselves, risks that cannot be dismissed as so improbable.'[3]

Rees is not alone in his assessment of the precariousness of human existence at this stage in history. Bill Joy, founder of the computer company Sun Microsystems, has warned that twenty-first century technology is threatening to make humans an endangered species.[4] Both Martin Rees and Bill Joy warn that present global threats are not simply more of the same that has already been experienced throughout the past millennia. Present threats are notably increased because of human impact upon the world. Rees ends *Our Final Century* with these words:

'The theme of this book is that humanity is more at risk than at any earlier phase in its history. The wider cosmos has a potential future that could even be infinite. But will these vast expanses of time be filled with life, or as empty as the Earth's first sterile seas? The choice may depend on us, this century.'[5]

Whether or not contemporary risks are greater than historical ones, and there certainly appear to be good reasons to suppose they have increased, the fact remains that our lives have always been fragile. Contemporary threats to our existence simply add to what has always been true, namely that our lives are in God's hands. It is wise to keep alert to risks around us and to take appropriate action in relation to them, yet we do not need to fear.

* * *

Monty Python's song *I'm So Worried* has already poked fun at our tendency to become nervous about countless details of life, including famously the baggage retrieval system they have at Heathrow! Many of us simply do not need more reasons to panic. Jesus called us not to worry about our needs being met, but to look to God to provide for us, and to focus on each day in turn.[6] God is well aware of the nature of risk within his creation, yet his most common message through the lips of angelic visitors is 'Do not be afraid'.[7] Human lives have always been vulnerable to forces beyond our own control yet because of the reality of God's love and of his activity, we do not need to fear.

Neither do we need to become paralysed into inactivity through acknowledging that what we set out to do may never bear fruit within this world. Martin Luther is famously attributed with saying, when asked what he would do if the world were to end tomorrow, that he would plant an apple seed. Whether or not Luther actually said these words, they do represent Christian hope in the value of life today.

Yes, we have a hope for the future but our life today matters too. There is real value in how we use the gifts of time and other resources which we have so generously been given.

We do not need to give up hope in the face of risks and threats. We can trust in God's goodness, his provision, and the ultimate outworking of his plans and purposes. Nonetheless, we will be wise to keep alert to what is happening around us. Not in order to take control of the future into our own hands, nor to despair, but to ensure our eyes are open to God's activity in and around us. Jesus called his disciples to keep watch,[8] to stay awake,[9] and to pray[10] in the face of concern about the future. It is right to pay attention to the reality of what is taking place around us.

Nick Bostrom and Milan Cirkovic have co-edited a substantial book exploring global catastrophic risks.[11] Bostrom is the Transhumanist who co-edited the 2009 book entitled *Human Enhancement* with Julian Savulescu. He has enormous hope in the ability of humans to make the world a better place in the future, yet he is realistic enough to want to be attentive to identifying future threats. *Global Catastrophic Risks* explores threats from three areas: nature, unintended consequences and hostile acts. Natural threats include super-volcanoes, comets and asteroids, and risks associated with radiation from the sun and beyond. Risks from unintended consequences include climate change, plagues and pandemics, artificial intelligence and social collapse. Hostile acts include those from nuclear war, terrorism, biotechnology, nanotechnology and totalitarianism.

Bostrom and Cirkovic want humanity 'to approach the global problems of the present era with greater maturity, responsibility, and effectiveness'.[12] They explore global risks in order to limit and control them. We may not all share their confidence in the human ability to dominate such threats but the research they present is illuminating. It is useful to have access to a scientific assessment of the risks we face, yet such research can also trigger unhelpful fear.

We live in a world in which fear is generated in order to manipulate and restrict. Businesses may exaggerate risk in order to sell protection of one kind or another. Similarly governments and other bodies may exaggerate risks in order to push through legislation or policies. A sober assessment of risk can help to liberate us from the fear of exaggerated concerns and to provide a realistic understanding of threats. Such insight is vital for it will determine how we engage with different threats and how we prioritise between them.

One chapter in Bostrom and Cirkovic's book focuses upon the significance of our emotional response to global risks. It is written by James Hughes and explores the ways in which our behaviour will be affected by our beliefs and expectations about the future.[13] Hughes warns against the ultimate hope for the future expressed within Christianity and Judaism, arguing that such hope can lead to equally unhelpful views of the near future as either a utopia or an apocalypse.

As we speak about the future we will need to heed Hughes' warnings. If we speak and think about future hope in a way which is disconnected from present realities we will risk misrepresenting the value of our present context. This was explored in Chapter Seven, by drawing upon Bonhoeffer's concepts of the ultimate and the penultimate. Yet if we do not speak out in relation to our future hope, the world will be unable to make sense of our present context in relation to the biblical promise of a new earth and a new heaven. We need to model what it means to be fully alive in the present, with our eyes open to all the reality of risks and threats in the world around us, and pointing towards our future hope without denying the significance of today. That's not an easy juggling act to perfect, but drawing upon scientific assessments of the context of risk in which we live can only help us with that task.

Jesus warned that heaven and earth will pass away, but he offered the comfort that his words will never pass away. Holding on to Bonhoeffer's message that we need to be focused both upon the present and the future, it is important for us to recognise that we cannot base our security upon an unfounded hope that tomorrow will look the same as today. We can expect change. We can not only expect change; we can rely upon there being change. Change is certain. We do not know what tomorrow will hold, but we can be assured that elements of it will surprise us. In such a context, we need to keep our wits about us and to cling to Jesus' promises about what is to come. Those promises include the assurance that in his Father's house are many rooms.[14] We can also rely on the fact that nothing can separate us from his love.[15]

It would be blinkered and short-sighted to become so obsessed by Human Enhancement that we forget about climate change and threats from nuclear war, terrorism, and economic collapse. We need to keep focused upon the forest as well as the individual trees. Yet it is important to go into the future aware of some of the challenges which lie ahead. Unless Christians are alert to these issues on the horizon, society will be unable to engage with them using the theological tools which the Church can make available. We can also declare with joy and confidence that our future hope is not based upon naive disengagement with the realities of life. The Church does not advocate burying one's head in the sand. Rather, despite the very real risks and threats which lie ahead, we have a sure and certain hope. Such hope is not in the avoidance of troubles, but is built on faith in God who works all things for good and who has already secured that ultimately, all shall be well.

* * *

Christians have been accused in the past, somewhat unfairly I believe, of not caring for the created world. The claim has been made that the Christian hope of life after death has meant that we have devalued the physical world of today. Whether or not such claims had any basis in fact in the past, it is exciting that in recent decades the Church has been at the forefront of moves to care for our creation. Organisations like *A Rocha*[16] have made it a priority to emphasise how central creation care is to biblical Christian faith.

As explored in more detail earlier in this book, the Bible teaches of a new earth and a new heaven, but this renewal does not imply that our treatment of the planet is of no consequence. Far from it. As our bodies are central to our identity and to God's gift of life, so too the physical world is central to God's purposes both for now and for the future. As a Christian engagement with Human Enhancement points to the significance of our human bodies, it also points beyond that to the value of the whole created world. It is right that the Church goes into the future with its eyes open, alert to the fragility of our own lives and of our world. Yet such awareness demands that we value the world around us more and not less.

* * *

About ten years ago my parent and I visited Chartwell, the home of Sir Winston Churchill from 1922 until his death in 1965. It was an inspiring and thought-provoking visit. The most powerful moment of the trip for me was walking out of the house to look out over the Kent countryside. I had just read a note in the dining room which explained that it was the view from the house out over that beautiful green landscape which inspired Churchill to work so tirelessly to defend England. Churchill seemed to be energised by the beauty of that landscape, and the very fact that it was threatened by invasion seemed to spur Churchill on to appreciate it more, and to work ever harder to preserve it.

We cannot know what threats the human body and the created world will face in years to come. Yet the fact that such threats lie ahead is no reason to give up on those precious gifts. Rather, we will be wise to cherish ever more deeply the treasure God has given us in our own bodies and in the world.[17] God has already determined their ultimate fate in resurrection bodies and a new heaven and a new earth. It is right to be realistic both about what lies soon ahead, and about our ultimate destiny. Both of those aspects of reality can rightly inspire us to prize the physical created world more highly than ever and to use it to point others to our loving, creating and redeeming Lord, Jesus Christ.

Questions for discussion

1. Which risks do you feel are most significant in relation to how you live your own life today?

2. What leaves you most anxious about the future? How might those anxieties be overcome?

3. Can you identify people or organisations that exaggerate risks and cause fear?

4. Which risks and threats do you feel are most significant in relation to the world as a whole over the coming decades?

5. How might the Church respond to issues of fear and reality in our climate of global risks?

6. What do you feel we need to do nationally and globally in order to prepare for future human needs?

7. In which situations do you need to hear God's words 'Do not be afraid' for yourself and for others?

8. What has God revealed about the future? What can we know and what remains unknown?

9. How does your hope for the future affect the way you live today?

10. What are your priorities in relation to caring for your own body? For the physical needs of others? And for the planet?

Notes

[1] See Martin Rees' 2003 book in which he explores threats to human existence, *Our Final Century: Will Civilisation survive the Twenty-First Century?*, p28-9.

[2] *Our Final Century.*

[3] *Our Final Century*, p2.

[4] Bill Joy's infamous article *Why the Future Doesn't Need Us* was first published in *Wired* magazine in the year 2000. It is available online through the *Wired* archive at http://www.wired.com/wired/archive/8.04/joy.html. Accessed 17 May 2011.

[5] *Our Final Century*, p188.

[6] Matthew 6:25-34

[7] Genesis 21:17; 2 Kings 1:15; Matthew 1:20, 28:5; Luke 1:13, 1:30, 2:10. The words 'Do not be afraid' are spoken by God on numerous other occasions from Genesis 15:1 to Revelation 2:10.

[8] Matthew 24:3, 25:13; Mark 13:35.

[9] Mark 13:33-7.

[10] Matthew 26:41; Mark 14:26-52.

[11] *Global Catastrophic Risks*

[12] *Global Catastrophic Risks*, p29.

[13] *Global Catastrophic Risks*, p73-90.

[14] John 14:2.

[15] Romans 8:38-9.

[16] www.arocha.org

[17] 2 Corinthians 4:7.

Chapter 15

BEING SALT AND LIGHT IN THIS CONTEXT

'You are the salt of the earth; but if salt has lost its taste, how can its saltiness be restored? It is no longer good for anything, but is thrown out and trampled underfoot. You are the light of the world. A city built on a hill cannot be hidden. No one after lighting a lamp puts it under the bushel basket, but on the lampstand, and it gives light to all in the house. In the same way, let your light shine before others, so that they may see your good works and give glory to your Father in heaven.' Matthew 5:13-16

I can still remember the childhood excitement of finding the small bag of salt in a packet of crisps and, after tearing open the dark blue bag, shaking its contents onto the crisps. As a young boy there was something wonderful about this opportunity to prepare the snack for oneself. The salt made all the difference. The plain crisps became tasty with the addition of the salt.

Today each packet of food I buy provides me with details about its salt content and what proportion of my recommended daily intake it contains. Salt brings out the flavour within food as well as acting as a preservative. It is because of our desire to enhance taste that we need to monitor our salt intake to ensure we do not have too much of a good thing. Humans are not the only species to be drawn to salt. Like us, other mammals need a certain amount of salt in their diet. Many animals will go far out of their way to find natural salt deposits, and artificial 'salt licks' are a well-known way of attracting wildlife.

Jesus' description of his disciples as 'the salt of the earth'[1] draws upon the properties of salt to preserve and to draw out flavour. How wonderful that this phrase has become used of those whom we admire most in society. When the Church responds to her call to be salt in the world she makes life better for all. She draws out the flavour of beauty, creativity and fullness of life within the created world. She models what is good and helps to preserve worldly enterprises from becoming rotten and corrupt.

Salt also makes us thirsty and we quickly reach for a drink if we eat a lot of salty food. Similarly, as we respond to our call to be the salt of the earth, we will promote spiritual thirst in others. As, through our saltiness, we generate that thirst, we will point others towards Jesus, the only One who can quench that thirst. He is the One who provides spiritual water which will become a spring of water gushing up to eternal life.[2] He is the One who invites everyone who is thirsty to come and to take the water of life as a gift.[3]

As the Church responds to Jesus' call to be salt within society in the context of Human Enhancement, we will preserve from decay, we will draw out the flavour of all that is good within our culture, and we will leave others thirsty for living water. As we drink deeply of that living water our eyes will look beyond life extension, and the enhancement of worldly powers, to the hope of resurrection life.

* * *

I also have childhood memories of light. I can think of light pouring through a round window in one of my early homes. I remember different lamps at my grandparents' home, used to illuminate evening card games and the reading of stories. I have memories of the colours of fireworks and of sunsets and sunrises. I remember the horror with which I first considered what it would be like to experience the darkness of an arctic winter. Being told about the blindness of Helen Keller, I remember being profoundly struck by the recognition that my life would be so very different if I were unable to see.

As we need salt in our diet, so too we need light in our world. Light reveals and illuminates. It enables colours to be displayed. It provides vision for decision and action. Light is a precious gift and the command for the Church to be light in the world[4] is both a challenge and also an inspiration in relation to what is possible. It is right that we seek to live with humility yet we are also called to live in such a way that our good deeds are visible to others and that they bring glory to God.

I have sometimes been reluctant to sing one of the lines within the worship song *Great is the Lord*. The lyric which thanks God 'for the work you've done in our lives' has often made me feel uncomfortable about pointing to my own life which is so far from perfect. I have not wanted to use any evidence from my own life as any basis upon which to say that 'Great is the Lord'. Surely it is better, within the context of praising God, to shy away from my own failings and mistakes. Pointing to all those issues in my life which are not yet the way I want them to be risks opening up a whole can-full of unhelpful distractions. Yet, I am finding that my thoughts are changing. My life is still far too full of mistakes and failure, yet God is at work in me and to deny that is not humility, it is to avoid acknowledging God's generosity.

It is only because God has formed me in my mother's womb[5] that I am here at all. It is only because God is a God of relationships that I find myself in a creation where I have the joyful opportunity to relate to others. It is only because God is a faithful God that I find myself in a world where I experience the gift of consciousness and the ability to engage with a world of sense and beauty in which science helps to reveal truth. It is only because God invites each of us into intimate and personal relationship with him that I can grow as a person and as a disciple of Jesus. To pretend that there is no evidence for God's goodness in the detail of each of our lives is futile. Of course I need to take responsibility for my own disobedience and selfishness, yet to pretend that God has not carried out his work within me is not humility, it would be hubristic arrogance. Flawed as I am, I cannot even maintain my own existence for a fleeting moment without God's generosity.

Letting our light shine before others[6] is not about boastful arrogance. It is about pointing to the One without whom none of us would exist. We are his awesome creation and, what is more, he invites us to join him in bringing about his good plans and purposes. There are limits to that invitation. To seek to bring about our own immortality within this life is to seek to go beyond those limits. Yet, to join in with Christ's work of healing, restoring, teaching and providing is part of the call to live as his body. Being light in the world is about recognising our nature as created beings and modelling what it is to be a creature who is fully alive, neither denying our creatureliness, nor devaluing the awesome potential within each of us to be used by God. We are called to live openly and visibly in the world, not safely tucked away. We are not to stay in a secure huddle but to live on the world's edges, flavouring, preserving, revealing and illuminating.

* * *

Engaging with Human Enhancement is just one of many ways in which we, the Church, need to respond to Jesus' call to be salt and light in the world. This will require speaking into the subject and modelling what it means to be human within our technological context. It will involve keeping alert to the ways in which those who advocate enhancement will call for society to act. It will mean being prepared to live differently to those around us if that is required in order to affirm our nature as creatures. It will mean praying for ourselves, the world, and the Church.

The call to be salt and light can provide us with profound hope in the context of a technological world which seems to move so rapidly down avenues we might not wish to enter. The image of salt and light remind us that in God's economy size and scale can be deceptive. A very small amount of salt can offer taste and preservation to a much larger quantity of food. A small flame can illuminate an entire room. When we feel surrounded by a world which is embracing technology in a way that seems to be placing trust in human accomplishment over divine gift, we can be encouraged by the call to be salt and light. When two or three of Jesus' followers are gathered together, he is there in the midst of us.[7]

The Church does not need to be powerful in the world's eyes to make a real difference for good. Indeed God sometimes seems drawn to using what is not powerful. God promised Abraham that had there been just ten righteous men in Sodom he would have saved the entire city on the basis of their righteousness.[8] When God was preparing to use Gideon and his men to rescue Israel from the Midianites, he deliberately whittled down the number of Gideon's troops.[9] This is the God whose power is made perfect in weakness.[10]

In the coming years and decades there may well be times when we will feel as if the world is changing for the worse so very quickly that we seem powerless to do anything about it. Yet, we are called to be salt and light and we can trust God to accomplish all that he sets out to achieve. He will use us to bring about his plans and purposes exactly as he chooses. We do not need to determine the future. We simply need to respond to God's call with trust and obedience, valuing the privilege of being used by him.

One key aspect of responding to God's call to be salt and light will be to pray and work for unity within the Church. Jesus himself prayed for that unity[11] and it is affirmed throughout the Bible.[12]

During my four years as a secondary school chemistry teacher, one of the areas which I loved introducing eleven and twelve year old pupils to was the difference between chemical elements and compounds. There are just fewer than one hundred naturally occurring elements and they include oxygen, hydrogen, carbon and aluminium. They combine chemically to form compounds including water, carbon dioxide and table salt.

It is possible to show school students how sodium and chlorine combine to form white crystals of sodium chloride, table salt. Sodium is a silvery metal. It can be cut with a knife. It will ignite with an orange flame when it is thrown into water. Chlorine is a pale green gas used as a nerve agent in the First World War. If a small piece of sodium is dropped into a glass jar full of chlorine gas, it will react immediately, producing a flash of light energy and white sodium chloride crystals. The chemical compound which is produced is so very different to the elements from which it is comprised. When the sodium and chlorine are separated they do not offer the goodness of salt. Alone, they comprise a poisonous gas and a reactive metal. Combined together they offer taste and preservation. As they react together they give out light.

White light is made up of a spectrum of colours. We see those constituent colours when they separate as sunlight passes through water droplets and a rainbow is formed, or when white light passes through a glass prism. Each particular colour of visible light has its own frequency and its own beauty, but it is white light which illuminates our world afresh each morning. White light reveals the beauty of God's creation and that light reveals and illuminates because of the component parts from which it is formed. It is only when the rainbow of differently coloured frequencies of light come together and combine that white light is formed. As in salt, and in the Church, light too is dependent upon unity.

If we as the Church, members of the body of Christ, are to respond to Christ's call to be salt and light in the world, we will need to obey his call to work for unity. Unless we are one in him, we will be unable to work together in the way to which we are called. Teamwork requires unity. Furthermore, speaking into our social context requires unity if we are to avoid being heard as a babble of competing sounds. Of course, each member of the body of Christ will have his or her own perspective, experience and character. Our insights into the reality of God and his activity in our world will not be exactly the same; neither will our understanding of what is required of each of us. Nonetheless, unless the Church finds a way to speak with some sense of unity, it will be terribly difficult for the world to hear and to assess what the Church has to say within our technological context.

The Church has too often been so concerned about discussing theological and ecclesiastical differences that we have failed to communicate our shared understandings. If we continue to behave in such a way we risk the world being unable to hear that which we need to be saying. This is not a call to abandon the task of continuing to articulate our understanding of who God is and how he is at work in the world. We need to keep on growing in wisdom and in faith. We need to continue to learn from one another as iron sharpens iron. Yet, unless we model and speak out that of which we are confident, we are failing to offer others the opportunity to make decisions on the basis of a Christian perspective. Of course we do not have all the answers. Of course we disagree amongst ourselves. Of course we are still in the process of learning and growing. Yet, in the meantime we have a sure and certain hope for the future. This truth needs to be spoken out into our society if the world is to be able to make sense of what is going on around us.

*   *   *

Our technological world provides a critical context within which to speak with unity and purpose. It is a challenge to speak out on these issues for they spring up rapidly and the Church can find that she does not have long to engage with them before the context has changed once more. Nonetheless, these technological issues also provide an opportunity to speak with unity, for the specific areas of discussion are so new that there is little baggage of past disagreement. We have a fresh chance to work out what it might mean for the Church to gather around an issue and to speak with clarity and unity for the benefit of society.

Such speech will always involve nuance and a variety of perspectives. We have been called to be members of a body, not to be clones of one another. Yet, if society is to hear the words of the Church today, we need to learn more about naming our agreements and our shared understandings, and to find better ways of exploring our differences within the light of those agreements.

If we can discipline ourselves and our discussions for the benefit of society we will discover we are more fully alive as the Church. As Jesus warned that those who seek to save their own lives will lose them, yet those who lose their life for his sake will find them,[13] we may discover as a Church that forsaking our own internal agendas and focussing instead upon the needs of the world, we will bring life to the Church as well as to the world.

Questions for discussion

1. What emotions do you have in response to Jesus' call to his followers to be salt and light in the world? Does any aspect of this call excite you? Does any aspect concern you?

2. Which needs within society today in relation to Human Enhancement and other issues of technology do you perceive to be most important?

3. What might it mean to be salt and light in these areas?

4. Are there good tastes in your society which require salt to bring out their flavour?

5. Are there any practical steps you feel God calling you to take to be salt and light in relation to these subjects?

6. How does your involvement with your local church relate to these challenges?

7. Do you observe unity within your local church?

8. Do you have any sense of how God is calling you to pray for the Church and the world in our technological context?

9. What sense do you have of being united to others? How might you nurture and work for appropriate unity with others?

10. What most concerns you about the world around you? Does any aspect of this concern require you to take action?

Notes

[1] Matthew 5:13.

[2] John 4:14.

[3] Revelation 22:17.

[4] Matthew 5:14.

[5] Psalm 139:13.

[6] Matthew 5:16.

[7] Matthew 18:20.

[8] Genesis 18:32.

[9] Judges 7:1-8.

[10] 2 Corinthians 12:9.

[11] John 17:23.

[12] Psalm 133:1; 1 Corinthians 1:10; Ephesians 4:3; Philippians 2:1-3.

[13] Matthew 16:25; Mark 8:35; Luke 17:33.

Chapter 16

RESPONDING PRACTICALLY

'Very truly, I tell you, the one who believes in me will also do the works that I do and, in fact, will do greater works than these, because I am going to the Father. I will do whatever you ask in my name, so that the Father may be glorified in the Son. If in my name you ask me for anything, I will do it.' John 14:12-14

During the last decade of the twentieth century I had the privilege of carrying out some chemical research using DNA. The techniques I was using were common in universities and laboratories around the world. Today, many of them will have been superseded by more developed procedures. Yet, had some of the world-renowned biologists of the nineteenth century seen what I was doing they would have been amazed. The everyday scientific methods and procedures which I was able to take for granted were undreamed of by scientists living and working one hundred years earlier. Yet those common experimental techniques only came about because of the ability of one generation of scientists to build upon the discoveries of those who had gone before. My own scientific research was made possible by the pioneering work of those who had preceded me, including that of those nineteenth century biologists who would have been so amazed by my work with DNA. Scientists do indeed stand on the shoulders of giants.

When Jesus told his disciples that those of us who believe in him will do even greater works than those his disciples saw him accomplish, he was not saying we would be greater than him in any way. Jesus Christ is our Lord and our God. Like John the Baptist, we are not worthy to stoop down and to untie the straps of his sandals.[1] Yet, through his grace and generosity he does offer us the gift of joining him in carrying out incredible works through the power of his Holy Spirit. God invites us to be used by him in the most amazing ways and to accomplish the most wonderful purposes, not because we are great, but because he is God and he chooses to invite us to be used by him.

In the face of the myriad challenges posed by technology in our society today, I find it easy to feel that there is little I can do to make any difference. To complicate matters further, I am often uncertain about how God is calling us to respond. Yet I do know that God accomplishes awesome things through his people. I am also convinced that our response needs to involve pointing to our own nature as created beings, and pointing to God as our loving Creator and Redeemer. As explored in the previous chapter, we have been called to let our light shine in the world. God is inviting each of us to offer ourselves to him that we might be used for his purposes. Let's join together to do that!

This book has been written in the hope that God might use it as part of his work in prompting the Church to pray and to engage with society around the issue of Human Enhancement. It has been written through a compulsion to respond to what I have sensed as a personal call to be part of this engagement. Writing this book was not the result of an objective decision based upon a rational calculation. Rather, it has been an action growing out of a sense that I would not be at peace until I had accomplished that which I felt called to do. I pray that God will take this book and use it as part of his purposes. I recognise that for it to be of any use, it needs to be taken by God and made a part of something larger. I am aware that this book raises more questions than it gives answers. Yet, I pray that it prompts others to join me in wrestling with these subjects and in being part of the Church's work of reaching out into society and engaging with these issues.

* * *

I expect that a number of practical steps will need to be taken next in order for the Church to continue to engage with this issue. Of course, as in all preparations for the future, we will need to plan with the understanding that circumstances will take us by surprise and that the unexpected will determine much of what we do. Nonetheless, it is surely prudent to begin to prepare for what is likely to be expected of us.

Next steps which are likely to be of value include the following:

1. Forming groups, teams and communities within which to explore these issues together;
2. Keeping alert to small choices within science, medicine and technology which may lead to significant shaping of our future society;
3. Working for the health of the Church in relation to love, unity, holiness and prayerfulness so as to be equipped to work for the needs of others;
4. Continuing to develop a mindset within the Church which is outward looking and which prioritises the needs of the world over internal disagreements;
5. Engaging with all those who work in the fields of science, medicine and technology, including paying careful attention to the insights they gain, so we can learn as much as possible concerning all that God is inviting us to discover through that work;

6. Continuing to prioritise showing love to all those who are weak, and discovering together the wonderful ways in which God invites us to be fully alive as human beings, with all the realities of our inherent human limitations;
7. Modelling what it means to face disability, aging and death in the context of the hope of resurrection life.

1. Forming groups, teams and communities

As I have begun to explore this area over the last few years I have been aware of an increasing amount being written which advocates Human Enhancement. Furthermore, people seem to be gathering around the subject, within face-to-face organisations and groups as well as within online communities. Yet the Church seems to have commented very little upon this area and there appears to be no significant gathering of Christians around the subject. My sense is that, unless we come together as a body to explore how we need to engage with Human Enhancement for the benefit of society, we will find it difficult to move beyond disconnected comments and projects. I pray that this book will prompt Christians to come together to work on these issues.

Practical next steps: I believe we need to begin to form such groups immediately. I encourage anyone reading this who feels prompted to do so, to take action to join with others in prayer and other forms of engagement with this subject. I pray that this book might be part of beginning to link people who wish to form part of such a network.

2. Keeping alert to small choices

Developments in science, medicine and technology come about incrementally and it is often only by looking back upon a longer period of change that we become aware of how those developments have affected our lives. Yet each of those small steps can influence the larger trend. We are not yet faced with opportunities to live for hundreds of years, to upload ourselves into a computer network or to exert significant control over our children's genetic identity, but we are able to influence how our current scientific, medical and technological context changes, at least in small ways.

We have the opportunity to speak into conversations with our doctors and other medical professionals which relate to views on aging and disability. We have the freedom to express our own understanding of what it is for us, our parents and our children to be human in the context of valuing healing whilst also holding onto the hope of resurrection life. We have the chance to vote for politicians who will have responsibility for shaping the legal and political framework within which technological developments will take place. We are able to use our time, money and other resources in such a way as demonstrates that we care both for our own needs and also for the needs of others.

Exploring the subject of Human Enhancement draws attention to dramatic future possibilities for radical life extension, genetic control and enhanced human powers and abilities. Yet we will not experience a single moment at which we as a society are invited to choose whether or not to embark upon such a path. Instead, we will face myriad small choices, each of which will influence whether we move closer or further from a future in which we put our hope in human ability rather than divine gift. It is the way in which we engage with those small choices which will influence the shape of our future society.

Practical next steps: Let's keep in mind these issues next time we visit our doctor or hospital, as we spend money on healthcare, and as we engage with our political leaders.

3.   Working for the health of the Church

Too often we hear stories of those who have to take time out to recover from the effects of overwork and stress. It is right that we work sacrificially for the benefit of others, yet if we do not remain alert to our own health we may suddenly find ourselves able to offer only very little to others. In the same way, unless we keep alert to our corporate health, the Church may find its ability to work for the good of others has become weakened. This corporate health requires a high level of love, unity, holiness and prayerfulness. We need to keep in good shape because the work we will be invited to contribute to in the coming years requires us to be fit for purpose.

We need to be disciplined in developing the characteristics of love, unity, holiness and prayerfulness. These are not optional extras which will leave us feeling better about ourselves. They are vital aspects of who we need to be if we are to be able to fulfil our calling to be salt and light in the world. It is such a privilege to have been called by God to join him in his work in the world. We need to ensure that nothing we do prevents us from responding to that call.

At the heart of the enhancement quest is the question of whether future hope is based upon human activity or divine gift. In prayer, Christians are continually being shaped into a people who look not to our own gifts, skills and accomplishments but to God's generosity. I am convinced that the more we model what it is to be a prayerful people the easier it will be for the world to imagine a future which does not depend upon human achievement. Unless we embody trust in God through living prayerful lives, we will not be able to speak with any integrity about basing our hope for the future upon God's provision.

I believe that the most appropriate response that anyone can make to this book is to grow in prayerfulness and gratitude to God, recognising that all good gifts come from him and that we are invited into the good future which he has already secured. Prayer will not only open us further to God's priorities, align our will with his, and focus us on being used by God in bringing about his plans and purposes, but it expresses the very dependence upon God which the enhancement quest challenges.

Practical next steps: Let's review our habits of prayer and amend them if necessary. Let's consider our connections to other Christians, within our local churches and beyond, and work to ensure these relationships model unity and love. Let's pray for all leaders within the Church.

4.   Looking outwards and prioritising the needs of others

It is understandable that church conversations often involve issues of worship, belief and leadership. These areas of church life are important and we need to ensure that the ways in which we attend to these areas are holy and pleasing to God. Nonetheless, we have not been given the opportunity to spend all our time discussing such matters. We have work to do in the world. Jesus sent us out to make disciples of all nations.[2] Such disciple-making involves pointing to God's activity in all areas of our lives, including technological areas.

It also involves helping those around us to make sense of how we live well as human beings in light of the fact that we are creatures, formed and redeemed by a loving God.

We need to ensure that our church life is focused upon responding to God's call to love him and to love others. That will require attending to our own internal health but that attention can never come at the cost of those outside. We worship Christ who laid down his life for the benefit of others. We too need to have the same attitude,[3] and the Church needs to demonstrate that we prioritise the needs of others. If ever we find ourselves caught up in pouring resources into projects which are neither about loving God, nor about showing love to others, we need to stop ourselves and turn around.

Practical next steps: Let's reflect upon the ways in which our own lives, and the life of the Church, model love for others. Let's revise our habits as necessary and seek to model an outward looking concern for others within our local churches.

5.   Engaging with those who work within the fields of science, medicine and technology

Those who work within the medical profession as doctors, nurses, researchers, managers and in other roles have particular responsibilities for helping us as a society to engage with issues of Human Enhancement. Many of the decisions which will shape our future society in relation to enhancement and technology will not be voted upon by the population at large. They will be taken by small groups of professionals as part of their day to day work. These include the ways in which the medical profession offer care when it is not possible to cure, the ways in which unborn children, the weak and the vulnerable are treated, and the ways in which the dying are enabled to face the reality of their own mortality. Medical professionals can help patients accept the inherent limits and finitude of being human. All of us need to be praying for these professionals, those who would call themselves Christians and those who would not.

Engaging with God's creation illuminates details of how the world has been made and reveals the beauty of God's creativity. If we seek to learn from those who are best placed to uncover these insights we will ensure that our engagement with Human Enhancement is informed by a rich understanding of God's creativity. This is not to say that we delegate all ethical decisions to those who work in the fields of science, medicine and technology. That would be to neglect our corporate responsibilities as a Church and a society. Yet the insights of those whose professional work offers them particular opportunities to understand our world are gifts to be treasured.

As we need those who work in these fields, so too they need us if they are to carry out their roles for the benefit of society. Stanley Hauerwas has written on a number of occasions about the need for the Church to be the sort of community which medicine requires if it is to fulfil its own potential.[4] If medicine is to function as the gift to society which it has the potential to be, it needs to be embedded within society in such a way that the care and cure which it makes possible is understood within the wider context of what it means to be human. The Human Enhancement debate draws attention to the fact that medicine within our society has begun to break away from those foundations. The Church needs to speak wisdom into society and the medical professions in order to offer appropriate boundaries for medical work. This will involve pointing to the value of all people as created in the image of God, to the value of care as well as of cure, and of understanding healing, aging and death within the context of the hope of resurrection life.

Practical next steps: Let's pray for all who work in the fields of science, medicine and technology. Let's take any appropriate opportunities to learn about their work. Let's reflect prayerfully upon the ways in which medicine shapes our society.

6. Showing love to and learning from all who are weak

Our nature as human beings involves both weakness and strength. Learning to accept the intrinsic limitations that help to shape who we are as human beings has been a key topic of this book. Recognising and embracing this reality will involve showing love to all those people whose weakness we see, as well as learning from the weaknesses within others and ourselves. Yet this perspective is threatened by the dangerous view that our potential will only be achieved by striving for ever greater power and control. If our society proceeds further down the road of seeking enhancement of human abilities we will run the danger of losing respect for those amongst us who are weakest.

In this context, it is vital that the Church keeps modelling and championing the importance of caring for those who are weak. In doing so, we will learn more about what it means for each of us to be fully human. This care of the weak needs to include caring for children, those born as well as those not yet born, and for the disabled, the sick, the elderly and the dying. This priority is no new innovation in response to our particular technological context. The gospels reveal the importance that Jesus gives to welcoming children[5] and to healing the sick.

Caring for children needs to involve welcoming *all* children, not just those we feel particularly connected to. Whenever we demonstrate that our love for our children is not determined by seeking for them

194

to gain at the expense of someone else's child, we will help to build a community which welcomes all children, regardless of ability or competence. Whenever we demonstrate a willingness to welcome a new child into the world without first checking that it meets certain health criteria, we challenge the assumption that we have a duty to have the 'best' possible child, whatever 'best' means in relation to children. Whenever we adopt a child, or support those who are doing so, we challenge the idea that parenting is dependent upon having a child 'of one's own'. Whenever we seek to care for children as part of a community of love, we help to demonstrate the fact that in Christ our relationships to one another are not determined by bloodline or genetics.

If the Church can model this unconditional welcome of all children, we will offer a profound perspective on valuing each and every human being that will help to illuminate all issues relating to our care for one another.

Practical next steps: Let's reflect upon all those close to us who may be in particular need and consider what love and support we may be called to offer. Let's pray for one another as we struggle with our own particular weaknesses and as we care for one another. Let's pray for each child and for all those who are caring for them.

7.   Modelling what it is to be human in the face of disability, aging and death

Living with disability, growing old and facing death each have their own real and profound challenges, yet most of us will be able to point to wonderful examples of people who demonstrate what it is to be fully human in these situations. Specific disabilities are different to aging and death, for each of us experiences our own unique pattern of ability, whilst all of us who avoid dying young face the same inevitability of aging and then death. Each one of us faces the challenge of coming to terms with the reality that we, like every other human being, is mortal and limited.

However old we are, we all have an opportunity to model the fact that we do not need to seek immortality in this life. In relation to the money which we invest in our own healthcare and the way in which we react to our own mortality, we are able to model a hope in life beyond death. If the Church can model what it means to live fully human lives in the context of all the realities of human mortality and limitation, we will embody a challenge to any who argue that shrugging off these conditions is necessary for us to flourish.

Practical next steps: Each of us has the opportunity to demonstrate love, grace, humour and hope in the face of our own inabilities and limitations. Let's encourage one another, affirming the gifts of others, offering our own gifts for the benefit of others, and delighting in the reality that God's power is made perfect in weakness. Let's embody what it means to live in the light of a vast horizon of resurrection hope.

* * *

I believe that it is important to have concluded this book with a chapter considering practical responses because our contemporary technological context demands our engagement. Nonetheless, in the light of this book's call to focus upon divine gift rather than human ability, it seems fitting to close this chapter with prayer and a focus upon the Bible, rather than upon advice about human action.

Father God, may the same mind be in us that was in Jesus. We bend our knee to him and we confess that he is Lord, to your glory, Amen.

'Let the same mind be in you that was in Christ Jesus, who, though he was in the form of God, did not regard equality with God as something to be exploited, but emptied himself, taking the form of a slave, being born in human likeness. And being found in human form, he humbled himself and became obedient to the point of death – even death on a cross. Therefore God also highly exalted him and gave him the name that is above every name, so that at the name of Jesus every knee should bend, in heaven and on earth and under the earth, and every tongue should confess that Jesus Christ is Lord, to the glory of God the Father.' Philippians 2:5-11

Questions for discussion

1. What aspects of the future are you left pondering most in light of this book?

2. Are there any next steps you feel God is calling you to take as part of his work in this area? If so, what are they?

3. Are there others around you to whom you need to be connected more deeply in order to respond to what God is calling you to do? If so, who are they?

4. Are there any skills, experience or resources which you have been given which may be needed by others within this work? If so, what are they?

5. Do you have a sense of how your particular role at work, your family situation and your local social context provide opportunities for you to engage with issues of Human Enhancement?

6. Are there obstacles preventing you from responding to God's call in these areas? If so, what help do you need in overcoming them?

7. Are you prompted to pray for others in relation to this subject? If so, who?

8. What are the most important needs of children you are aware of, both close to home and further afield?

9. Is there anything you are being called to do in relation to caring for children?

10. What is the next step you are being called to take in relation to our wider technological context?

Notes

---

[1] Matthew 3:11; Mark 1:7; Luke 3:16; John 1:27.

[2] Matthew 28:19-20.

[3] Philippians 2:5.

[4] Hauerwas describes 'the community of and required by medicine' within his 1986 book *Suffering Presence*, p51-54.

[5] Matthew 19:14; Mark 10:14; Luke 18:16.

BIBLIOGRAPHY

Bonhoeffer, D. (2005) *Dietrich Bonhoeffer Works, Volume 6: Ethics* (Minneapolis, MN: Fortress Press)

Bostrom, N. (2003b) *Transhumanist Values.* Available from: www.nickbostrom.com [Accessed 20 May 2011].

Bostrom, N. (2005) *The Fable of the Dragon-Tyrant.* Available from: www.bostrom.org [Accessed 21 March 2011].

Bostrom, N. & Cirkovic, M. M. Editors (2008) *Global Catastrophic Risks* (Oxford: Oxford University Press)

Brock, B. (2010) *Christian Ethics in a Technological Age* (Grand Rapids, MI: W. B. Eerdmans Publishing Co.)

Brown, G. (2008) *The Living End: The Future of Death, Aging and Immortality* (London: Macmillan)

Campbell, H. & Walker, M. (2005) *Religion and Transhumanism: Introducing a Conversation.* Journal of Evolution and Technology 14(2). Available from: http://jetpress.org/volume14/specialissueintro.html [Accessed 21 March 2011].

Cole-Turner, R. Ed. (2008) *Design and Destiny: Jewish and Christian Perspectives on Human Germline Modification* (London: The MIT Press)

Cooper, J. W. (2000) *Body, Soul & Life Everlasting: Biblical Anthropology and the Monism-Dualism Debate* (Grand Rapids, MI: W. B. Eerdmans Publishing Co.).

Daly, T. T. (2008) *A Theological Analysis of Life Extension via Aging Attenuation with particular reference to Ascetic Practice in the Desert Fathers.* Unpublished University of Edinburgh PhD Thesis. Available from: http://hdl.handle.net/1842/2588 [Accessed 1 April 2011].

de Grey, A. with Rae, M. (2007) *Ending Aging: The Rejuvenation Breakthroughs that could reverse Human Aging in our lifetime* (New York: St Martin's Press)

Deane-Drummond, C. Editor (2003) *Brave New World?: Theology, Ethics and the Human Genome* (London: T & T Clark)

Deane-Drummond, C. & Scott, P. M. Editors (2010) *Future Perfect? God, Medicine and Human Identity* (London: T & T Clark)

Ellul, J. (1964) *The Technological Society* (Translated from the French by John Wilkinson)(Toronto: Vintage Books)

European Parliament STOA Report (2009) *Human Enhancement Study*. Available from: http://www.itas.fzk.de/deu/lit/2009/coua09a.pdf [Accessed 3rd August 2011].

Fukuyama, F. (2002) *Our Post-Human Future: Consequences of the Biotechnology Revolution* (New York: Profile Books)

Fuller, S. (2011) *Humanity 2.0: What it means to be Human Past, Present and Future* (Basingstoke: Palgrave Macmillan)

Garreau, J. (2005) *Radical Evolution: The Promise and Peril of Enhancing Our Minds, Our Bodies – and What it Means to Be Human* (New York: Broadway Books)

Goodman, D. C. Ed (1973) *Science and Religious Belief 1600-1900* (Dorchester: John Wright & Sons)

Greenfield, S. (2003) *Tomorrow's People: How 21st-Century Technology is Changing the Way We Think and Feel* (London: Allen Lane)

Haldane, J. B. S. (1923) *Daedalus: Science and the Future*. Available from: http://www.cscs.umich.edu/~crshalizi/Daedalus.html [Accessed 25th May 2011].

Harris, J. (2007) *Enhancing Evolution – The Ethical Case for Making Better People* (Princeton: Princeton University Press)

Hauerwas, S. (1981b) *A Community of Character: Towards a Constructive Christian Social Ethic* (Notre Dame, IN: University of Notre Dame Press)

Hauerwas, S. (1998) *Suffering Presence: Theological Reflections on Medicine, the Mentally Handicapped and the Church* (Edinburgh: T. & T. Clark)

Hauerwas, S. (2001) *The Hauerwas Reader* (Durham: Duke University Press)

Hauerwas, S. (2001) *Wilderness Wanderings* (London: SCM Press)

Hays, R. B. (1996) *The Moral Vision of the New Testament: A Contemporary Introduction to New Testament Ethics* (Edinburgh: T & T Clark)

Huxley, A. (2007) *Brave New World* (London: Vintage Books)

Jones, D. G. (2005) *Designers of the Future: Who Should Make the Decisions?* (Oxford: Monarch Books)

Joy, B. (2000) *Why the Future Doesn't Need Us.* Wired Issue 8.04 Available from: http://www.wired.com/wired/archive/8.04/joy.html [Accessed 17 May 2011].

Kelly, K. (2010) *What Technology Wants* (London: Viking)

Kurzweil, R. (1999) *The Age of Spiritual Machines: When Computers Exceed Human Intelligence* (New York: Viking Press)

Kurzweil, R. (2005) *The Singularity is Near* (New York: Penguin)

Kurzweil, R. & Grossman, T. (2005) *Fantastic Voyage: Live Long Enough to Live Forever* (London: Rodale)

Kurzweil, R. & Grossman, T. (2009) *TRANSCEND: Nine Steps to Living Well Forever* (New York: Rodale)

Lammers, S. E. & Verhey, A. Eds. (1998) *On Moral Medicine: Theological Perspectives in Medical Ethics* (Grand Rapids, MI: W. B. Eerdmans Publishing Co.)

Lewis, C. S. (1978) *The Abolition of Man* (London: Fount Paperbacks)

Lewis, C. S. (2004) *The Collected Letters of C. S. Lewis Volume II: Books, Broadcasts, and the War 1931-1949* (New York: HarperCollins)

McKibben, B. (2003) *Enough: Genetic Engineering and The End of Human Nature* (London: Bloomsbury Publishing Plc)

Messer, N. (2002) *Theological Issues in Bioethics* (London: Darton, Longman & Todd)

Messer, N. (2011) *Respecting Life: Theology and Bioethics* (London: SCM Press)

Metaxas, E. (2010) *Bonhoeffer: Pastor, Martyr, Prophet, Spy* (Nashville: Thomas Nelson)

Middleton, J. R. (2005) *The Liberating Image: The Imago Dei in Genesis 1* (Grand Rapids MI: Brazos Press)

Moore, P. (2000) *Babel's Shadow – Genetic Technologies in a Fracturing Society* (Oxford: Lion Publishing plc)

Moore, P. (2008) *Enhancing Me – The Hope and Hype of Human Enhancement* (Chichester: John Wiley & Sons)

Murphy, N. (2008) *Nonreductive Physicalism and Free Will.* Available from: http://www.metanexus.net/Magazine/tabid/68/id/10501/Defaul t.aspx [Accessed 9th June 2011].

O'Donovan, O. (1984) *Begotten or Made?* (Oxford: Oxford University Press)

Outka, G. (1972) *Agape: An Ethical Analysis* (New Haven & London: Yale University Press)

President's Council on Bioethics (2003) *Beyond Therapy: Biotechnology and the Pursuit of Happiness* (New York: Regan Books)

Ramsey, P. (1970a) *Fabricated Man – The Ethics of Genetic Control* (New Haven & London: Yale University Press)

Rees, M. (2003) *Our Final Century: Will Civilisation Survive the Twenty-First Century?* (London: Arrow Books)

Sandel, M. J. (2007) *The Case against Perfection* (Cambridge, MA: Belknap Press)

Savulescu, J. (2002) *Procreative Beneficence: Why We Should Select the Best Children.* Abstract available from: http://onlinelibrary.wiley.com/doi/10.1111/1467-8519.00251/abstract [Accessed 12th March 2011].

Savulescu, J. & Bostrom, N. (2009) *Human Enhancement* (Oxford: Oxford University Press)

Silver, L. M. (1999) *Remaking Eden – Cloning, Genetic Engineering and the Future of Humankind?* (London: Phoenix Giant)

Singer, P. (1995) *Rethinking Life and Death: The Collapse of Our Traditional Ethics* (Oxford: Oxford University Press)

Song, R. (2002) *Human Genetics: Fabricating the Future* (London: Darton, Longman & Todd)

Sutton, A. (2008) *Christian Bioethics: A Guide for the Perplexed* (London: T & T Clark)

Waters, B. (2001) *Reproductive Technology – Towards a Theology of Procreative Stewardship* (London: Darton, Longman & Todd Ltd)

Waters, B. (2006) *From Human to Posthuman: Christian Theology and Technology in a Postmodern World* (Aldershot, Hants: Ashgate Publishing Co.)

Wells, S. (2004) *Improvisation: The Drama of Christian Ethics* (London: SPCK)

Wright, N. T. (1992) *The New Testament and the People of God* (London: SPCK)

THE WI B

JAMS
and Other Preserves

PAT HESKETH

EBURY
PRESS

ACKNOWLEDGEMENTS

Illustrated by Vanessa Luff
Edited by Sue Jacquemier and Rosemary Wadey
Designed by Clare Clements
Cover photography by James Jackson
The publishers would like to thank the dozens of WI
members who tested the recipes in this book.
Some of the recipes on pages 14–16, 18–19, 22, 24, 26,
30, 36–40, 47–8, 50–1, 56–8, 63, 68–70, 72, 76, 80,
82–3, 85, 87, and 90–1 are based on recipes from *Bulletin
21 – Home Preservation of Fruit and Vegetables* (HMSO
1971) with the kind permission of the Controller of Her
Majesty's Stationery Office. The author wishes also to
acknowledge the advice given by the staff of the Home
Preservation section of the Long Ashton Research
Station, Bristol.

Published by Ebury Press
National Magazine House
72 Broadwick Street
London W1V 2BP

ISBN 0 85223 307 8

First impression 1984

Filmset by
D. P. Media Limited, Hitchin, Hertfordshire

Reproduced, printed and bound in Great Britain by
Hazell Watson & Viney Limited,
Member of the BPCC Group,
Aylesbury, Bucks

CONTENTS

INTRODUCTION

Foods have been preserved by many methods over the centuries, but in particular by drying, salting and freezing. Traditionally this has enabled housewives to provide a varied menu throughout the year. Modern growing methods and air freight have meant that most fruits and vegetables are always available in the supermarkets, but when locally grown fruits and vegetables are at their peak, they are relatively cheap to purchase, and great personal satisfaction can be achieved from the making of preserves, and from seeing a larder containing a good selection of home-produced preserves.

Three types of preserves are relatively easy and cheap to make and are eaten by most families: jams, marmalades and, to a lesser extent, some vinegar preserves such as chutneys. Using fruits and vegetables in season means they are at their best and their least expensive, and will bring welcome variety to meals at other times of the year.

To ensure that fruits and vegetables keep well when preserved, it is necessary to understand a little about enzyme action and about the control of spoilage organisms – yeasts, moulds and bacteria.

The action of enzymes brings about the natural ripening of fruits and also, given time, their decay. So it is necessary to stop enzyme action when fruits are ripe. This can be done by heat, as when making jams and bottling fruit, and also by low temperatures, as in the freezing of foods.

Yeasts, moulds and bacteria are micro-organisms which can be killed by high temperatures and also have their growth inhibited by high concentrations of sugar and high acid content. Methods of making preserves take these principles into account.

Jams, jellies and marmalades should have a sufficiently high sugar content to prevent fermentation, but they must also, after making, be covered in a manner which prevents the re-entry of airborne micro-organisms (see page 11).

Vinegar preserves should have a sufficiently high

acid content to prevent the action of micro-organisms, and they should also be covered in a manner that prevents the vinegar from evaporating (see page 65).

The type of vinegar to use is stated in the introduction to chapter 5. If in doubt, use malt vinegar unless it is a very pale coloured preserve or pickle, when a white, distilled vinegar is preferable.

Equipment
Preserves need very little special equipment and can be made quite satisfactorily with the equipment found in most kitchens. Here is a check-list:

preserving pan and/or	scales
large saucepan	measuring jug
mixing bowl	measuring spoons
small basin	large wooden spoons
plates	(one preferably a
colander	preserving spoon)
sieve (nylon)	tablespoon
small vegetable knife	vegetable parer
large chopping knife	mincer
chopping board	juice extractor

Further equipment which may be useful:

juicer	slow cooker
liquidiser/	microwave oven
food processor	pressure cooker

Preserves in the microwave oven
Microwave ovens are particularly useful for making small batches of preserves. Jams, marmalades and chutneys can all be cooked in a microwave oven. They require less time and less attention than when cooked conventionally, but the container used for cooking must be about three times as large as the amount of ingredients being used. This will allow for the preserve to 'boil up' without spilling. It is recommended that the advice in the instruction book for each microwave oven be followed, but many of

the recipes in this book can be made successfully using a microwave oven, providing it is remembered that only small quantities may be cooked at a time.

Measurements
All spoon measures are level unless otherwise stated.
3 tsp = 1 tbsp
8 tbsp = ¼ pint = 5 fl oz = 150 ml

All eggs used are size 2 or 3 unless otherwise stated.

Use either the metric measures or the imperial in the recipes; do not mix them. They are not always equivalent to one another, because they have been tested and balanced separately.

All can sizes are approximate.

All weights referred to in lists of ingredients for fruit, vegetables, etc. are unprepared weights unless stated otherwise.

Presentation of preserves for showing
When entering a competition or show, it is necessary to read the schedule carefully so that the rules and instructions are fully understood.

It may help competitors to know that although only one mark out of twenty is given for the appearance of the container – that is, the cover, cleanliness of the jar and the label – if the cover is not suitable for the preserve and will not keep it in good condition, the judge may not judge the preserve at all.

The container must be suitable for the preserve and it must have the appropriate cover (see pages 11, 12, 65, 66 and 89 for further details). The jar should be well filled, and the glass can be polished with methylated spirits to remove fingerprints. For carrying to the show, place the jar in a polythene bag and wrap it in either newspaper or corrugated card and pack it in a box.

The label must be straight and should be parallel

to the bottom of the jar and placed as low as possible without wrinkling. The label should state: type of fruit, e.g. raspberry; type of preserve, e.g. jam; date of making, e.g. 3rd July 1984. If frozen fruit has been used, this should be stated, and also the date of making, e.g.:

Raspberry Jam
(frozen fruit)
10th January 1984

For bottled fruit the label should state the strength of the syrup or the usage to which the fruit may be put, e.g.:

Bottled Gooseberries		*Bottled Gooseberries*
(light syrup)	or	*(for pies)*
30th June 1984		*30th June 1984*

The label on chutneys should state whether they are mild or hot.

The colour should be good, and appropriate to the fruit the preserve was made from. In jams, jellies and marmalades the colour should be bright, even and sparkling. A dullness and slight darkening indicates overboiling of the preserve after the sugar was added. In chutneys, although the colour will be dark-ish, it should be bright, not muddy-looking.

The jar should be full – a low quantity in jams means that the cover is not able to do its job properly and that moulds may develop. A low quantity in vinegar may indicate shrinkage which is caused by evaporation of the vinegar due to an incorrect cover.

The consistency of jams should show a good gel, and if whole fruits are present, as with black-currants, or peel shreds as in marmalade, these should be soft. Check that they are before adding the sugar. In chutneys, if there is 'free' vinegar floating on top of the preserves, this indicates that the chut-ney was insufficiently cooked before potting.

The flavour should be characteristic of the fruit, not spoilt by the use of inferior quality fruit, nor by overboiling or burning on the base of the pan.

JAMS AND CONSERVES

In this chapter are some of the more traditional
jam recipes using unusual fruits, and also
exciting combinations of ingredients such as
rhubarb with rose petals or angelica. If you like
preserves with whole fruit in them, you will
find here recipes for conserves, but remember
that these will not set as well as jam does.

A good jam should: keep well; be clear and bright; be characteristic in colour; be well set, but not too stiff; have a distinct fruity flavour.

Jam is a mixture of fruit and sugar cooked together to form a gel. To obtain a good gel (set), acid, pectin and sugar should be present in the correct proportions. Fruits vary in their acid content and the amount of fruit used when making jam varies according to whether or not it is rich in pectin. Extra acid is often added to fruit to help release the pectin present. If frozen fruit is used, increase the amount of fruit in the recipe by 10%.

Good pectin content

Black and Redcurrants	Gooseberries
Cooking Apples	some Plums
Crab Apples	Quince
Damsons	

Medium pectin content

Early Blackberries	Loganberries
Fresh Apricots	Raspberries
Greengages	

Poor pectin content

Late Blackberries	Medlars
Cherries	Pears
Elderberries	Rhubarb
Marrow	Strawberries

Pectin Test
A test for *pectin* should be carried out after the initial cooking of the fruit with water.
1. Take 5 ml (1 tsp) juice, place it in a small glass. Cool.
2. Add 15 ml (3 tsp) methylated spirits.

3. Shake gently together.

If a well formed jelly-like clot is apparent, this shows a good pectin content.

If several small clots appear, this shows a medium pectin content.

If no clot appears, then no pectin is present.

If, after further cooking, still no recognisable clot appears, the addition of extra pectin will be necessary. This may be either juice from pectin-rich fruits, or commercial pectin. Use 50–100 ml per 450 g (2–4 fl oz per 1 lb) of fruit.

| Very little or no pectin content | Medium pectin content | Good pectin content |

Acid helps to give a bright colour and prevent crystallization. It must be added at the beginning of cooking to fruits low in acid and to any vegetable jam, in the following proportions:

To 1.8 kg (4 lb) fruit:

30 ml (2 tbsp) lemon juice (1 average lemon) or

5 ml (½ level tsp) citric acid or tartaric acid or

150 ml (¼ pint) redcurrant or gooseberry juice

Sugar. Granulated or preserving sugar may be used, but it must be thoroughly dissolved before the jam is brought to the boil. Many recipes are based on 60% sugar content, therefore if 2.7 kg (6 lb) sugar is used, a 4.5 kg (10 lb) yield could be expected.

Fruit should be dry, clean and fresh, and preferably slightly underripe.

Stages in jam-making
1. Initial cooking of fruit either on its own (e.g.
strawberries) or with water. Fruit should *simmer*
gently to break down the cell walls to release the
pectin.
2. Carrying out the pectin test. A good result means
that the cooking time with the sugar will not be
prolonged and therefore the finished jam will have a
good colour.
3. Addition of sugar, off the heat, stirring to ensure
that it is completely dissolved.
4. Returning pan to the heat, bringing to the boil,
and boiling rapidly until setting point is reached.
5. Putting into clean jars and covering immediately
with either a wax circle or a pliable plastic top or a
metal twist top. The jars should be filled to within
3 mm (⅛ inch) of the rim. A cover should be placed
on each jar as it is filled.

The cellophane dust-covers used in conjunction
with wax circles may be dampened on the upperside
and placed over the jar when either hot or cold, but
never when warm.

Tests for setting point
Saucer test (also known as plate, or wrinkle test).
Have a plate cooling in the refrigerator. Place 5 ml
(1 small tsp) jam on the plate and return to the
refrigerator to cool for 1 minute. If the surface
wrinkles as the finger is pushed through the jam, the
jam has reached setting point. *It is important to keep
the jam pan away from the heat during the test otherwise
the jam may go beyond setting point.*

Flake test. Dip the spoon into the boiling jam.

Holding the spoon above the pan, twist it horizontally to cool the jam on the surface. Allow the jam to drop from the surface. If it has reached setting point the jam will run together and form a flake on the edge of the spoon before breaking off cleanly.

Temperature test. Place a sugar thermometer into the jam. Boil the jam until it reaches a temperature of 105°C (220°F).

Labelling
Clean the jars and label with details of contents and date of making (see page 7).

Storage
All jams are best stored in cool, dry, dark, well ventilated places. Storage is a problem in centrally heated homes. Therefore jars with metal twist tops are recommended, because when properly used these form an airtight seal.

Conserves
A conserve is very similar to a jam in its making but the result is different in that the set is much softer and some fruits remain whole in a thick syrup.

Sugar thermometer
and preserving pan

APPLE AND PINEAPPLE JAM

Makes about 6.5 kg (11 lb)

3 kg (6 lb) cooking apples
1.25 litres (2 pints) unsweetened
pineapple juice
juice of 2 lemons
450-g (16-oz) can crushed pineapple
3 kg (6 lb) sugar

Peel, core and slice the apples. Place in a preserving pan with the pineapple juice and lemon juice. Simmer gently until the fruit is soft. Test for pectin. Remove from the heat.

Add the sugar and stir until dissolved. Add the drained crushed pineapple and return to the heat. Bring to the boil, and boil rapidly until setting point is reached. Pour into warmed jars, cover and label.

SEEDLESS BLACKBERRY AND APPLE JAM

Makes about 2.5 kg (5 lb)

2 kg (4 lb) sour green apples
juice of 1 orange
juice of 1 lemon
300 ml (½ pint) water
3 kg (6 lb) blackberries
sugar

Peel, core and slice the apples. Place in a preserving pan with the fruit juices and water. Simmer until tender. Add the blackberries, and simmer again until quite tender, stirring frequently.

Rub the mixture through a hair or nylon sieve and return to a clean preserving pan. To each litre of pulp add 750 g sugar or to each pint of pulp add 1 lb sugar. Stir until the sugar is dissolved. Return the pan to the heat, bring to the boil, and boil rapidly until setting point is reached. Pour into warmed jars, cover and label.

MARROW AND PINEAPPLE JAM

Makes about 3 kg (5½ lb)

2 kg (4 lb) prepared marrow
1.5 kg (3 lb) sugar
450-g (16-oz) can pineapple pieces

Peel the marrow, remove seeds and cut into small neat dice. Place in a bowl and sprinkle with the sugar. Leave overnight.

Next day, transfer to a preserving pan, add the pineapple pieces, chopping roughly if rather large and the juice. Bring to the boil, and boil until clear (about 1 hour). Pour into warmed jars, cover and label.

RASPBERRY JAM

Makes about 5 kg (10 lb)

3 kg (6 lb) raspberries
3 kg (6 lb) sugar

Place the fruit in a preserving pan and cook slowly to extract some of the juices, then simmer gently until the fruit is tender. Remove from the heat. Add the sugar, and stir until dissolved. Return the pan to the heat, bring to the boil and boil rapidly until setting point is reached. Pour into warmed jars, cover and label.

PEACH AND RASPBERRY JAM

Makes about 3.5 kg (7 lb)

1 kg (2 lb) ripe peaches (weight after stoning)
1 kg (2 lb) raspberries
150 ml (¼ pint) water
2 kg (4 lb) sugar

Skin, stone and chop the peaches into small pieces; crack a few stones to remove the kernels. Place the peaches, raspberries and water in a preserving pan and simmer gently until tender. Remove from the heat.

Add the sugar, and stir until dissolved, then a few peach kernels. Return to the heat, bring to the boil, and boil rapidly until setting point is reached. Pour into warmed jars, cover and label.

BLACKBERRY AND RHUBARB JAM

Makes about 5 kg (10 lb)

4 kg (8 lb) blackberries
1 litre (1½ pints) water
2 kg (4 lb) prepared rhubarb
sugar

Simmer the blackberries in the water until tender. Rub through a hair or nylon sieve. Cut the rhubarb into 2.5-cm (1-inch) pieces, place in a preserving pan with the sieved blackberry pulp, and simmer until tender. Remove from the heat.

To each 1 kg (2 lb) fruit pulp and 1 kg (2 lb) warmed sugar. Stir until the sugar is dissolved. Return to the heat, bring to the boil, and boil rapidly until setting point is reached. Pour into warmed jars, cover and label.

STRAWBERRY AND GOOSEBERRY JAM

Makes about 2.5 kg (5 lb)

750 g (1½ lb) gooseberries or 500 g
(1 lb) gooseberries and 250 g
(8 oz) redcurrants
150 ml (¼ pint) water
750 g (1½ lb) strawberries
1.5 kg (3 lb) sugar

Place the gooseberries (or gooseberries and redcurrants) in a preserving pan with the water, and cook gently until beginning to soften. Add the prepared strawberries and continue cooking gently until the fruit is soft. Remove from the heat. Test for pectin.
Add the sugar and stir until dissoved. Return to the heat, bring to the boil and boil rapidly until setting point is reached. Pour into warmed jars, cover and label.

GOOSEBERRY JAM

Makes about 5 kg (10 lb)

2.2 kg (4½ lb) gooseberries
1 litre (1½ pints) water
3 kg (6 lb) sugar

Wash, and top and tail the gooseberries. Place in a preserving pan with the water. Simmer gently until quite tender. Test for pectin. Remove from the heat.
Add the sugar and stir until dissolved. Return to the heat, bring to the boil and boil rapidly until setting point is reached. Pour into warmed jars, cover and label.

The degree of greenness of the jam will depend on the variety and maturity of the fruit, and the length of time of cooking with the sugar.

GOOSEBERRY AND ORANGE JAM

Makes about 2.5 kg (5 lb)

1.5 kg (3 lb) gooseberries
finely grated rind and juice of 2
oranges
300 ml (½ pint) water
1.5 kg (3 lb) sugar

Wash and top and tail the gooseberries and place in a preserving pan. Add the orange rind and juice, together with the water. Simmer gently until the fruit is tender. Test for pectin. Remove from the heat. Add the sugar, and stir until dissolved. Return to the heat, bring to the boil and boil rapidly until setting point is reached. Pour into warmed jars, cover and label.

RHUBARB AND ORANGE JAM

Makes about 2.5 kg (5 lb)

6 sweet oranges
1 kg (2¼ lb) rhubarb, trimmed and
finely sliced
sugar

Scrub the oranges in warm water. Pare the zest from the oranges with a potato peeler and cut into thin strips, or grate finely. Squeeze the juice from the fruit, allowing flesh to go with juice. Place both fruits and rind in a preserving pan and cook gently until tender.

Weigh the pulp and to each 1 kg (1 lb) fruit add 1 kg (1 lb) sugar. Stir until the sugar is dissolved. Return the pan to the heat, bring to the boil and boil rapidly until setting point is reached. Pour into warmed jars, cover and label.

RHUBARB AND GINGER JAM

Makes about 2.5 kg (5 lb)

1.5 kg (3 lb) rhubarb
1.5 kg (3 lb) sugar
130 ml (4 fl oz) lemon juice
25 g (1 oz) root ginger, bruised

Wipe the rhubarb and cut into chunks. Place in a bowl layered up with the sugar. Add the lemon juice and leave to stand overnight. Transfer to a preserving pan, and add the ginger tied in muslin. Bring to the boil and boil rapidly until setting point is reached. Remove the root ginger. Pour into warmed jars, cover and label.

RHUBARB AND ELDERFLOWER JAM

Makes about 5 kg (10 lb)

3 kg (6 lb) rhubarb
12–18 heads of elderflower
3 kg (6 lb) sugar
grated rind and juice of 2 lemons

Wipe the rhubarb and cut into 1-cm (½-inch) chunks. Place in a bowl, layering up with the sugar. Tie the elderflowers in a muslin bag and place in the middle of the rhubarb. Leave to stand for 24 hours.

Transfer the contents of the bowl to a preserving pan, bring to the boil, boil for 2–3 minutes, and return all to the bowl. Leave to stand for another 24 hours.

Remove the elderflowers. Add the grated rind and juice of the lemons to the jam and transfer to the preserving pan. Bring to the boil and boil rapidly until setting point is reached. Pour into warmed jars, cover and label.

This jam has rather a soft set.

RHUBARB AND ROSE PETAL JAM

Makes about 900 g (1¾ lb)

500 g (1 lb) rhubarb, trimmed
500 g (1 lb) sugar
juice of 1 lemon
2 handfuls of scented rose petals (red if possible)

Wipe the rhubarb, cut into small pieces and place in a bowl. Cover with the sugar, add the lemon juice, and leave to stand overnight.

Chop the rose petals and add to the rhubarb. Transfer all to a preserving pan, bring to the boil and boil until setting point is reached. Pour into warmed jars, cover and label.

50 g (2 oz) finely chopped angelica (fresh or crystallized) can be used as an alternative to rose petals.

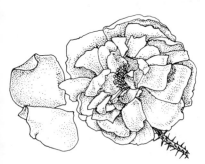

BLACKBERRY JAM

Makes about 5 kg (10 lb)

3 kg (6 lb) blackberries
150 ml (¼ pint) water
60 ml (4 tbsp) lemon juice or
   300 ml (½ pint) apple pectin
   stock or 1 level tsp citric or
   tartaric acid
3 kg (6 lb) sugar

Place the blackberries in a preserving pan with the water and the lemon juice or acid. Simmer until the fruit is cooked and reduced by about one-third. Remove from the heat.

Add the sugar, and pectin stock (if being used) and stir until sugar is dissolved. Return to the heat, bring to the boil and boil rapidly until setting point is reached. Pour into warmed jars, cover and label.

APPLE AND BLACKBERRY JAM

Makes about 2.5 kg (5 lb)

500 g (1 lb) blackberries
600 ml (1 pint) water
juice of 1 small lemon
1 kg (2 lb) cooking apples
1.5 kg (3 lb) sugar

Wash and drain the blackberries. Place in a pan with the water, and the lemon juice. Simmer gently until tender.

Peel, core and slice the apples and place in a pan. Strain the juice from the blackberries on to the apples and simmer until quite soft. Remove from the heat, add the sugar and stir until dissolved, then add the blackberries.

Return to the heat, bring to the boil and boil rapidly until setting point is reached. Pour into warmed jars, cover and label.

PUMPKIN/MARROW AND BLACKBERRY JAM

Makes about 3 kg (5½ lb)

2 kg (4 lb) pumpkin (or marrow)
1 kg (2 lb) blackberries
600 ml (1 pint) water
2 lemons
1.7 kg (3½ lb) sugar

Peel the pumpkin (or marrow) and remove the seeds. Cut into small neat dice and place in a preserving pan. Wash and stalk blackberries, add to the pumpkin, together with the water and grated rind of one lemon. Simmer gently until soft, then rub through a hair or nylon sieve.

Return to a clean pan, add the sugar and

stir until dissolved. Add the juice of the 2 lemons. Return the pan to the heat, bring to the boil, and boil rapidly until setting point is reached. Pour into warmed jars, cover and label.

APRICOT JAM (FRESH FRUIT)

Makes about 5 kg (10 lb)

3 kg (6 lb) fresh apricots
600 ml (1 pint) water
3 kg (6 lb) sugar

Wash the fruit, cut in halves and remove the stones. Crack a few stones, remove the kernels and blanch them by dipping in boiling water.

Place the fruit, kernels and water in a preserving pan, bring to simmering point, and simmer gently until the fruit is tender, and the contents of the pan reduced by one-third. Test for pectin.

Remove pan from the heat, add the sugar and stir until dissolved. Return pan to the heat, bring to the boil and boil rapidly until setting point is reached. Pour into warmed jars, cover and label.

APRICOT JAM (DRIED FRUIT)

Makes about 2.5 kg (5 lb)

500 g (1 lb) dried apricots
1.75 litres (3 pints) water
juice of 1 lemon
1.5 kg (3 lb) sugar
75 g (3 oz) blanched almonds

Wash the apricots and cut into small pieces, or chop coarsely in a food processor. Soak in the water for 12 hours. Place the fruit and water in a preserving pan, together with the lemon juice. Simmer until tender, about 30 minutes.

Remove from the heat, add the sugar and stir until dissolved, then add the almonds. Return to the heat, bring to the boil, and boil rapidly until setting point is reached. Pour into warmed jars, cover and label.

DRIED APRICOT AND GINGER JAM

Makes about 2.5 kg (5 lb)

500 kg (1 lb) dried apricots
1.75 litres (3 pints) water
125 g (4 oz) crystallized ginger
7 g (¼ oz) root ginger (bruised)
juice of 1 lemon
1.5 kg (3 lb) sugar

Wash the apricots and cut into small pieces or chop coarsely in a food processor. Soak in the water for 12 hours.

Place the apricots and soaking water in a preserving pan. Cut the ginger into small strips and add to the apricots, together with the bruised root ginger (tied in a muslin bag) and lemon juice. Simmer until tender, about 30–40 minutes.

Remove from the heat, add the sugar and stir until dissolved. Return to the heat, bring to the boil and boil rapidly until setting point is reached. Remove root ginger. Pour into warmed jars, cover and label.

AMBROSIA JAM

Makes about 3.1 kg (7¼ lb)

1 kg (2 lb) dried apricots
1 orange
2 lemons
Two 450-g (16-oz) cans crushed
   pineapple
sugar

Wash the apricots and cut into small pieces or chop coarsely in a food processor. Cover with cold water and leave to soak for 12 hours. After soaking, add the finely grated rind and juice of the orange and lemons, together with the contents of the cans of pineapple. Weigh the contents.

Place in a preserving pan, bring to simmering point, and simmer gently until the apricots are soft. Remove from the heat, add 1 kg (1 lb) sugar to each 1 kg (1 lb) fruit and juice (as weighed previously); stir until dissolved.

Return to the heat, bring to the boil and boil rapidly until setting point is reached. Pour into warmed jars, cover and label.

BANANA AND LEMON JAM

Makes about 900 g (1¾ lb)

500 g (1 lb) firm, ripe bananas, peeled
finely grated rind and juice of 3 lemons
500 g (1 lb) caster sugar

Peel and slice the bananas and place in a bowl. Add the grated rind and juice of the lemons, sprinkle the sugar over the fruit, cover the bowl with a plate and leave to stand until the sugar dissolves (about 1½ hours).

Transfer the contents of the bowl to a preserving pan, and simmer gently, stirring initially to ensure sugar is dissolved, until setting point is reached (about 15–20 minutes). Pour into warmed jars, cover and label.

BILBERRY JAM

Makes about 1.7 kg (3 lb)

1.5 kg (3½ lb) bilberries
150 ml (¼ pint) water
1 tsp tartaric or citric acid
1 kg (2 lb) sugar

Wash the fruit and place in a preserving pan with the water and acid. Simmer gently until the fruit is tender. Test for pectin. Remove from the heat.

Add the sugar and stir until dissolved. Return to the heat and bring to the boil, boil rapidly until setting point is reached. Pour into warmed jars, cover and label.

The set in this jam is never very firm.

GLENCAR JAM

Makes about 3.2 kg (7 lb)

500 g (1 lb) dried figs
2 kg (4 lb) rhubarb
finely grated rind and juice of 1 lemon
2 kg (4 lb) sugar

Chop the figs very finely and place in a large bowl with the finely sliced rhubarb and grated rind and juice of the lemon. Add the sugar, mix well. Allow to stand for 24 hours.

Transfer the mixture to a preserving pan, bring to the boil and boil rapidly until setting point is reached. Pour into warmed jars, cover and label.

PLUM JAM

Makes about 5 kg (10 lb)

3 kg (6 lb) plums
300–900 ml (½–1½ pints) water
3 kg (6 lb) sugar

Wash the fruit and place in a preserving pan with the water. Simmer gently until the fruit is tender, and the contents of the pan reduced by one-third. Test for pectin. Remove from the heat. Remove as many stones as possible as they rise to the surface.

Add the sugar and stir until dissolved. Return to the heat, bring to the boil and boil rapidly until setting point is reached. Pour into warmed jars. Cover and label.

PLUM AND ELDERBERRY JAM

Makes about 3.2 kg (7 lb)

1 kg (2 lb) elderberries
300 ml (½ pint) water
1.25 kg (2½ lb) plums
2 kg (4 lb) sugar

Remove the stalks from the elderberries and place in a saucepan with half the water. Simmer gently until tender; strain through a jelly bag. Stone the plums and cook in a preserving pan in the remaining water until tender. Add the elderberry juice; remove from the heat. Add the sugar, and stir until dissolved. Return the pan to the heat, bring to the boil, and boil rapidly until setting point is reached. Pour into warmed jars, cover and label.

DAMSON JAM

Makes about 5 kg (10 lb)

2.4 kg (4¾ lb) damsons
750 ml–1.25 litres (1¼–2 pints)
water
3 kg (6 lb) sugar

Wash the fruit and place in a preserving pan with the water. Simmer gently until tender, and the contents of the pan are reduced by one-third. Remove as many stones as possible as they rise to the surface. Remove from the heat and test for pectin.

Add the sugar and stir until dissolved. Return to the heat, bring to the boil, and boil rapidly until setting point is reached.

BULLACE (OR DAMSON) AND PEAR JAM

Makes about 5 kg (10 lb)

1.5 kg (3 lb) prepared pears
1.5 kg (3 lb) bullaces or damsons
600 ml (1 pint) water
1 tsp citric acid
3 kg (6 lb) sugar

Peel and finely dice the pears. Remove the stones from bullaces or damsons. Place each fruit in a separate pan with 300 ml (½ pint) water in each, and add the citric acid with the pears. Simmer gently until both fruits are tender. Combine the two fruits in one pan and test for pectin. Add the sugar and stir until dissolved. Return to the heat, bring to the boil, and boil rapidly until setting point is reached. Pour into warmed jars, cover and label.

MILLIONAIRE'S MARROW JAM

Makes about 3 kg (6 lb)

2 kg (4 lb) prepared marrow
2 kg (4 lb) sugar
40 g (1½ oz) root ginger
finely grated rind and juice of 2
lemons
25 g (1 oz) glacé cherries, finely
chopped
small can pineapple pieces (optional)
1 tsp cayenne pepper
100 ml (4 fl oz) whisky

Peel the marrow, remove seeds and cut into small, neat dice. Place in a bowl and sprinkle with half the sugar. Leave overnight.

Next day, bruise the ginger and tie in a muslin bag. Transfer the marrow to a preserving pan and add the grated rind and juice of the lemons, the ginger, cherries, drained pineapple, cayenne pepper, whisky, muslin bag and the remaining sugar.

Heat gently, stirring until the sugar is dissolved, bring to the boil, and boil until setting point is reached. Remove the ginger. Pour into warmed jars, cover and label.

The jam should be dark brown and firm.

PEAR, APPLE AND QUINCE JAM

Makes about 5 kg (10 lb)

1 kg (2 lb) cooking apples
1 kg (2 lb) cooking pears
750 g (1½ lb) quinces
pared rind and juice of 1 lemon
1.4 litres (2½ pints) water
3 kg (6 lb) sugar

Peel and core the fruits, and cut into pieces. Retain the peel and cores and tie them in a muslin bag with lemon rind. Place the fruits and water in a preserving pan with the muslin bag and simmer until tender. Remove muslin bag and squeeze out the juice. Remove the pan from heat.

Add the sugar and stir until dissolved then add the lemon juice. Return the pan to the heat, bring to the boil and boil rapidly until setting point is reached. Pour into warmed jars, cover and label.

JAPONICA JAM

Makes about 4 kg (10 lb)

2 kg (4 lb) japonica quinces
4 litres (7 pints) water
1 heaped tsp ground cloves
sugar

Wash the fruit, cut into eighths and place in a preserving pan with the water. Simmer gently until tender. Sieve.

Weigh the pulp. To each 1 kg (1 lb) of pulp add 1 kg (1 lb) sugar. Stir until sugar is dissolved then add the ground cloves. Return to the heat, bring to the boil and boil rapidly until setting point is reached. Pour into warmed jars, cover and label.

BLACKCURRANT JAM

Makes about 5 kg (10 lb)

2 kg (4 lb) blackcurrants
1.75 litres (3 pints) water
3 kg (6 lb) sugar

Remove the stalks and wash the fruit. Place in a preserving pan with the water. Simmer gently until the fruit is quite tender, and the contents of the pan reduced by one-third. Test for pectin. Remove from the heat.

Add the sugar and stir until dissolved. Return to the heat, bring to the boil and boil rapidly until setting point is reached. Pour into warmed jars, cover and label.

TUTTI-FRUTTI JAM

Makes about 3 kg (6 lb)

500 g (1 lb) blackcurrants
water
500 g (1 lb) redcurrants
500 g (1 lb) strawberries
500 g (1 lb) raspberries
2 kg (4 lb) sugar

Prepare the fruits by hulling, strigging etc. Place the blackcurrants in a pan and add sufficient water to barely cover. Simmer gently until tender. Add all the other fruits, and continue to simmer gently until all the fruits are tender. Test for pectin. Remove from the heat.

Add the sugar and stir until dissolved. Return to the heat, bring to the boil and boil rapidly until setting point is reached. Pour into warmed jars, cover and label.

MULBERRY JAM

Makes about 3 kg (6 lb)

1.5 kg (3 lb) ripe mulberries
500 g (1 lb) apples
water
1.75 kg (3½ lb) sugar

Place the mulberries in a preserving pan, and allow to simmer in their own juices until tender. Peel, core and slice the apples, place in a small amount of water in another pan and cook until soft. Mix the two fruit pulps together in the preserving pan. Add the sugar and stir until dissolved. Return to the heat, bring to the boil and boil rapidly until setting point is reached. Pour into warmed jars, cover and label.

WHORTLEBERRY JAM

Makes about 1.5 kg (2½ lb)

1 kg (2 lb) whortleberries
juice of 1 lemon
750 g (1½ lb) sugar

Wash the fruit, and drain thoroughly. Place in a preserving pan, crush with a wooden spoon, add the lemon juice, and simmer gently until the fruit is tender. Remove from the heat.

Add the sugar and stir until dissolved. Return to the heat, bring to the boil and boil rapidly until setting point is reached. Pour into warmed jars, cover and label.

HIGH DUMPSIE DEARIE JAM

Makes about 4.5 kg (9 lb)

1 kg (2 lb) apples
1 kg (2 lb) pears
1 kg (2 lb) plums
300 ml (½ pint) water
finely grated rind of 2 lemons
7–15 g (¼–½ oz) dried root ginger
300 ml (½ pint) water
sugar

Wash the fruit. Peel, core and finely dice the apples and pears. Remove stones from the plums. Place the fruits in a preserving pan with the water and lemon rind. Bruise the ginger and tie in a muslin bag; add to the fruit. Simmer gently until the fruit is tender, then remove the ginger.

Measure the pulp and to each litre add 600 g sugar or to each pint add 12 oz sugar. Stir until the sugar is dissolved. Return to the heat, bring to the boil and boil rapidly until setting point is reached. Pour into warmed jars, cover and label.

MATRIMONY JAM

Makes about 2.5 kg (5 lb)

500 g (1 lb) cooking apples
500 g (1 lb) pears
500 g (1 lb) Victoria plums
150 ml (¼ pint) water
1 tsp citric acid
sugar

Prepare the fruit. Peel, core and dice the apples and pears and stone the plums. Place the fruits in a preserving pan with the water and citric acid. Simmer gently until quite tender.

Measure the pulp, and to each litre of pulp add 750 g sugar or to each pint of pulp add 1 lb sugar. Stir until the sugar is dissolved. Return to the heat, bring to the boil and boil rapidly until setting point is reached. Pour into warmed jars, cover and label.

STRAWBERRY JAM (1)

Makes about 5 kg (10 lb)

3.5 kg (7 lb) strawberries
juice of 2 lemons
3 kg (6 lb) sugar

Prepare the fruit, and place in a preserving pan with the lemon juice. Heat gently and stir constantly until the volume is reduced by about one-third. Add the sugar and stir until dissolved. Bring to the boil, and boil

rapidly until setting point is reached.
Remove any scum immediately, then let
the jam cool until a skin forms on the
surface. Stir gently, and pour the jam
quickly into warmed jars, cover and label.

Lemon juice is not necessary with the more
acid varieties of strawberries.

STRAWBERRY JAM (2)

Makes about 2.5 kg (5 lb)

225 g (8 oz) gooseberries or
 redcurrants
300 ml (½ pint) water
1.5 kg (3 lb) strawberries
1.5 kg (3 lb) sugar

Place the gooseberries or redcurrants in a
pan with the water and cook gently until
soft. Strain off the juice.
 Place the prepared strawberries in a
preserving pan, add the strained juice and
cook gently, stirring constantly, until the
fruit is soft. Remove from the heat.
 Add the sugar and stir until dissolved.
Return to the heat, bring to the boil and boil
rapidly until setting point is reached.
Remove any scum immediately. Allow the
jam to cool slightly until a skin forms. Pour
into warmed jars, cover and label.

RHUBARB AND RASPBERRY JAM

Makes about 3.5 kg (7 lb)

1.5 kg (3 lb) rhubarb, trimmed
2 kg (4 lb) sugar
1 kg (2 lb) raspberries

Wash the rhubarb and cut into small cubes.
Place in layers with the sugar in a bowl.
Leave overnight.
 Transfer the contents of the bowl to a
preserving pan and bring slowly to the boil.
Add the lightly crushed raspberries and
bring to the boil. Boil until setting point is
reached. Pour into warmed jars. Cover
and label.

SWISS JAM

Makes about 5 kg (10 lb)

500 g (1 lb) redcurrants
3 kg (6 lb) Morello cherries
200 ml (¼ pint) water
juice of 2 lemons
3 kg (6 lb) sugar

Place the redcurrants in a pan with the water and simmer gently until tender. Strain off the juice. Stone the cherries and place in a preserving pan; crack the stones and tie them in a muslin bag. Add to the pan together with the lemon juice and the strained redcurrant juice. Simmer gently until the cherries are soft. Remove the pan from the heat.

Add the sugar and stir until it is dissolved. Return the pan to the heat, bring to the boil, and boil rapidly until setting point is reached. Pour into warmed jars, cover and label.

MORELLO CHERRY AND REDCURRANT JAM

Makes about 2.5 kg (5 lb)

500 g (1 lb) Morello cherries
  (weighed after stoning)
300 ml (½ pint) redcurrant juice
1.5 kg (3 lb) sugar

Wash the fruit, remove stones and place in a preserving pan with the redcurrant juice. Bruise the cherry stones, tie in a muslin bag, and add to the fruit. Simmer the fruit gently until tender. Test for pectin, remove from the heat. Remove the bag of stones.

Add the sugar and stir until dissolved. Return to the heat, bring to the boil and boil rapidly until setting point is reached. Pour into warmed jars, cover and label.

BLACKCURRANT AND RHUBARB JAM

Makes about 5.5 kg (11 lb)

2 kg (4 lb) blackcurrants
1.5 kg (3 lb) rhubarb
1 litre (1½ pints) water
3.5 kg (7 lb) sugar

Wash the fruit. Remove stalks from the blackcurrants and cut the rhubarb into 1-cm (½-inch) slices. Place the fruit and water in a preserving pan, bring to the boil and simmer gently until the fruit is quite soft (about 20 minutes). Test for pectin (see pages 9–10). Remove from the heat. Add the sugar and stir until dissolved. Return to the heat, bring to the boil, and boil rapidly until setting point is reached. Pour into warmed jars, cover and label.

PLUM AND APPLE JAM

Makes about 3 kg (5 lb)

1.5 kg (3 lb) cooking apples
water
1.5 kg (3 lb) plums
sugar

Peel, core and slice the apples. Place in a preserving pan with water to barely cover and simmer until tender. Have and stone the plums and add to the apples. Continue cooking gently until the fruit is soft. Rub through a hair or nylon sieve.

Measure the purée into a pan. To each 600 ml (1 pint) add 350 g (12 oz) sugar. Stir until the sugar is dissolved. Return the pan to the heat, bring to the boil, and boil rapidly until setting point is reached. Pour into warmed jars, cover and label.

GOOSEBERRY AND ELDERFLOWER JAM

Makes about 4.2 kg (8 lb)

2 kg (4 lb) firm green gooseberries
10–15 heads elderflowers
600 ml (1 pint) water
2.5 kg (5 lb) sugar

Wash and top and tail the gooseberries. Place in a preserving pan with the water. Gently rinse the elderflower heads, tie loosely in a muslin bag, and place in the pan with the gooseberries. Simmer gently until tender. Test for pectin (see pages 9–10). Remove from the heat. Squeeze the juice from the muslin bag and discard it.

Add the sugar and stir until dissolved. Return to the heat, bring to the boil and boil rapidly until setting point is reached. Pour into warmed jars, cover and label.

STRAWBERRY CONSERVE

Makes about 2.7 kg (6 lb)

2 kg (4 lb) hulled strawberries
2 kg (4 lb) sugar

Place the strawberries in layers with the sugar in a bowl and leave for 24 hours.

Transfer the contents of the bowl to a pan, bring to the boil and boil for 5 minutes. Return to the bowl and leave for 48 hours.

Again transfer the mixture to a preserving pan, bring to the boil and boil for 10–20 minutes until setting point is reached. Cool slightly until a skin forms. Stir gently. Pour into warmed jars, cover and label.

BLACK CHERRY CONSERVE

Makes about 1.25 kg (2½ lb)

1 kg (2 lb) stoned black or dark cherries
1 kg (2 lb) sugar
300 ml (½ pint) redcurrant juice

Wash and stone the cherries. Dissolve the sugar in the redcurrant juice and bring to the boil. Add the cherries and boil for 10 minutes, stirring constantly. Drain the syrup from the cherries and return the syrup to the pan and boil hard until it begins to thicken.

Return the cherries to the syrup and boil again until setting point is reached. Remove any scum. Cool slightly until a skin forms. Stir gently and pour into warmed jars, cover and label.

PEAR AND GINGER CONSERVE

Makes about 2.5 kg (5 lb)

2 kg (4 lb) hard pears
1.5 kg (3 lb) sugar
50–100 g (2–4 oz) stem ginger
2 lemons

Peel, core and cut into quarters (eighths, if large) the pears and place in a bowl in layers with the sugar. Cover and leave to stand for 24 hours.

Chop the ginger and add to the pears with the grated rind and juice of the lemons.

Transfer all to a preserving pan and heat gently, stirring constantly, until all the sugar is dissolved. Bring to the boil and boil gently until the fruit is transparent and setting point is reached. Cool slightly before pouring into warmed jars. Cover and label.

PEAR AND GRAPE CONSERVE

Makes about 1.5 kg (3 lb)

750 g (1½ lb) black grapes
2.5-cm (1-inch) piece cinnamon stick
water
juice of 3 lemons
750 g (1½ lb) dessert pears
  (barely ripe)
sugar

Wash the grapes and place in a pan with the cinnamon stick and 4 tablespoons water. Simmer gently until soft. Sieve and make up to 600 ml (1 pint) with water, if necessary. Add the lemon juice and place in a preserving pan.

Peel and core the pears and slice thinly. Add to the grape purée and cook gently until tender and the pears appear transparent. Measure the pulp and to each 600 ml (1 pint) add 350 g (12 oz) sugar. Stir over a low heat until the sugar is dissolved. Bring to the boil and boil rapidly until setting point is reached. Pour into warmed jars, cover and label.

RHUBARB CONSERVE

Makes about 3.6 kg (8 lb)

2 kg (4 lb) rhubarb
500 g (1 lb) raisins, coarsely
  chopped
1.7 kg (3½ lb) sugar
2 oranges
1 lemon

Wipe the rhubarb and cut into 2.5-cm (1-inch) lengths. Place in a preserving pan with the sugar and raisins. Cook gently for 20 minutes. Add the juice of the oranges and lemon. Remove the white pith from the orange peel and shred the peel finely; add to the pan. Bring to the boil and boil gently until the syrup is thick and jelly-like. Pour into warmed jars, cover and label.

APRICOT AND ORANGE CONSERVE

Makes about 2.8 kg (6 lb)

500 g (1 lb) dried apricots
1.75 litres (3 pints) water
2 oranges
1.5 kg (3¼ lb) sugar
juice of 2 lemons
50 g (2 oz) walnuts, chopped

Wash the apricots and if large, cut up roughly. Place in a bowl and cover with the water. Scrub the oranges and remove the peel as for eating. Remove as much white pith as possible and slice the peel thinly. Chop the flesh coarsely. Place pith and pips in a muslin bag. Place all these with the apricots. Cover and leave to soak for 24 hours.

Transfer to a preserving pan, cover and simmer gently until soft. Remove muslin bag after squeezing out the juice. Remove from the heat, add the sugar and lemon juice, and stir until sugar is dissolved.

Return to the heat, bring to the boil and boil rapidly until setting point is reached. Stir in the chopped walnuts. Pour into warmed jars, cover and label.

APPLE AND PEAR CONSERVE

Makes about 3.8 kg (9 lb)

1.5 kg (3½ lb) cooking apples
1.5 kg (3½ lb) dessert pears
100 g (4 oz) chopped candied peel
grated rind and juice of 2 lemons
2.25 kg (5 lb) sugar

Peel and core the apples and pears, cut into neat small dice. Place in acidulated water to prevent browning.

Drain the prepared fruit and place in a preserving pan with the candied peel and the grated rind and juice of the lemons. Cover the pan and cook very gently for 20 minutes, until the fruit is softened. Remove the pan from the heat, cover with a clean cloth and leave to stand for 24 hours.

Next day, add the sugar, place over a gentle heat and stir to dissolve the sugar. Bring to the boil and boil rapidly until setting point is reached. Remove any scum and leave to cool slightly until a skin forms. Stir gently and pour into warmed jars, cover and label.

SPICED QUINCE CONSERVE

Makes about 1.7 kg (3½ lb)

about 450 g (1 lb) quinces
about 450 g (1 lb) oranges
1 lemon
1.25 kg (2½ lb) sugar
1 cinnamon stick
water

Peel and core the quinces and cut into small pieces. Place in a pan with sufficient water to cover, and cook gently until soft, adding more water if necessary to prevent burning. Rub through a sieve.

Place sieved pulp in a preserving pan together with the grated rinds and juice of the oranges and lemon. Add the sugar and cinnamon stick and stir until dissolved. Bring to the boil and boil rapidly until setting point is reached. Remove cinnamon stick. Pour into warmed jars, cover and label.

TOMATO AND APPLE CONSERVE

Makes about 1.5 kg (2¼ lb)

500 g (1 lb) ripe tomatoes
500 g (1 lb) apples
1 lemon
750 g (1½ lb) sugar
100 g (4 oz) cut mixed peel
100 g (4 oz) stem ginger, chopped

Skin and slice the tomatoes. Peel, core and slice the apples. Scrub the lemon, then mince it. Place all of these in a preserving pan and cook for 15 minutes.

Remove from the heat. Add the sugar and stir until dissolved. Return to the heat and simmer gently until the mixture thickens. Add the peel and ginger and stir well. Continue to simmer gently for a further 10 minutes. Pour into warmed jars, cover and label.

CHERRY CONSERVE

Makes about 1.4 kg (2½ lb)

1.2 kg (2½ lb) sugar
300 ml (½ pint) water
1 kg (2 lb) stoned cherries

Place the sugar and water in a pan and boil for 10 minutes. Add the prepared cherries, bring to the boil and boil for 25 minutes. Leave to stand for 24 hours.

Bring to the boil again and boil for 10 minutes. Pour into warmed jars, cover.

JELLIES

Jellies add variety to all meals, particularly as interesting accompaniments to many meats; for a change, when having roast pork, why not try sage jelly?

Jellies should be clear and sparkling. They are similar to jams in the principles of making, but as only the juice is used (all traces of pulp, skin, pips being removed) considerably more fruit is required than in jam making. Damaged and windfall fruit, providing it is underripe, can be used (the damaged parts being cut away). Economical and interesting jellies can be made by using fruits from hedgerows.

Jellies were traditionally potted in sloping sided jars, so that they could be turned out on to a plate for serving, but as these jars are virtually unobtainable nowadays, jellies are potted in small jars. not exceeding 450 g (1 lb) – the small jars aid setting. Jellies should be covered in the same way as jams.

It is misleading to give approximate yields for each jelly recipe as results depend on the type and quality of the fruit used and also on the growing season.

General Method

1. Fruits should be washed and any unsound parts removed. It is not necessary to stalk currants or peel apples, etc., but large fruits should be cut into smaller pieces.

2. Place prepared fruit in a large pan, adding sufficient water just to cover. (The quantity of water used depends on the kind of fruit – those with tough skins or hard fruits require longer cooking to soften, and therefore need more water).

3. Place the pan on the heat and simmer gently until the fruit is quite tender (about ¾–1 hour).

4. Pour into a scalded jelly bag and allow to drip (about 1 hour) until there is barely any liquid dripping from it. Do *not* squeeze the jelly bag. (Fruits rich in pectin can be extracted a second time – return the pulp to the pan with more water (half the original

amount used) and simmer again for 30 minutes –
pour into the jelly bag and allow to drip for a further
hour).
5. Test for pectin (see page 9).
6. Measure the strained juice into a preserving pan,
and bring to the boil.
7. To each 600 ml (1 pint) of juice add 450 g (1 lb)
sugar. Fruits rich in pectin will set 575 g (1¼ lb)
sugar to each 600 ml (1 pint).
8. Remove the pan from the heat, add sugar, and stir
until dissolved.
9. Return pan to the heat, bring to the boil and boil
rapidly until setting point is reached. Recommended
tests for setting point are the flake test and the temperature test (see pages 11–12).
10. Remove pan from the heat, remove any scum
immediately and pour into warmed jars. Gently
pouring the jelly into slightly tilted jars will help to
avoid air bubbles.
11. Cover the jars immediately as for jam (see page
11). Do not move the jars until the jelly has cooled.

BLACKBERRY JELLY

4 kg (8 lb) blackberries
juice of 3 large (4 small) lemons or
2 tsp citric or tartaric acid
1 litre (1½ pints) water
sugar

Wash the fruit, place in a preserving pan
with the lemon juice or acid and water.
Simmer until tender.

Mash the fruit well and proceed from
stage 4 of the General Method (see page 35).

BLACKCURRANT JELLY

2 kg (4 lb) blackcurrants
1.85 litres (3 pints) water
sugar

Wash the fruit and place in a preserving pan with 1.25 litres (2 pints) water. Simmer until tender and mash well. Strain through a scalded jelly bag for 10–15 minutes.

Return the pulp to the pan, add another 600 ml (1 pint) water and simmer for a further 30 minutes. Then strain again.

Mix the two extracts together and proceed from stage 5 of the General Method (see above).

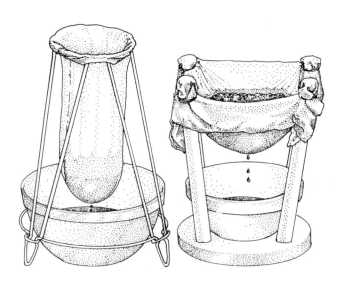

Jelly bag and stand, available from manufacturers of kitchen equipment

Several layers of scalded muslin tied to legs of a stool (as an alternative to jelly bag)

REDCURRANT JELLY

3 kg (6 lb) redcurrants
1.25–1.75 litres (2–3 pints) water
sugar

Prepare the fruit. Follow the method of making as for Blackcurrant Jelly (see page 37).

APPLE OR CRAB APPLE JELLY

apples
ginger or cloves
water
sugar

Choose apples with a definite flavour, or add flavourings such as ginger or cloves. Windfall apples can be used provided the damaged portions are cut out.

Wash and cut up the fruit and proceed as for the General Method (see pages 35–6).

If spices are used, these should be whole (not ground) and cooked with the apples.

APPLE AND SLOE JELLY

1.5 kg (3 lb) green apples
1.5 kg (3 lb) sloes
water
sugar

Rinse the fruit and cut the apples into quarters. Proceed as for the General Method (see pages 35–6).

CRAB APPLE AND DAMSON JELLY

3 kg (6 lb) crab apples
2 kg (4 lb) damsons
juice of 1 lemon
water
sugar

Rinse the fruit and cut the apples in halves. Place in a preserving pan with the lemon juice and water. Proceed as for the General Method (see pages 35–6).

RASPBERRY AND APPLE JELLY

1 kg (2 lb) cooking apples
  (windfalls will do)
2 kg (4 lb) raspberries
water
sugar

Cut up the apples and place in a large pan with the raspberries and sufficient water to barely cover. Simmer until the fruit is soft. Strain through a scalded jelly bag.
  Proceed from stage 5 of the General Method (see page 36).

RASPBERRY JELLY

4 kg (8 lb) raspberries
sugar

Place the fruit in a large pan and heat gently until the juice runs, then mash well. Strain through a scalded jelly bag.
  Measure the juice and add 450 g (1 lb) sugar to each 600 ml (1 pint) juice. Stir until dissolved. Return to the heat, bring to boil and boil rapidly until setting point is reached. Remove scum. Pour quickly into warmed jars, cover and label.

MINT JELLY (1)

3 kg (6 lb) green apples
juice of 4 lemons or 2 tsp citric or
  tartaric acid
water
sugar
bunch of fresh young mint
green liquid food colouring
  (optional)

Wash and cut the fruit roughly, place in a pan with lemon juice or acid and a few sprigs of the mint. Cover with water. Simmer to a soft pulp. Strain through a jelly bag. Test for pectin. Place the extract in a pan, bring to the boil. Add 500 g (1 lb) sugar to each 600 ml (1 pint); stir until it is dissolved. Boil rapidly for 5 minutes. Suspend the bunch of mint in the jelly and boil until setting point is reached. Remove mint, add colouring (if used). Remove any scum. Pour quickly into jars, cover and label.

MINT JELLY (2)

2.7 kg (6 lb) green apples
water
vinegar
sugar
fresh young mint
green food colouring

Wash and cut up the fruit. Place in a large pan with sufficient liquid to barely cover. To each 600 ml (1 pint) water add 150 ml (¼ pint) white vinegar.

Simmer gently to produce a soft pulp. Proceed as for Mint Jelly (1) (see page 39), but instead of suspending the bunch of mint in the boiling jelly, just before setting point is reached, add approximately 2 tablespoons finely chopped mint and a few drops of green colouring.

DAMSON JELLY

3 kg (6 lb) damsons
1.75 litres (3 pints) water
sugar

Prepare the fruit. Follow the method of making as for Blackcurrant Jelly (see page 37).

SAGE JELLY

1 kg (2 lb) crab apples or windfall
  apples
water
12 stems fresh sage
sugar
green liquid food colouring

Follow the method of making as for Mint Jelly (1) (see page 39). This jelly is excellent served with pork.

MULBERRY JELLY

3 kg (6 lb) mulberries
600 ml (1 pint) water
sugar

Follow the method of making as for the General Method (see pages 35–6).

LOGANBERRY JELLY

4 kg (8 lb) loganberries
water
sugar

Prepare the fruit. Follow the method of making as for Blackberry Jelly (see page 37).

LOGANBERRY AND REDCURRANT JELLY

1 kg (2 lb) loganberries
1 kg (2 lb) redcurrants
water
sugar

Prepare the fruit. Follow the method of making as for Blackberry Jelly (see page 37).

QUINCE JELLY

2 kg (4 lb) quinces
3.5 litres (6 pints) water
sugar
15 g (½ oz) citric or tartaric acid, if fruit is fully ripe

Wash the quinces, cut up finely and place in a large pan with 2 litres (4 pints) of the water. Cover and simmer until tender (about 1 hour). Strain through a scalded jelly bag. Return the pulp to a pan with the remaining water and make a second extract. Combine the two extracts and continue from stage 5 of the General Method (see page 36).

ROWAN JELLY

1 kg (2 lb) rowan berries
1 kg (2 lb) crab apples or windfall apples
water
sugar

Wash the berries thoroughly removing all leaves and twigs. Wash the apples and cut up roughly. Place both fruits in a preserving pan with sufficient water to barely cover. Simmer gently to produce a pulp. Strain through a scalded jelly bag.

Proceed from stage 5 of the General Method (see page 36).

GOOSEBERRY AND ELDERFLOWER JELLY

2 kg (4 lb) gooseberries
12 heads of elderflowers
1.25–1.75 litres (2–3 pints) water
sugar

Wash the gooseberries, but do not top and tail. Place in a preserving pan with water and proceed as for the General Method (see pages 35–6).

Tie the elderflower heads in a muslin bag. At stage 9, plunge the heads into the boiling jelly for a few minutes. This will be sufficient to impart a muscatel flavour to the jelly.

MEDLAR JELLY

2 kg (4 lb) medlars
2.5 litres (4 pints) water
sugar
lemon juice

Wash the fruit well, place in a preserving pan with the water and simmer slowly until fruit is soft and mushy. Pour into a scalded jelly bag and allow to drip for a few hours. Test for pectin (see pages 9–10).

Measure the strained juice into a preserving pan and add 1 tablespoon lemon juice to each 600 ml (1 pint) juice. Bring to the boil.

To each 600 ml (1 pint) juice add 350 g (12 oz) sugar. Stir until dissolved. Return to the heat, bring to the boil and boil rapidly until setting point is reached. Remove any scum. Pour quickly into warmed jars, cover and label.

ROSEHIP AND APPLE JELLY

600 ml (1 pint) fully ripe rosehips
1.5 kg (3 lb) green apples
water
juice of 1 lemon
sugar

Wash the rosehips thoroughly. Place in a pan and cover with water. Simmer gently until soft, then mash with a wooden spoon.

Wash the apples and cut up roughly. Place in a pan and barely cover with water. Simmer gently until soft. Strain the two

fruits together through a scalded jelly bag.
Proceed from stage 5 of the General
Method (see page 36) adding the strained
lemon juice with the sugar.

HIP AND HAW JELLY

1 kg (2 lb) rosehips
1 kg (2 lb) hawthorn berries
Juice of 4 lemons
water

Proceed as for the General Method (see
pages 35–6), adding the strained lemon
juice at stage 6.

If haws are ripe before the hips, they can be
frozen until required.
　　As the berries absorb a lot of water whilst
softening, extra water may be required
during the cooking period.

RHUBARB AND ORANGE JELLY

1.5 kg (3 lb) rhubarb
1 kg (2 lb) oranges
2.5 litres (4 pints) water
sugar

Wash the fruits. Cut the rhubarb into
2.5-cm (1-inch) pieces; cut the oranges into
2.5-cm (1-inch) cubes. Place in a bowl with
the water and leave to soak overnight.
　　Transfer the contents of the bowl to a
large pan and simmer, covered, until the
peel is tender (1½-2 hours). Strain through
a scalded jelly bag.
　　Proceed from stage 5 of the General
Method (see page 36).

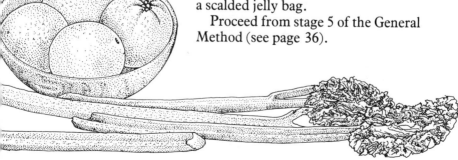

MARMALADES

It is difficult to find the origin of marmalade.
Nowadays a jam-like preserve made from citrus
fruits, where the peel is shredded, is called
marmalade. However, some other recipes use a
combination of citrus fruits and other fruits e.g.
apples and apricots. Some of these recipes have
been included.

The principles of making marmalade are essentially the same as those for making jam, with the exception that the peel of citrus fruits takes considerably longer to cook than the softer fruits used for jam, therefore more water is required for cooking.

Pectin. Much of the pectin necessary for a good set is found in the pith and pips of citrus fruits, and although in all finished marmalade, no pips are wanted and in some, the absence of pith and pips makes a far more appetising result, it is essential that the pith and pips are cooked to extract pectin.

Acid. As citrus fruits contain a much higher proportion of pectin than other fruits, extra acid must be added to obtain a good set. The quantity of acid to add is as follows: to 1.5 kg (3 lb) fruit add the juice of 2 lemons or 1 tsp citric acid or tartaric acid.

General Method
1. Scrub the fruit – dipping in boiling water for 1–2 minutes will help the skin to peel off.
2. Prepare the fruit according to the recipe. Simmer the fruit with the water and acid until the peel is tender (about 2 hours). Remove from the heat. Remove the bag containing the pips. Carry out the pectin test (see pages 9–10).
3. Add the sugar and stir until dissolved. Return to the heat, bring to the boil and boil until setting point is reached. (Tests for setting point – see page 11).
4. Remove from the heat and carefully skim off any scum. Allow to cool for 15–20 minutes until a skin forms. This cooling helps prevent the shreds from rising in the jar when potted. Gently stir in the skin. Pour into warmed jars and cover as for jams (see page 11). Label with type and date. Store in a cool, dry, dark, well-ventilated place.

GRAPEFRUIT MARMALADE

Makes about 5 kg (10 lb)

Either 1 kg (2¼ lb) grapefruit and
* 350 g (12 oz) lemons*
or 1.5 kg (3 lb) grapefruit and 2 tsp
* citric or tartaric acid*
2.75–3.5 litres (4½–6 pints) water
3 kg (6 lb) sugar

Scrub and scald the fruit, then peel the fruit as for eating. Remove the pith from the skins and shred the peel finely. Place the shredded peel in a preserving pan with the acid if used and half the water. Simmer gently until the peel is tender, about 2 hours.

Coarsely chop the rest of the fruit and the pith and place with the remaining water in a pan. Cover and simmer gently for about 1½ hours. Strain through a colander, or rub through a sieve to make a thick marmalade. Add the strained pulp to the peel. Carry out a pectin test.

Add the sugar and stir until dissolved. Return to the heat, bring to the boil and boil rapidly until setting point is reached. Remove any scum. Allow to cool until a skin forms. Stir gently. Pour into warmed jars, cover and label.

SEVILLE ORANGE MARMALADE (1)

Makes about 5 kg (10 lb)

1.5 kg (3 lb) Seville oranges
2.75–3.5 litres (4½–6 pints) water
juice of 2 lemons or 1 tsp citric or
*   tartaric acid*
3 kg (6 lb) sugar

Either follow the method of making as for Grapefruit Marmalade (see page 46) noting that it is not necessary to remove any pith from the peel unless very thick.

or

Scrub the fruit, cut in half and squeeze out the juice. Tie the pips in a muslin bag. Slice the peel thinly, without removing the pith. Place in a preserving pan with the juice, the muslin bag and the water. Simmer gently until the peel is quite soft and the contents reduced by about one-third, about 2 hours.

Remove from the heat, squeeze the muslin bag to extract the juice then remove the bag. Test for pectin. Add the sugar and stir until dissolved. Return the pan to the heat, bring to the boil and boil rapidly until setting point is reached. Remove any scum, allow to cool slightly until a thin skin forms, then stir gently. Pour into warmed jars, cover and label.

PUMPKIN MARMALADE

Makes about 3 kg (6 lb)

2 kg (4 lb) ripe pumpkin, peeled
3 Seville oranges
600 ml (1 pint) water
2 kg (4 lb) sugar

Cut the pumpkin in to small cubes, place in a bowl and cover with the sugar. Scrub the oranges, remove the peel and shred finely. Cut up the pulp roughly and tie the pips in a muslin bag. Place all these in another bowl and cover with the water. Leave both to stand for 24 hours.

Transfer the oranges to a pan and cook gently for about 1 hour until shreds are tender. Add the pumpkin and sugar, bring the mixture to the boil and boil gently until tender and setting point is reached. Remove any scum. Pour into warmed jars, cover and label.

JELLY MARMALADE

Makes about 2.25 kg (5 lb)

1 kg (2 lb) Seville oranges
2.75 litres (4½ pints) water
juice of 2 lemons
1.5 kg (3 lb) sugar

Scrub and scald the fruit, then peel the oranges as for eating. Remove the pith from the skins and shred the peel finely. Place the peel in a closed pan with 750 ml (1¼ pints) water and cook gently until quite tender (about 1½ hours).

Coarsely chop the rest of the fruit and place in another pan with the lemon juice and remaining water. Simmer gently for 2 hours. Drain the liquid from the shreds on to the pulp and strain through a scalded jelly bag. Do not squeeze. (A second extraction can be made as for jelly – see page 35). Carry out a pectin test.

Place the strained juice in a pan with the sugar and stir until dissolved. Add the shreds. Return the pan to the heat, bring to the boil and boil rapidly until setting point is reached. Remove any scum and allow to cool until a thin skin forms. Stir gently. Pour into warmed jars, cover and label.

SEVILLE ORANGE MARMALADE (2)

Makes about 2.5 kg (5 lb)

750 g (1½ lb) Seville oranges
juice of 1 lemon
1 litre (1½ pints) water
1.5 kg (3 lb) sugar

Prepare the fruit as for Seville Orange Marmalade (1) (see page 47). Place the prepared fruit and lemon juice in the pressure pan with the water. Put on the lid, leaving the vent open. Heat gently and when steam appears, close the vent and bring to 15 lb (H) pressure. Maintain pressure for 20 minutes, then allow pan to cool at room temperature for 10 minutes. Remove the bag of pips after extracting the juice. Test for pectin (see pages 9–10).

Add the sugar and stir until dissolved. Return the open pan to the heat, bring to the boil and boil rapidly until setting point is reached. Remove any scum. Allow to cool until a skin is formed. Stir gently. Pour into warmed jars, cover and label.

PINEAPPLE MARMALADE

Makes about 3 kg (6 lb)

1 lemon
3 large Jaffa oranges
525-g (1 lb 3-oz) can pineapple
1.5 litres (2½ pints) water
2 kg (4 lb) sugar

Scrub the lemon and oranges and peel as for eating. Cut the peel into small cubes. Coarsely chop the fruit, tying any pips in a muslin bag. Place all in a preserving pan, cover with the water and the strained pineapple juice. Simmer gently until the peel is tender. Squeeze the muslin bag to extract the juice, then remove the bag. Carry out a pectin test (see pages 9–10). Remove the pan from the heat.

Add the sugar and stir until dissolved then add the pineapple cut into small cubes. Return the pan to the heat, bring to the boil and boil rapidly until setting point is reached. Remove any scum. Allow to cool until a skin is formed. Stir gently. Pour into warmed jars, cover and label.

DARK THICK MARMALADE

Makes about 5 kg (10 lb)

1 kg (2 lb) Seville or bitter oranges
2 lemons
2.75–3.5 litres (4½–6 pints) water
3 kg (6 lb) sugar
25 g (1 oz) black treacle

Follow the method as for Seville Orange
Marmalade (1) (see page 47) but the lemons
should be sliced and included in the pulp.
Add the treacle with the sugar.

THREE FRUIT MARMALADE

Makes about 5 kg (10 lb)

2 grapefruit
4 lemons
2 sweet oranges
  total weight of fruit 1.5 kg (3 lb)
2.75–3.5 litres (4½–6 pints) water
3 kg (6 lb) sugar

Follow the method of making as for
Grapefruit Marmalade (see page 46).

LEMON AND WHISKY MARMALADE

Makes about 2.5 kg (5 lb)

750 g (1½ lb) lemons
1.5 litres (2½ pints) water
1.5 kg (3 lb) sugar
1 miniature bottle whisky

Scrub the lemons, cut in half and squeeze
out the juice. Place the pips in a muslin bag.
Slice the fruit finely and place in a
preserving pan with the juice, muslin bag
and the water. Simmer gently until tender
(about 2 hours). Squeeze the muslin bag to
extract the juice, then remove the bag. Test
for pectin. Remove from the heat.
Add the sugar and stir until dissolved.
Return to the heat. Bring to the boil and
boil rapidly until setting point is reached.
Stir in the whisky. Remove any scum.
Allow to cool slightly until a skin is formed.
Stir gently. Pour into warmed jars, cover
and label.

THICK LEMON AND GINGER MARMALADE

Makes about 5 kg (10 lb)

1.5 kg (3 lb) lemons
3 litres (5–6 pints) water
3 kg (6 lb) sugar
100–175 g (4–6 oz) stem ginger

Scrub the fruit, place in a covered pan with the water and simmer gently for about 1 hour, until the lemons are soft. Retaining the liquid in the pan, remove the lemons and cut the fruit in half. Remove the pips, tie these in a muslin bag and return to the pan. Slice the fruit and return it to the pan.

Return the uncovered pan to the heat and simmer gently for about 30 minutes, or until the original volume has been reduced by about one-third. Remove the pan from the heat and carry out a pectin test (see pages 9–10).

Add the sugar and stir until dissolved. Chop the ginger finely and add to the pan. Return the pan to the heat, bring to the boil and boil rapidly until setting point is reached. Remove any scum. Cool slightly until a skin is formed. Stir gently. Pour into warmed jars, cover and label.

LEMON OR LIME MARMALADE

Makes about 5 kg (10 lb)

1.5 kg (3 lb) lemons or limes
2.75–3.5 litres (4½–6 pints) water
3 kg (6 lb) sugar

Follow the method of making as for Grapefruit Marmalade (see page 46).

WINDFALL MARMALADE

Makes about 4 kg (8 lb)

2 grapefruit
4 lemons
1 kg (2 lb) windfall apples
(weighed after preparation)
3 litres (5 pints) water
2.5 kg (5 lb) sugar

Scrub the citrus fruits, remove the zest from the fruit thinly using a potato peeler and then shred. Remove the pith from the fruit and chop the flesh roughly.

Roughly cut up the pith. Chop the prepared apples and place in a preserving pan with the prepared citrus fruits and the water. Tie the pith, pips and apple parings in a muslin bag and add to the pan. Simmer gently until the peel is tender and the quantity reduced by half. Squeeze the muslin bag to extract the juice then remove the bag. Carry out a pectin test. Remove from the heat.

Add the sugar and stir until dissolved. Return the pan to the heat, bring to the boil and boil rapidly until setting point is reached. Remove any scum. Allow to cool until a thin skin is formed, then stir gently. Pour into warmed jars, cover and label.

APRICOT MARMALADE

Makes about 4.5 kg (9 lb)

500 g (1 lb) dried apricots
750 g (1½ lb) Seville or sweet
oranges
grated rind and juice of 1 lemon
1.8 litres (3 pints) water
3 kg (6 lb) sugar
25 g (1 oz) split almonds (optional)

Wash the apricots. Place in bowl and cover with 1.2 litres (2 pints) water, leave to soak for 24 hours. Transfer contents of the bowl to a preserving pan, add the grated rind and juice of the lemon and simmer gently until tender, stirring occasionally.

Meanwhile, scrub the oranges, cut in half and squeeze out the juice. Remove the pith from the peel and shred the peel finely. Place the peel and juice in a pressure cooker, together with the roughly chopped pith and pips tied in a muslin bag and 600 ml (1 pint) water. Bring slowly to 15 lb pressure (H) and cook for 20 minutes. Allow to cool 10 minutes before opening.

(Alternatively, cook in an open pan with at least 1.2 litres (2 pints) water for about 2 hours or until the peel is soft).

Squeeze the muslin bag to extract the juice, then remove the bag from the pan. Combine the two fruit pulps. Carry out a pectin test (see pages 9–10).

Add the sugar and stir until dissolved. Return to the heat, bring to the boil and boil until setting point is reached. Stir in the almonds. Pour into warmed jars, cover and label.

CARROT MARMALADE

Makes about 4.5 kg (9 lb)

500 g (1 lb) peeled carrots
500 g (1 lb) oranges
500 g (1 lb) lemons
3.5 litres (6 pints) water
3 kg (6 lb) sugar
1 tsp ground cinnamon

Finely chop the carrots and place in a preserving pan. Scrub the fruit, cut in half and squeeze out the juice. Remove the pith from the peel and shred the peel finely. Chop the pith roughly and place with the pips in a muslin bag. Place the finely shredded peel, juice and muslin bag in the pan with the carrots. Add the water and simmer gently for 1½–2 hours, until the peel is soft.

Squeeze the muslin bag to extract the juice and remove the bag. Remove from the heat and test for pectin (see pages 9–10).

Add the sugar and stir until dissolved, then stir in the cinnamon. Return the pan to the heat, bring to the boil and boil rapidly until setting point is reached. Remove scum. Allow to cool until a skin begins to form. Stir gently. Pour into warmed jars, cover and label.

BUTTERS, CHEESES AND CURDS

Butters and cheeses are an ideal way of using up an excess of fruit. Fruit cheeses are served in exactly the same way as dairy cheeses – cut into wedges. Curds are familiar in the lemon form, but in this chapter are some different combinations of fruits. Curds are not true preserves and should not be entered, when showing, in a class for 'any preserve'. Recipes for mincemeat and Cumberland rum butter are also included; again they are not true preserves.

Fruit butters and cheeses are made when there is a glut of fruit. Although they contain a large quantity of sugar, the proportion is less than that in jams.

Fruit butters are of a softer consistency than cheeses and are usually spiced and should be hermetically sealed. They are usually served as a spread.

Cheeses are cooked to a stiff consistency and set in small moulds so that they can be turned out for serving and cut into wedges.

Curds contain eggs and butter in addition to the fruit and sugar, and are not intended to keep. Strictly speaking they are not a true preserve. As the temperature reached during cooking is low, curds should only be covered with a wax circle and cellophane cover.

Unusual preserves, some of which are strictly speaking not preserves, all have their place on the larder shelf; they are also fun to make.

General Method
Wash the fruit, cut up if necessary, and place in a saucepan with sufficient water to barely cover. Simmer gently until soft. Sieve.

To make a cheese To each 500 g (1 lb) pulp add 500 g (1 lb) sugar. Stir until the sugar is dissolved. Boil gently for ¾–1 hour, stirring occasionally to prevent burning until a clean line is left when a spoon is drawn across. Pour into a mould which has been smeared with glycerine so that the cheese will turn out.

To make a butter To each 500 g (1 lb) pulp add 250–375 g (8–12 oz) sugar. Stir until the sugar is dissolved, add any spices and cook gently until a thick creamy consistency is reached. Pour into jars with airtight covers. Then process by immersing in a deep pan of hot water. Bring to the boil and boil for 5 minutes.

CUMBERLAND RUM BUTTER

450 g (1 lb) soft brown sugar
225 g (8 oz) butter
½ tsp ground nutmeg
2 tbsp rum

Ensure there are no lumps in the sugar by rolling between two sheets of greaseproof paper, or rubbing through a sieve. Place the sugar in a bowl.

Put the butter in a pan, heat gently until melted then heat until very hot but not disintegrating. Pour the butter on to the sugar, add the nutmeg, and stir until the butter is fully incorporated. Add the rum and stir again until well blended and a smooth texture.

Pour into an old-fashioned china bowl and allow to set.

APPLE BUTTER

3 kg (6 lb) crab apples or windfalls
1.25 litres (2 pints) water
1.25 litres (2 pints) cider
sugar
1 tsp ground cinnamon
1 tsp ground cloves

Wash the apples and chop roughly, removing any damaged parts. Place in a pan with the water and cider. Cook gently until soft. Sieve. Return the sieved pulp to the pan and simmer to obtain a thick consistency. To each 500 g (1 lb) pulp add 350 g (12 oz) sugar. Stir until the sugar is dissolved. Boil, stirring frequently until a thick creamy consistency is obtained. Pour into warmed jars, seal and process (see page 55).

MARROW ORANGE CREAM

Makes about 2.1 kg (3¾ lb)

1.5 kg (3 lb) prepared marrow
2 oranges
750 g (1½ lb) sugar

Peel and de-seed the marrow. Cut into large pieces and steam until tender (1–1½ hours depending on the age of the marrow). Leave to drain for several hours or overnight if possible to ensure that it is dry. Rub through a sieve or purée in a blender or food

135 g (4½ oz) butter
2 eggs (size 4)

processor. Place in a pan. Add the finely grated rind and juice of the oranges, together with the sugar and butter.

Cook over a low heat, stirring until the sugar has dissolved then simmer gently until the mixture thickens. Remove from the heat. Beat the eggs well, and strain on to the other ingredients. Mix well, return the pan to the heat and cook gently for 2–3 minutes. Pour into warmed jars, cover and label.

BRAMBLE CHEESE

1.5 kg (3 lb) blackberries
1.5 kg (3 lb) cooking apples
water
sugar

Wash the blackberries. Wipe the apples and chop up roughly. Place both in a pan with sufficient water to barely cover. Cover and cook gently until reduced to a pulp. Rub through a sieve. Return the sieved pulp to an open pan and cook further, if necessary, to reduce the pulp until thick. Weigh the pulp.

To each 500 g (1 lb) pulp add 500 g (1 lb) sugar and cook over a low heat to dissolve the sugar. Continue cooking until a thick consistency is obtained. When a spoon is drawn across the base of the pan, it should leave a clean line. Pour into prepared moulds. Cover as for jam (see page 11).

QUINCE CHEESE

quinces
water
sugar

Prepare quinces by washing and cutting into small pieces. Follow the method as for Bramble Cheese (see page 57).

DAMSON CHEESE

3 kg (6 lb) damsons
300 ml (½ pint) water
sugar

Follow the method for Bramble Cheese (see page 57).

PLUM AND APPLE CHEESE

1.5 kg (3 lb) cooking apples
500 g (1 lb) plums
water
sugar

Wash and cut up the apples without peeling. Wash the plums, and halve or quarter if large. Place both the fruits in a closed pan with sufficient water to barely cover.

Proceed as for Bramble Cheese (see page 57).

LEMON CURD (1)

Makes about 1.1 kg (2¼ lb)

4–5 lemons (225 ml/8 fl oz juice)
175 g (6 oz) butter
550 g (1¼ lb) sugar
4 eggs (225 ml/8 fl oz))

Wash the fruit and finely grate the rind from the lemons. Squeeze the juice and use 225 ml (8 fl oz). Place the butter, sugar, grated lemon rind and the juice in the top of a double saucepan, or in a bowl over a pan containing hot water. Cook gently until the sugar is dissolved. Strain and return to a clean pan or bowl.

Beat the eggs well, measure and strain on to the other ingredients. Return the pan to the heat and continue cooking over a low heat until the mixture thickens sufficiently to coat the back of a wooden spoon. Pour into warmed jars, cover and label.

APPLE LEMON CURD

Makes about 1.1 kg (2¼ lb)

450 g (1 lb) cooking apples
grated rind and juice of 2 lemons
4 tbsp water
450 g (1 lb) sugar
4 eggs (size 4)
125 g (4 oz) butter

Peel, core and roughly chop the apples. Cook in a closed pan with the grated lemon rind and the water until reduced to a pulp. Beat well to remove any lumps (or purée in a food processor).

Add the lemon juice and sugar and stir until the sugar is dissolved. Beat the eggs well and strain on to the apple pulp. Add the butter. Cook over a low heat, stirring occasionally, until a thick creamy consistency is obtained. Pour into warmed jars, cover and label.

GOLDEN CURD

Makes about 630 g (1½ lb)

50 g (2 oz) butter
2 oranges
1 lemon
225 g (8 oz) sugar
4 eggs (size 3)

Place the butter in the top of a double saucepan, or in a bowl standing over a pan containing hot water, to melt. Scrub the oranges and lemons and then finely grate the rinds. Cut the fruit in half and squeeze out the juice. Add the rinds, juice and sugar to the butter and stir until sugar dissolves.

Beat the eggs and strain on to the fruit mixture. Cook gently, stirring occasionally until the mixture thickens sufficiently to coat the back of the wooden spoon. Pour into warmed jars, cover and label.

LEMON CURD (2)

Makes about 300 g (10 oz)

150 g (5 oz) unsalted butter
225 g (8 oz) sugar
2 lemons
2 eggs

Follow the method as for Lemon Curd (1) (see page 58).

GOOSEBERRY CURD

Makes about 1.8 kg (4 lb)

1.5 g (3 lb) green gooseberries
600 ml (1 pint) water
750 g (1½ lb) sugar
750 g (4 oz) butter
4 eggs

Wash the gooseberries and place in a pan with the water. Simmer gently until tender then sieve. Place the sieved pulp in the top of a double saucepan, or in a bowl over a pan containing hot water, add the sugar and stir until dissolved.

Add the butter. Beat the eggs well and strain on to the other ingredients. Stir well. Cook gently, stirring occasionally, until the mixture thickens sufficiently to coat the back of a wooden spoon. Pour into warmed jars, cover and label.

ORANGE AND LEMON CURD

Makes about 500 g (1 lb)

150 g (5 oz) butter
225 g (8 oz) sugar
1 lemon
1 orange
2 eggs (size 4)

Follow the method as for Lemon Curd (1) (see page 58).

MARROW LEMON CREAM

Makes about 2.3 kg (6 lb)

2 kg (4 lb) prepared marrow
225 g (8 oz) butter
1.75 kg (3½ lb) sugar
6 lemons

Peel and de-seed the marrow. Cut into large pieces and steam until tender (1–1½ hours depending on age of marrow). Leave to drain for several hours, or overnight if possible, to ensure that it is completely dry. Mash into a smooth mixture or purée in a blender or food processor. Place in a pan with the butter, sugar and finely grated rind and juice of the lemons.

Cook over a low heat, stirring until the sugar has dissolved. Bring to the boil and

simmer, stirring occasionally, for
20–30 minutes. Pour into warmed jars,
cover and label.

PEAR HARLEQUIN

Makes about 2 kg (4 lb)

1.5 kg (3 lb) pears
450-g (1-lb) can pineapple pieces
grated rind and juice of 1 orange
sugar
150-ml (¼-pint) bottle maraschino
cherries

Cut the pears into 1-cm (½-inch) cubes.
Add the pineapple pieces, and the grated
rind and juice of the orange. Weigh the
fruits and add three-quarters of their weight
in sugar. Sprinkle over the fruits and leave
overnight in a bowl.

Transfer the contents of the bowl to a pan
and simmer gently until thick. Meanwhile
cut the cherries in half and add to the fruit,
together with the maraschino syrup. Stir
well. Pour into wide-necked bottles
and seal.

This is excellent served with ice cream.

MINCEMEAT (1)

Makes about 3 kg (6 lb)

500 g (1 lb) cooking apples
(prepared weight)
500 g (1 lb) currants
500 g (1 lb) seedless raisins
500 g (1 lb) sultanas
250 g (8 oz) chopped mixed peel
500 g (1 lb) suet, finely chopped or
grated
500 g (1 lb) sugar (granulated or
demerara)
grated rind and juice of 2 lemons
50 g (2 oz) almonds, blanched and
shredded
½ tsp mixed spice (or to taste)
150 ml (¼ pint) whisky, rum or
brandy (optional)

Mince the apples, currants, raisins and sultanas coarsely. Mix all the ingredients together (with the exception of the alcohol) and leave covered with a clean cloth or cling film at room temperature for three days, stirring two or three times daily.

Stir in the alcohol (if used) and pack the mincemeat into clean jars. Cover with a wax disc and cellophane circle. Store in a cool dry place.

A firm hard apple e.g. Wellington is preferable to a Bramley seedling for good keeping.

MINCEMEAT (2)

Makes about 800 g (1½ lb)

125 g (4 oz) Valencia raisins
125 g (4 oz) currants
125 g (4 oz) cooking apples, peeled
125 g (4 oz) demerara sugar
50 g (2 oz) sultanas
grated rind and juice of 1 lemon and
1 orange
50 g (2 oz) suet, finely chopped or
grated
40 g (1½ oz) chopped mixed peel
25 g (1 oz) blanched almonds,
grated
1 tbsp brandy
1 tbsp rum
1 tsp mixed spice

Mince together all the fruits except the currants. Add all the remaining ingredients and stir well. Pack into clean jars and cover with wax discs and cellophane circles. Store in a cool dry place.

CRANBERRY AND ORANGE PRESERVE

Makes about 700 g (1½ lb)

225 g (8 oz) cranberries
1 medium orange
300 ml (½ pint) water
350 g (12 oz) sugar
50 g (2 oz) raisins
50 g (2 oz) walnuts, chopped

Wash the cranberries, finely chop the orange and place both in a pan with the water. Bring to boil and simmer for about 40 minutes. Add the sugar, the raisins and walnuts. Stir until the sugar is dissolved, return the pan to the heat, bring to the boil, and boil until setting point is reached (10–15 minutes).
   Pour into warmed jars, cover and label.

The walnuts and raisins may be omitted to produce a variation.

AMERICAN PLUM GUMBO

1.5 kg (3 lb) plums
300–600 ml (½–1 pint) water
2 small oranges
1.5 kg (3 lb) sugar
500 g (1 lb) seedless raisins

Wash the plums, and if very large, halve or quarter. Place in pan with the water and simmer until a pulp is formed. Scrub the oranges, and slice thinly, removing the pips. Sieve the plums and place the sieved purée in a pan with all the other ingredients.
   Cook over a low heat to dissolve the sugar. Continue cooking, stirring occasionally, until a thick pulp is obtained. Pour into warmed jars, cover and label.

VINEGAR PRESERVES

Here is a varied choice of pickles, some of the old favourites and also some interesting new ones. Flavoured vinegars are also included – fruit vinegars to help fight that tickling cough in winter and herb vinegars to give additional flavour to mayonnaise, and salad dressings.

Vinegar preserves allow for great individual scope. These preserves are mixtures of fruits and vegetables flavoured with spices, with sugar and vinegar acting as the preservatives. The vinegar used must be a good quality one containing not less than 5% acetic acid. Owing to the nature of vinegar great care must be taken in the choice of containers and covers. The cover must be one which will prevent vinegar from evaporating and yet also be unaffected by the acidity in the vinegar. The most suitable tops today are twist tops which have a plastic lining. Pliable plastic tops are available but these must be checked to ensure that they are a good fit on the jar. Porosan preserving skin is also suitable as it is vinegar-proof. Wax circles and cellophane tops are *not* suitable.

As vinegar preserves have such a variety of ingredients mixed together, it is necessary to keep them for a few weeks before using to ensure a good blend of flavours. It is recommended that pickles should be kept for six weeks before using, and chutneys for up to three months. There are a few, however, which can be used almost immediately but they will also improve further if allowed to mature.

The spices that can be used are many, and the personal choice of these adds greatly to the individuality of the finished preserve. Both whole and ground spices can be used, but if a clear, bright result is required, you must use whole spices tied in a muslin bag which can be removed before the preserve is potted. Whatever spices are used, remember that they should be fresh each year as their strength diminishes during storage.

Vinegars
Flavoured vinegars are often required in cookery, and it is very easy, and usually cheaper, to make these at home. Remember that top quality vinegar,

containing 5% acetic acid, is required. Brown malt vinegar is usually used, but some light-coloured pickles require the use of white, or distilled, malt vinegar. Cider or wine vinegars can be used but their flavour is often masked by strong flavours in some pickles and they are expensive.

Spiced Vinegars

These can be purchased, but it is more fun to spice your own. Recommended quantities: to each 1 litre (2 pints) malt vinegar add 25 g (1 oz) mixed whole spices (cloves, cinnamon sticks, blade mace, allspice in equal amounts).

If a hotter flavoured vinegar is required a few peppercorns and 2–4 chillies may be added.

Cold Spiced Vinegar gives the best results (but needs plenty of forethought). Place the whole spices in the cold vinegar in the bottle and allow to steep for 4–8 weeks. Occasional shaking helps the full flavour to be extracted.

Hot Spiced Vinegar. Place vinegar and whole spices in a bowl covered with a plate, over a saucepan of cold water. Bring the water slowly to the boil, then remove the pan from the heat. Allow the spices to steep in the vinegar for 2 hours. Strain before use.

Herb vinegars

Half-fill a wide-necked jar with freshly gathered leaves, picked just before flowering. Fill to the top with white vinegar and allow to steep for at least 14 days before use. The herbs may be left longer if desired.

Fruit vinegars

Use equal quantities of fruit – usually soft fruit (e.g. blackberries, raspberries) and a good malt vinegar i.e. 500 g (1 lb) fruit to 600 ml (1 pint) vinegar.

Place in a bowl, cover and leave to steep for 3–5 days, stirring occasionally. Strain off the liquid, measure, and to each 600 ml (1 pint) add 500 g (1 lb) white sugar. Stir over a gentle heat until the sugar is dissolved, bring to the boil, and boil for 10 minutes. Put into bottles.

Pickles
There are two types: clear pickles, like pickled onions, and sweet pickles, like pickled damsons.

Clear pickles
It is necessary when making clear pickles to salt or brine the vegetables for 12–48 hours to extract some of the water from them. Block salt is preferable to vacuum-packed salt as it is less dense, but it is advisable to weigh salt to ensure that the vegetables are not oversalted.

For a cold brine use 500 g (1 lb) salt to 4.5 litres (1 gallon) water. The method is as follows:
1. Prepare the vegetables, cut into bite-sized pieces and place in a bowl. Cover with the brine, or alternatively sprinkle layers with salt. Cover the vegetables with a plate to ensure that they are under the liquid. Leave 12–48 hours in a cool place.
2. Rinse the vegetables carefully. Drain thoroughly.
3. Pack into jars and cover with spiced vinegar ensuring that there is at least 1 cm (½ inch) vinegar over the vegetables.
4. Cover the jars tightly with a vinegar-proof top (see page 65).

Sweet pickles
These are made from fruit and/or sweet vegetables. The fruit is stewed gently in sweetened, spiced vinegar until tender. Whole fruits need to be pricked before cooking to avoid shrivelling during storage.

PICKLED ONIONS

small onions
salt
water
spiced vinegar (see page 66)

Choose small, even-sized onions and place in a bowl. Make a brine using 500 g (1 lb) salt to 4.5 litres (1 gallon) water, pour over the onions and leave for 12 hours. Drain. Peel the onions and place in some freshly made brine and leave for 24 hours. They will float, so put a plate on top to keep them submerged. Drain and rinse thoroughly, removing surplus moisture. Pack into bottles and cover with cold spiced vinegar. Cover and label.

PICKLED RED CABBAGE

red cabbages
salt
spiced vinegar (see page 66)

Choose cabbages which are firm and a good red colour. Remove the core and slice finely. Place in a bowl, sprinkling salt between each layer. Leave to stand for 24 hours. Drain under cold running water and rinse well. Drain again, ensuring all surplus water is removed. Pack loosely into jars and cover with cold spiced vinegar. Cover securely and label.

This pickle is ready for eating in one week, and at its best if eaten before three months, after which it will lose its crispness.

MIXED PICKLE

A selection of:
   onions
   cauliflower
   cucumber
   marrow
   runner beans
brine
spiced vinegar (see page 66)

Prepare the vegetables and cut into bite-sized pieces, place in a bowl and cover with brine (see page 67). Leave to stand for 24–48 hours. Wash and drain very thoroughly. Pack neatly into jars and cover with cold spiced vinegar. Cover securely and label.

CUCUMBER PICKLE

Makes about 2.3 kg (5 lb)

*3 kg (6 lb) sliced cucumber,
 unpeeled
250 g (8 oz) salt
2.5 litres (4 pints) water
1.8 litres (3 pints) white vinegar
1 tbsp celery seed
2 tbsp mustard seed
1½ tsp curry powder
1 kg (2 lb) sugar*

Place the prepared cucumber in a bowl. Mix the salt and water, pour over the cucumber and leave for at least 6 hours, or preferably overnight. Rinse and drain thoroughly.

Place the remaining ingredients in a pan, heat gently until the sugar is dissolved, stirring frequently. Bring to the boil. Add the cucumber slices, return to the boil, and simmer gently for 4–5 minutes, stirring constantly. Pack into warmed jars, cover securely and label.

SHARP HOT PICCALILLI

Makes about 3 kg (6 lb)

*3 kg (6 lb) prepared vegetables –
 diced cucumber, marrow, beans,
 small onions, cauliflower florets,
 green tomatoes (if liked)
500 g (1 lb) cooking salt
4.5 litres (1 gallon) water (optional)
15 g (½ oz) turmeric
25–40 g (1–1½ oz) dry mustard
25–40 g (1–1½ oz) ground ginger
150 g (6 oz) white sugar
1.2 litres (2 pints) white vinegar
20 g (¾ oz) cornflour or plain flour*

Prepare the vegetables and brine or salt them as described on page 67. Rinse thoroughly under cold running water and drain. Mix the spices and the sugar in a large pan, and stir in most of the vinegar. Add the prepared vegetables and simmer gently until the desired texture is obtained – either crisp or tender. Do *not* cook until soft.

Blend the cornflour or flour with rest of the vinegar and add to the other ingredients. Bring back to the boil and, stirring carefully, boil for 2–3 minutes. Pack into warmed jars, cover securely and label.

BEETROOT PICKLE

Makes about 3.2 kg (7 lb)

1.5 kg (3 lb) boiled beetroot
750 g (1½ lb) cooking apples
  (prepared weight)
250 g (8 oz) onions, peeled
½ tsp ground ginger or 15 g (½ oz)
  mixed pickling spice
375 g (12 oz) brown sugar
750 ml (1 pint) vinegar
1 tsp salt

Prepare the beetroot by either dicing finely or mincing. Peel and core the apples and mince with the onions. If using pickling spice, tie in a muslin bag.

Place all the ingredients in a preserving pan, bring to the boil and simmer gently until the desired consistency is reached, stirring occasionally. Remove the bag of spices, pour into jars, cover and label.

PICKLED NASTURTIUM SEEDS

3 peppercorns
1 bay leaf
½ tsp salt
300 ml (½ pint) white vinegar
unripe nasturtium seeds

Place the spices and vinegar in a pan and simmer gently for 30 minutes. This vinegar may be prepared in advance and stored in a securely covered bottle.

Pick unripe nasturtium seeds on a fine day, wash and dry thoroughly. Place on greaseproof paper on a tray and leave in the sun for 3–5 days to dry thoroughly or place in a cool oven. Place in small jars and cover with the prepared vinegar. Cover the jars securely, label and leave for 2 months. Use as a substitute for capers.

SWEET PICKLED PRUNES

Makes about 1.5 kg (3 lb)

500 g (1 lb) dried prunes
1.25 litres (2 pints) sweetened spiced
  vinegar

Soak the prunes in water overnight.

Prepare the sweetened spiced vinegar as for pickled damsons (see page 71). Place the drained prunes in a pan with the vinegar and simmer until tender (take care not to break the prunes).

Remove the prunes from the vinegar and pack into jars. Boil the vinegar until

reduced to a syrup consistency, and pour
into the jars to cover the prunes. Cover
securely, label and store for at least 4 weeks
before eating.

PICKLED APRICOTS

1 kg (2 lb) sugar
600 ml (1 pint) white spiced vinegar
  (see page 66)
1 kg (2 lb) fresh apricots

Dissolve the sugar in the vinegar. Prepare
the fruit by cutting in half, removing the
stones, and cooking in a little water until
just beginning to soften. Drain well.

Place in the sweetened spiced vinegar and
simmer gently for about ¾ hour, until just
tender – great care must be taken not to
overcook. Drain from the syrup and pack
neatly into jars.

Place the syrup back on the heat and boil
to reduce to a thick syrup. Pour over the
fruit in the jars. Cover and label.

PICKLED DAMSONS

4 kg (8 lb) damsons
rind of ½ lemon
2 kg (4 lb) sugar
15 g (½ oz) whole cloves
15 g (½ oz) whole allspice
15 g (½ oz) root ginger
15 g (½ oz) stick cinnamon
1.25 litres (2 pints) vinegar

Wash the damsons, prick thoroughly and
place in a bowl. Heat the rest of the
ingredients together gently in a pan until
the sugar is dissolved then pour over the
damsons. Leave to stand for 5–7 days.

Strain off the vinegar, place in a pan,
bring to the boil, pour over the damsons
and leave to stand for another 5–7 days.
Repeat once more.

Strain off the vinegar, place in a pan and
simmer gently to reduce to a thick syrup.
Meanwhile pack the damsons into jars.
Cover with the hot syrup. Cover jars
securely and label.

SWEET MILD PICCALILLI

Makes about 3 kg (6 lb)

3 kg (6 lb) prepared vegetables –
diced cucumber, marrow, beans,
small onions, cauliflower florets,
green tomatoes (optional)
500 g (1 lb) cooking salt
4.5 litres (1 gallon) water (optional)
15 g (½ oz) turmeric
20 g (¾ oz) dry mustard
1½ tsp ground ginger
275 g (9 oz) white sugar
1.8 litres (3 pints) white vinegar
40 g (1½ oz) cornflour or plain flour

Prepare the vegetables and brine or salt them as described on page 67. Rinse thoroughly under cold running water and drain. Continue in the same way as for Sharp Hot Piccalilli (see page 69).

MILITARY PICKLE

Makes about 4 kg (8 lb)

1 marrow
1 cucumber
1 cauliflower
500 g (1 lb) runner beans
500 g (1 lb) onions
salt
7 chillies
15 g (½ oz) turmeric
15 g (½ oz) ground ginger
75–100 g (3–4 oz) plain flour
2.5 litres (4 pints) vinegar
500 g (1 lb) demerara sugar

Prepare the vegetables, and cut into bite-sized pieces. Place in a bowl, sprinkle with salt and leave overnight. Rinse in cold water and drain very thoroughly. Blend the spices and flour together with a little vinegar to form a smooth paste. Place the vegetables, vinegar and sugar in a pan, heat gently until the sugar is dissolved then bring to the boil and boil for 5 minutes. Add the blended spices, return to the boil, stirring constantly, and boil for 30 minutes. Pack into warmed jars, cover securely and label.

SPICED ORANGES

Makes about 700 g (1¾ lb)

6 oranges
water

Scrub the oranges and slice thickly. Place in a pan with sufficient water to cover. Bring to the boil and simmer gently until tender, about 1½–2 hours. Drain.

575 g (1¼ lb) white sugar
450 ml (¾ pint) white vinegar
1 tsp whole cloves
5-cm (2-inch) stick of cinnamon
1 tsp blade mace

Dissolve the sugar in the vinegar over a gentle heat and add the spices and lemon rind (tied in a muslin bag). Simmer for 10 minutes. Add the drained oranges, and simmer gently for about 1 hour.

Strain off the vinegar. Pack the oranges into warmed jars. Return the vinegar to the pan and boil rapidly to reduce to a syrup. Pour over the oranges. Cover securely, label and store.

SPICED CRAB APPLES

Makes about 1.5 kg (3 lb)

1.5 kg (3 lb) crab apples
600 ml (1 pint) vinegar
1 kg (2 lb) sugar
5-cm (2-inch) piece cinnamon stick
6 cloves
1 heaped tsp pickling spice

Place the vinegar and sugar in a pan with the spices (tied in a muslin bag). Heat gently to dissolve the sugar, stirring occasionally and then allow to simmer gently for 10 minutes.

Prepare the fruit by washing and de-stalking. Prick thoroughly, and if large, cut in half. Place in the sweetened vinegar and simmer gently until tender.

Strain off the vinegar, and pack the fruit into bottles. Return the vinegar to the pan and reduce to half by rapid boiling. Pour over the fruit. Cover the jars, label and store.

PICKLED BEETROOT

beetroots
water
salt
cold spiced vinegar (see page 66)

Choose small young beets, and prepare as for eating. Wash, place in a pan and cook in boiling salted water for 1–1½ hours. Cool, peel and slice. Pack the slices into bottles and cover with cold spiced vinegar. Cover and label.

CHUTNEYS

Chutneys add greatly to the choice of accompaniments to serve with cold meats and cheese. Spicy tomato chutney is superb with cheese, and a homemade mango chutney is excellent with curry.

A chutney is a vinegar preserve which offers great scope for individuality by the maker. It is a mixture of fruits, fresh and dried, vegetables, sugar, vinegar and spices, cooked slowly together to form a thick jam-like consistency. In a finished chutney, although some vegetables may retain a slightly crisp texture, there should be no 'free' vinegar floating at the top of the jar.

Care should be taken towards the end of cooking time to avoid the chutney burning on the base of the pan; occasional stirring and a low temperature help.

Chutneys should be poured into jars, filled to within 5 mm (¼ inch) of the top and covered as for other vinegar preserves (see page 65).

Vinegar has a slight hardening effect on some ingredients, especially onions and apples, so it is advisable to cook these ingredients in a little water to soften them before adding the rest of the ingredients.

Chutneys should be stored for two to three months before eating, although some of the present-day recipes which tend to be rather mild will be ready for eating almost at once. However, they lack character compared with the well-matured chutneys.

Chutneys after one year's storage

Covered only   Covered with a
with cellophane   metal twist-top

SPICY TOMATO CHUTNEY

Makes about 1.8 kg (4 lb)

500 g (1 lb) ripe tomatoes
500 g (1 lb) onions, peeled
500 g (1 lb) cooking apples
2 cloves garlic
1 large green pepper
300 ml (½ pint) vinegar
375 g (12 oz) brown sugar
1 tbsp salt
1 tbsp paprika
2 tsp prepared mustard
1 tsp chilli powder
1 tsp Worcestershire sauce
175 g (6 oz) tomato purée
¼–1 tsp cayenne pepper (to taste)

Dip the tomatoes in boiling water for ½–1 minute. Remove the skins and chop the flesh. Place in a saucepan. Chop or coarsely grate the onions; peel, core and slice the apples; crush the garlic and de-seed and chop the green pepper.

Add the onions, apples, garlic and peppers to the tomatoes with half the vinegar. Cover and simmer until the onions are soft. Add the remaining ingredients, bring to the boil and stir until the sugar is dissolved. Simmer uncovered until the desired consistency is reached. Pour into warmed jars, cover and label.

GREEN TOMATO CHUTNEY

Makes about 3 kg (7¼ lb)

2 kg (4 lb) green tomatoes
500 g (1 lb) apples
250 g (8 oz) stoned raisins
625 g (1¼ lb) shallots
15 g (½ oz) root ginger
8–10 chillies
2 tsp salt
500 g (1 lb) brown sugar
600 ml (1 pint) vinegar

Chop the tomatoes, peel and chop the apples and shallots and chop the raisins, *or* mince all the fruit. Bruise the ginger and tie in a muslin bag with the chillies.

Place all the ingredients in a preserving pan, bring to the boil, stirring until the sugar is dissolved, and simmer until the desired consistency is reached. Remove the muslin bag. Pour into warmed jars, cover and label.

RED AND GREEN PEPPER CHUTNEY

Makes about 3 kg (6 lb)

500 g (1 lb) red and green peppers,
mixed
1 kg (2 lb) sour apples

Cut the peppers in half, and remove the stalks and seeds. Peel and core apples; peel the onions. Mince or finely chop the peppers, tomatoes, apples and onions. Place in a preserving pan.

750 g (1½ lb) onions
1 kg (2 lb) green tomatoes
25 g (1 oz) salt
40 g (1½ oz) bruised ginger,
  chillies, whole cloves, whole
  allspice, mustard seed and
  peppercorns, mixed
1 litre (1½ pints) vinegar
500 g (1 lb) sugar

Tie the spices in a muslin bag. Add to the pan with half the vinegar. Bring to the boil and simmer gently until thick. Add the remaining vinegar and the sugar, bring back to the boil, stirring until the sugar is dissolved and continue simmering until the desired consistency is reached. Remove the muslin bag. Pour into warmed jars, cover and label.

MANGO CHUTNEY

Makes about 2 kg (4 lb)

1 kg (2 lb) mangoes (fresh or
  canned)
750 g (1½ lb) cooking apples
125 g (4 oz) onions
125 g (4 oz) tamarinds
250 g (8 oz) stoned dates
125 g (4 oz) raisins
juice of 1 large lemon
600 ml (1 pint) vinegar
25 g (1 oz) salt
7 g (¼ oz) cayenne pepper
¼ tsp nutmeg
3 bay leaves
1½ tbsp lime juice
1 kg (2 lb) demerara or Barbados
  sugar

Peel and quarter the mangoes, if fresh. Peel, core and chop the apples. Peel and chop the onions. Stone and chop the tamarinds. Roughly chop the dates and raisins. Place all the ingredients except the lime juice and sugar in a large bowl, mix thoroughly and leave to stand for at least 3 hours.

Transfer to a preserving pan, bring to the boil and simmer gently until tender, stirring frequently. Add the sugar and lime juice, stir until the sugar is dissolved and continue to simmer until thick and of the desired consistency. Pour into warmed jars, cover and label.

RHUBARB CHUTNEY

Makes about 2.2 kg (4 lb)

1 kg (2 lb) rhubarb
2 lemons
25 g (1 oz) garlic
25 g (1 oz) root ginger
500 g (1 lb) sultanas
1 kg (2 lb) brown sugar
1 tsp curry powder
½ tsp cayenne pepper
600 ml (1 pint) vinegar

Slice the rhubarb finely and place in a preserving pan. Squeeze the juice from the lemons and strain on to the rhubarb. Crush the garlic and add to the pan. Bruise the ginger and tie in a muslin bag with the lemon skin.

Place the remainder of ingredients in the pan, and bring to the boil, stirring until the sugar is dissolved. Simmer gently until the desired consistency is reached. Remove the muslin bag. Pour into warmed jars, cover and label.

MARROW CHUTNEY

Makes about 1.5 kg (3 lb)

500 g (1 lb) marrow (prepared
  weight)
1 tbsp salt
500 g (1 lb) onions
500 g (1 lb) tomatoes
125 g (4 oz) sultanas
250 g (8 oz) sugar
3 chillies
3 cloves
1 pinch mixed spice
300 ml (½ pint) vinegar

Prepare the marrow and cut into small cubes, place in a bowl, sprinkle with the salt and leave for 24 hours. Drain.

Peel and chop the onions and tomatoes. Place all the ingredients in a preserving pan including the marrow and bring to the boil. Stir until the sugar is dissolved and then simmer gently until tender and the desired consistency is reached. Pour into warmed jars, cover and label.

PEAR, APPLE AND MARROW CHUTNEY

Makes about 3 kg (5½ lb)

1 kg (2 lb) marrow
75 g (3 oz) salt
1 kg (2 lb) cooking apples
1 kg (2 lb) cooking pears

Prepare the marrow and cut into small cubes, place in a bowl and sprinkle with the salt. Leave to stand for 24 hours. Drain. Place marrow in a steamer and cook until soft. Peel, core and slice the apples and pears and place in a covered pan with a little

125 g (4 oz) onions, chopped
1 tbsp plain flour
1 tbsp dry mustard
15 g (½ oz) cayenne pepper
25 g (1 oz) turmeric
25 g (1 oz) ground ginger
1.25 litre (2 pints) vinegar
500–700 g (1–1½ lb) sugar

water and the onions and cook gently until soft.

Mix the fruits and vegetables together, place in a preserving pan with the flour and spices and half the vinegar. Simmer gently until thick. Add the remaining vinegar and sugar, bring back to the boil, stirring until the sugar is dissolved and then continue simmering until the desired consistency is reached. Pour into warmed jars, cover and label.

PUMPKIN CHUTNEY

Makes about 1.8 kg (4 lb)

1.1 kg (1½ lb) pumpkin
600 ml (1 pint) vinegar
900 g (2 lb) sugar
225 g (8 oz) seedless raisins
125 g (4 oz) onion, chopped
25 g (1 oz) salt
1 tsp ground ginger
1 tsp pepper
¼ tsp ground nutmeg
juice of 1 lemon
1½ tbsp grape juice
4 bay leaves

Prepare the pumpkin and chop into small dice. Place in a bowl with 300 ml (½ pint) vinegar and the other ingredients, mix well, cover and leave for 3 hours.

Transfer to a preserving pan, bring to the boil, stirring until the sugar is dissolved and then simmer gently for about 1 hour. Add the remaining vinegar and continue cooking until the desired consistency is reached. Pour into warmed jars, cover and label.

CUCUMBER AND APPLE CHUTNEY

Makes about 2.7 kg (5 lb)

1 kg (2 lb) cooking apples
675 g (1½ lb) onions
900 g (2 lb) cucumber
600 ml (1 pint) vinegar
450 g (1 lb) demerara sugar
15 g (½ oz) salt
½ tsp cayenne pepper

Peel, core and chop the apples. Peel and finely chop the onion. De-seed the cucumber. If ridge variety, peel as well. Chop finely. Place the apple, onion and cucumber in a pan with the vinegar, bring to the boil and simmer gently until soft.

Add the sugar, salt and cayenne. Heat gently, stirring until the sugar is dissolved, then continue simmering until the desired consistency is reached. Pour into warmed jars, cover and label.

APPLE CHUTNEY (1)

Makes about 4.5 kg (10 lb)

3.5 kg (7 lb) sour apples
30 g (1 oz) garlic
1.2 litres (2 pints) vinegar
250 g (8 oz) crystallized ginger
1.5 g (3 lb) brown sugar
500 g (1 lb) sultanas
1 tsp mixed spice
1 tsp cayenne pepper
1 tsp salt

Peel, core and slice the apples. Place in a pan with the finely chopped garlic and a small amount of water and cook, covered, until soft.

Add half the vinegar, the chopped ginger and all the other ingredients.

Bring to the boil, stirring until the sugar is dissolved then cook, uncovered, until beginning to thicken. Add the remaining vinegar and continue cooking until the desired consistency is reached. Pour into warmed jars, cover and label.

FRESH APRICOT CHUTNEY

Makes about 1.8 kg (3 lb)

250 g (8 oz) onions
750 g (1½ lb) apricots, prepared
    weight
1 clove garlic
2 tsp salt

Peel and mince the onions, place in a pan with a little water and cook, covered, until soft. Wash and de-stone the apricots and chop roughly. Crush the garlic in the salt. Crush the mustard seeds and tie with the allspice in a muslin bag.

Place all the ingredients in a large pan,

25 g (1 oz) mustard seed
½ tsp whole allspice
1 tsp turmeric
grated rind and juice of 1 orange
250 g (8 oz) sultanas
500 g (1 lb) demerara sugar
750 ml (1 pint) vinegar

bring to the boil, stir until the sugar is dissolved and then simmer gently until the desired consistency is reached. Remove the bag of spices. Pour into warmed jars, cover and label.

ORANGE CHUTNEY

Makes about 2.5 kg (5 lb)

500 g (1 lb) onions
1 kg (2 lb) cooking apples
2 kg (4 lb) sweet oranges
500 kg (1 lb) sultanas/seedless
  raisins
1 tbsp salt
2 tsp ground ginger
2 tsp cayenne pepper
2.5 litres (4 pints) vinegar
1 kg (2 lb) sugar

Peel and chop the onions, place in a covered pan with a little water and cook gently until tender. Peel, core and chop the apples and add to the pan. Continue cooking gently. Scrub the oranges and peel, removing as much white pith as possible. Mince the peel and pulp.

Place all the ingredients except the sugar with half the vinegar in a preserving pan and simmer gently until the orange peel is tender. Add the sugar and remaining vinegar, bring to the boil, stirring until the sugar is dissolved and continue simmering until the desired consistency is reached. Pour into warmed jars, cover and label.

LEMON CHUTNEY

Makes about 1.75 kg (3½ lb)

4 large lemons
450 g (1 lb) onions
25 g (1 oz) salt
600 ml (1 pint) vinegar
125 g (4 oz) raisins
15 g (½ oz) mustard seed, crushed
¼ tsp cayenne pepper
450 g (1 lb) demerara sugar
1 tsp ground ginger

Wash the lemons, cut into quarters, remove pips and slice finely. Peel and chop the onions. Place in a bowl, sprinkle with the salt and leave for 12–24 hours.

Place in a preserving pan with all the other ingredients. Bring to the boil, stirring until the sugar is dissolved and then simmer gently until tender and the desired consistency is reached. Pour into warmed jars, cover and label.

GOOSEBERRY CHUTNEY

Makes about 2 kg (4¼ lb)

1.5 kg (3 lb) gooseberries, topped
  and tailed
250 g (8 oz) onions, peeled
300 ml (½ pint) water
500 g (1 lb) sugar
15 g (½ oz) salt
1 tbsp ground ginger
½ tsp cayenne pepper
600 ml (1 pint) vinegar

Mince or finely chop the gooseberries and onions. Place in a covered pan with the water and cook until soft.

Add the rest of the ingredients, bring to the boil, stirring until the sugar is dissolved and continue cooking until the desired consistency is reached. Pour into warmed jars, cover and label.

BANANA CHUTNEY

Makes about 1.8 kg (4 lb)

450 g (1 lb) onions
125 g (4 oz) crystallized ginger
225 g (8 oz) stoned or block dates
8 ripe bananas (medium-sized)
15 g (½ oz) mixed pickling spice
2 tsp salt
300 ml (½ pint) vinegar
225 g (8 oz) black treacle

Peel the onions and mince together with the ginger and dates. Place in a preserving pan. Mash the bananas and add to the pan. Tie the pickling spices in a muslin bag and add to the pan together with the rest of the ingredients. Bring to the boil, stir until the sugar is dissolved and then simmer gently until the desired consistency is reached. Remove the bag of spices. Pour into warmed jars, cover and label.

PLUM CHUTNEY

Makes about 3 kg (6 lb)

1.5 kg (3 lb) plums
500 g (1 lb) onions
500 g (1 lb) apples
500 g (1 lb) sultanas
250 g (8 oz) sugar
25 g (1 oz) salt
tsp ground cinnamon
tsp ground allspice
tsp ground ginger
pinch cayenne pepper
litre (1½ pints) vinegar

Stone the plums and chop roughly. Peel and chop the onions. Peel, core and chop the apples and chop the sultanas. Place all the ingredients in a preserving pan, bring to the boil, stirring until the sugar is dissolved and then simmer gently until tender and the mixture has reached the desired consistency. Pour into warmed jars, cover and label.

MIXED FRUIT CHUTNEY

Makes about 3.5 kg (7 lb)

kg (4 lb) apples
500 g (1 lb) gooseberries and
500 g (1 lb) green tomatoes or
1 kg (2 lb) green tomatoes
500 g (1 lb) onions
1.5 litres (2 pints) vinegar
25 g (1 oz) pickling spice
250 g (8 oz) sultanas
750 g (1½ lb) brown sugar
25 g (1 oz) salt

Peel, core and chop the apples. Prepare the gooseberries and chop. Slice the tomatoes and peel and chop the onions. Place these ingredients in a preserving pan with half the vinegar and simmer gently until soft.
Tie the pickling spice in a muslin bag and add with the remaining ingredients to the fruit pulp and bring back to boil. Stir until the sugar is dissolved and then simmer gently until the desired consistency is reached. Remove the muslin bag. Pour into warmed jars, cover and label.

THREE FRUIT CHUTNEY

Makes about 2.3 kg (5 lb)

250 g (8 oz) dried apricots
1 kg (2 lb) marrow, prepared weight
20 g (¾ oz) salt
1 kg (2 lb) apples, prepared weight
15 g (½ oz) mustard seed
750 g (1½ lb) demerara sugar
75 g (3 oz) preserved ginger,
   chopped
1 tsp turmeric
2 tsp cornflour
½ tsp garlic, finely chopped
½ tsp cayenne pepper
1 litre (1½ pints) vinegar

Place the apricots in a bowl, cover with water and soak for 24 hours. Prepare the marrow, cut into small cubes, place in a bowl, sprinkle with the salt and leave to stand overnight. Drain well.

Drain the apricots and chop finely. Peel, core and chop the apples and place in a preserving pan with the apricots, marrow and a little water. Cover and simmer until a pulp is obtained. Tie the mustard seed in a muslin bag.

Add all the remaining ingredients and the muslin bag to the pan, bring to the boil, stirring until the sugar is dissolved, then continue to simmer, uncovered, until the desired consistency is reached. Remove the muslin bag. Pour into warmed jars, cover and label.

DAMSON CHUTNEY

Makes about 2.7 kg (6 lb)

2 kg (4 lb) damsons
750 g (1½ lb) apples
4 onions
750 g (1½ lb) raisins
3 cloves garlic
2 tbsp salt
2 litres (3 pints) vinegar
1 kg (2 lb) demerara sugar
25 g (1 oz) root ginger
25 g (1 oz) whole allspice
2 tsp whole cloves

Wash the damsons, place in a covered pan with a little water and cook until soft; remove the stones. Meanwhile, peel the apples and onions and either chop finely or mince. Mince the raisins. Crush the garlic with the salt. Bruise the ginger and tie in a muslin bag with the other spices.

Place all the ingredients in a preserving pan, bring to the boil, stirring until the sugar is dissolved, and then simmer gently until the desired consistency is reached. Pour into warmed jars, cover and label.

MARROW AND APPLE CHUTNEY

Makes about 3.5 kg (7 lb)

2 kg (4 lb) marrow
75 g (3 oz) salt
1 kg (2 lb) sour apples
500 g (1 lb) shallots
30 g (1 oz) bruised ginger, chillies and peppercorns, mixed
500 g (1 lb) sugar
2 litres (3 pints) vinegar

Peel and cut the marrow into small pieces; layer up in a bowl with the salt between the layers. Leave for 12 hours, then drain.

Peel, core and chop the apples. Peel and chop the shallots. Tie the spices in a muslin bag. With the exception of the sugar and vinegar, place all the ingredients in a preserving pan. Bring to the boil and simmer gently until tender. Add the sugar and vinegar, stir until the sugar is dissolved and simmer until the desired consistency is reached. Remove the muslin bag. Pour into warmed jars, cover and label.

APPLE CHUTNEY (2)

Makes about 2.5 kg (5 lb)

1.5 kg (3 lb) sour apples
1 kg (2 lb) onions
500 g (1 lb) seedless raisins
750 g (1½ lb) brown sugar
finely grated rind and juice of 2 lemons
2 tsp ground ginger
1 tbsp mustard seed
1 tsp salt
¼ tsp pepper
1.25 litres (2 pints) vinegar

Peel and core the apples. Peel the onions. Mince the apples, onions and raisins and place in a preserving pan. Add the grated lemon rind and strained juices and the rest of the ingredients.

Bring to the boil and simmer gently, stirring occasionally, until the desired consistency is reached. Pour into warmed jars, cover and label.

PEAR, DATE AND NUT CHUTNEY

Makes about 1.5 kg (3½ lb)

1.5 kg (3 lb) pears
125 g (4 oz) seedless raisins
125 g (4 oz) stoned dates
250 g (8 oz) walnut halves
350 ml (½ pint) wine vinegar
250 g (8 oz) brown sugar
juice of 3 lemons
2 tsp salt

Peel, core and chop the pears. Chop the raisins, dates and walnuts. Place all the ingredients in a preserving pan, bring to the boil, stirring until the sugar is dissolved, and then simmer gently until tender and the desired consistency is reached. Pour into warmed jars, cover and label.

BENGAL CHUTNEY

Makes about 2 kg (4 lb)

1 kg (2 lb) cooking apples, or green
  gooseberries
250 g (8 oz) onions
1 clove garlic
500 g (1 lb) raisins
500 g (1 lb) stoned dates
125 g (4 oz) preserved ginger
1 tbsp salt
¼ tsp cayenne pepper
1 litre (1½ pints) vinegar

Peel, core and chop the apples or top, tail and chop the gooseberries. Peel and slice the onions and garlic. Place these ingredients in a pan with a little water and cook, covered, until soft.

Mince the raisins and dates and chop the ginger. Place all the ingredients in a preserving pan, bring to the boil and stir until the sugar is dissolved. Simmer gently until the desired consistency is reached. Pour into warmed jars, cover and label.

APPLE AND APRICOT CHUTNEY

Makes about 3.1 kg (7 lb)

250 g (8 oz) dried apricots
2 kg (4 lb) cooking apples
500 g (1 lb) onions
500 g (1 lb) sultanas
500 g (1 lb) soft brown sugar
750 ml (1 pint) vinegar
1 tbsp salt
¼ tsp cayenne pepper

Place the apricots in a bowl with sufficient cold water to cover and leave to soak overnight. Peel, core and chop the apples. Peel and chop the onions. Drain and chop the apricots and sultanas.

Place all the ingredients in a preserving pan, bring to the boil, stirring until the sugar is dissolved, and then simmer gently until the desired consistency is reached. Pour into warmed jars, cover and label.

RIPE TOMATO CHUTNEY

Makes about 3.6 kg (8 lb)

6 kg (12 lb) ripe tomatoes
500 g (1 lb) onions, peeled
40 g (1½ oz) salt
2 tsp paprika
pinch of cayenne pepper
600 ml (1 pint) distilled spiced
vinegar (see page 66)
750 g (1½ lb) sugar

Dip the tomatoes into boiling water for ½–1 minute, remove the skins and chop the flesh. Chop or mince the onions, place in a preserving pan with the tomatoes and cook until a thick pulp is obtained. Add the spices and half the vinegar and simmer until thick. Add the remaining vinegar and the sugar, bring back to the boil and stir until dissolved. Simmer again untitil the desired consistency is reached. Pour into warmed jars, cover and label.

APPLE CHUTNEY (3)

Makes about 3.6 kg (7 lb)

1.5 kg (3 lb) sour apples, prepared
weight
500 g (1 lb) onions
500 g (1 lb) green tomatoes
250 g (8 oz) raisins
50 g (2 oz) crystallized ginger
1 litre (1½ pints) vinegar
500 g (1 lb) demerara sugar
25 g (1 oz) salt
½ tsp ground cloves
¼ tsp cayenne pepper

Peel and core the apples. Peel the onions. Finely chop (or coarsely mince) the apples, onions, tomatoes and raisins. Place in a preserving pan. Chop the crystallized ginger and add together with the remaining ingredients to the pan. Bring to the boil, stirring until the sugar is dissolved and then simmer gently until the desired consistency is reached. Pour into warmed jars, cover and label.

SAUCES AND RELISHES

As an accompaniment to any meal or as an extra ingredient in casseroles, homemade sauces are ideal. Relishes have arrived from the United States – they offer interesting textures and flavours and many may be eaten immediately.

Sauces

Sauces are made from similar ingredients to those in chutneys, but they are sieved part-way through cooking, to obtain a purée. If a good bright colour is required, as in a ripe tomato sauce, the sugar is not added until a short time before the end of cooking.

Sauces made from ingredients with a low acid content, such as ripe tomatoes, require to be sterilised after potting, to avoid fermentation.

Fill the bottles to within 2.5 cm (1 inch) of the top and screw the tops lightly into place. Place the bottles in a large deep pan with hot water reaching up to their necks, bring to the boil and allow to simmer for 30 minutes. After removing from the water, tighten up the tops, cool and label.

Relishes

Relishes are a mixture of fruit and/or vegetables with spices and vinegars. The method of preparation of relishes is such that the vegetables retain some of their crispness, through little or no cooking. Because the quantity of vinegar used is low, relishes *cannot* be considered as true preserves. They can be eaten immediately and most should not be kept longer than 6–8 weeks. They are a delightful accompaniment to salads and cold meats.

KEEPING MINT SAUCE

young mint, cleaned and chopped
vinegar
sugar
water

Fill a jar with mint. Cover with cold vinegar. Cover and store in a dark place. When required, remove the desired amount and place in a sauceboat. Add a little sugar; dilute with more vinegar and/or water. Sugar added to the stored sauce would cause fermentation.

RIPE TOMATO SAUCE

Makes about 3 litres (5 pints)

5-cm (2-inch) stick of cinnamon
7 g (¼ oz) whole allspice
7 g (¼ oz) blade mace
600 ml (1 pint) distilled or
  white vinegar
5.5 kg (12 lb) fully ripe tomatoes
40 g (1½ oz) salt
pinch of cayenne pepper
7 g (¼ oz) paprika
500 g (1 lb) sugar
3 tbsp tarragon or chilli vinegar

Tie the whole spices loosely in a muslin bag, place in a pan with the distilled vinegar and bring slowly to the boil. Remove from the heat, cover, and allow to infuse for 2 hours.

Wash and slice the tomatoes, place in a pan and cook until the skins are free. Rub the pulp through a sieve and return to a clean pan. Add the salt, cayenne pepper and paprika and cook until it begins to thicken. Add the sugar and flavoured vinegars and cook until a thick creamy consistency is obtained. Pour into warmed sauce bottles, cover and sterilise (see page 89).

MUSHROOM KETCHUP

Makes about 1.1 litres (2 pints)

1.8 kg (4 lb) mushrooms
100 g (4 oz) salt
1½ tsp allspice
1½ tsp black peppercorns
1½ tsp ginger
1 tsp cloves
1 tsp mustard seed
600 ml (1 pint) vinegar

Break the mushrooms into pieces, sprinkle with salt and leave to stand overnight. Rinse carefully. Mash with a wooden spoon. Place all the ingredients in a pan, cover, bring to the boil and cook for about 30 minutes. Strain into bottles and seal.

Sterilise, as described on page 89.

BLACKBERRY KETCHUP

blackberries
water
To each 600 ml (1 pint) pulp add:
½ tsp salt
125 g (4 oz) sugar
¼ tsp dry mustard
⅛ tsp ground cinnamon
⅛ tsp ground cloves
⅛ tsp ground nutmeg
300 ml (½ pint) vinegar

Place the blackberries in a pan with sufficient water to reach halfway up the fruit. Simmer until quite soft then sieve through a nylon sieve, and measure the pulp. Place the measured pulp in a saucepan with all the other ingredients and simmer for about 30 minutes or until the desired pouring consistency is reached. Pour into warmed bottles, cover and label.

GOOSEBERRY SAUCE

Makes about 1.3 litres (2 pints)

1.5 kg (3 lb) gooseberries
350 g (12 oz) onions
1 tsp ground ginger
1 tsp cayenne pepper
½ tsp salt
600 ml (1 pint) vinegar
500 g (1 lb) sugar

Wash the gooseberries. Peel and slice the onions. Place together in a pan with the spices, salt and half the vinegar, bring to the boil and cook until soft.

Sieve the pulp and return to a clean pan. Stir in the sugar and the rest of the vinegar. Cook gently until a creamy consistency is obtained, stirring occasionally. Pour into bottles, seal and label.

PLUM SAUCE

Makes about 2 litres (3½ pints)

4 kg (8 lb) plums
500 g (1 lb) onions
250 g (8 oz) currants
15 g (½ oz) root ginger, bruised
15 g (½ oz) whole allspice
7 g (¼ oz) chillies
7 g (¼ oz) peppercorns
7 g (¼ oz) mustard seed
1.2 litres (2 pints) vinegar
500 g (1 lb) sugar
50 g (2 oz) salt

Cut up the plums, peel and chop the onions. Place together in a pan with the currants, spices and 600 ml (1 pint) vinegar. Bring to the boil and simmer for 30 minutes.

Rub the pulp through a sieve and return to a clean pan. Add the sugar, salt and remaining vinegar, bring back to the boil, and simmer for 1 hour or until a creamy consistency is obtained. Pour into warmed bottles, seal and label.

WINTER RELISH

Makes about 3 kg (4½ lb)

500 g (1 lb) cooking apples
375 g (12 oz) onions
1.5 kg (3 lb) blackberries
500 ml (1 pint) vinegar
1 tsp ground cinnamon
1 tsp ground allspice
15 g (½ oz) ground ginger
2 tbsp salt
6 cloves
6 peppercorns
500 g (1 lb) white sugar

Peel, core and chop the apples. Peel and chop the onions. Place apples, onions and blackberries in a pan with the vinegar and spices, bring to the boil and simmer for 15–25 minutes.

Rub through a nylon sieve or a mouli-mill and return to a clean pan. Add the sugar, and stir until dissolved. Bring back to the boil and allow the mixture to boil rapidly until it thickens – about 20–30 minutes. Pour into warmed jars, cover and label.

TOMATO AND PINEAPPLE RELISH

Makes about 1.7 kg (3½ lb)

4 large cooking apples
525-g (1 lb 3-oz) can tomatoes
400-g (14-oz) can crushed pineapple
1.1 kg (2½ lb) sugar
½ tsp ground allspice
½ tsp ground cloves
½ tsp ground cinnamon
2 tsp Yorkshire relish (or brown sauce)
50 g (2 oz) salt
300 ml (½ pint) vinegar

Peel, core and chop the apples. Place all the ingredients in a saucepan and mix thoroughly. Bring to the boil and simmer gently until mixture thickens, stirring occasionally. Pour into warmed jars, cover and label.

CUCUMBER AND GREEN PEPPER RELISH

Makes about 1.1 kg (2¼ lb)

750 g (1½ lb) ridge cucumbers
250 g (8 oz) onion
1 green pepper
18 g (¾ oz) salt

Peel and dice the cucumbers, finely slice the onions and de-seed and shred the pepper. Place in a bowl with the salt. Leave to stand for 3 hours. Drain, rinse in cold water and drain again thoroughly.

Place the remaining ingredients in a pan,

300 ml (½ pint) white vinegar
150 g (5 oz) sugar
1 tsp turmeric
1 tsp mustard seed
1 tsp ground allspice
½ tsp ground mace

stir until the sugar is dissolved, then bring to the boil and simmer for 2 minutes. Add the drained vegetables, bring to the boil, and simmer for 4–5 minutes, stirring constantly. Pour into jars, cover securely and label.

This relish is ready to eat in a week.

CORN AND PEPPER RELISH

Makes about 1.75 kg (3½ lb)

750 g (1½ lb) sweetcorn kernels
2 large onions
2 red peppers
2 green peppers
2 tsp salt
2 tsp plain flour
1 tsp turmeric
2 tsp dry mustard
250 g (8 oz) white sugar
600 ml (1 pint) white vinegar

Place the sweetcorn in a pan containing 1 cm (½ inch) lightly salted, boiling water. Bring to the boil and boil for 3 minutes. Drain well. Peel and chop the onions. De-seed and chop the peppers.

Mix the salt, flour, turmeric, mustard and sugar together in a pan and blend in the vinegar. Add the sweetcorn, peppers and onions and stir well. Bring to the boil, and simmer gently for 30 minutes, stirring occasionally. Pour into jars, cover and label.

BEETROOT AND HORSERADISH RELISH

Makes 1.5 kg (3 lb)

500 g (1 lb) beetroot
250 g (8 oz) horseradish
pinch of salt
125 g (4 oz) sugar
300 ml (½ pint) white wine vinegar

Boil the beetroot until tender, peel and shred. Wash the horseradish and grate across the sticks to avoid getting long shreds.

Mix together the beetroot, horseradish, salt and sugar. Add the wine vinegar and mix thoroughly. Place in jars, cover and label.

This relish is ready for immediate use and will keep for about 4 weeks.

WHAT IS THE WI ?

If you have enjoyed this book, the chances are that you would enjoy belonging to the largest women's organisation in the country — the Women's Institutes.

We are friendly, go-ahead, like-minded women, who derive enormous satisfaction from all the movement has to offer. This list is long — you can make new friends, have fun and companionship, visit new places, develop new skills, take part in community services, fight local campaigns, become a WI market producer, and play an active role in an organisation which has a national voice.

The WI is the only women's organisation in the country which owns an adult education establishment. At Denman College, you can take a course in anything from car maintenance to paper sculpture, from book binding to yoga, or cordon bleu cookery to fly-fishing.

All you need to do to join is write to us here at the **National Federation of Women's Institutes, 39 Eccleston Street, London SW1W 9NT**, or telephone 01-730 7212, and we will put you in touch with WIs in your immediate locality. We hope to hear from you.

ABOUT THE AUTHOR

Pat Hesketh, a trained home economics teacher, has taught both cookery and crafts in schools, further education and adult education. Before joining the WI as Home Economics and Specialised Crafts Adviser in 1977, she was head of department of Rural Home Economics at the Staffordshire College of Agriculture.

As Adviser to the National Federation of Women's Institutes, Pat Hesketh has acted as consultant on several published craft and cookery books, and now travels extensively lecturing and tutoring WI members in all aspects of home economics and crafts.

INDEX